BRUTALLY HONEST

BRUTALLY HONEST

—

MELANIE BROWN
WITH LOUISE GANNON

quadrille

Publishing Director Sarah Lavelle
Commissioning Editor Susannah Otter
Copy Editor Andrea Belloli
Designer Maeve Bargman
Jacket Photographer Malachi Banales
Typesetter seagulls.net
Cover lettering Arielle Gamble
Production Director Vincent Smith
Production Controller Tom Moore

Published in 2018 by Quadrille, an imprint of Hardie Grant Publishing

Quadrille
52–54 Southwark Street
London SE1 1UN
quadrille.com

Cataloguing in Publication Data: a catalogue record for this book is available from the British Library.

Reprinted in 2018
10 9 8 7 6 5 4 3 2
Hardback: ISBN 978 1 78713 352 5
Export Trade Paperback: ISBN 978 1 78713 355 6
Printed in United States

You may write me down in history
With your bitter, twisted lies
You may trod me in the very dirt
But still, like dust, I rise

from *Still I Rise* by Maya Angelou

THANK YOU

—

To my writer and collaborator, Louise Gannon, who spent so much time with me in London and Los Angeles. I know I am really difficult but thank you for your endless patience and kindness and for somehow putting into words all those emotions and feelings I could never properly express myself. To Gary Madatyan, there aren't enough thanks I can say for sticking by me through thick and thin, making me laugh and sitting with me as I cried. You are my forever and ever friend. To Dr Charles Sophy for never giving up on me. Thank you Simon Cowell, my TV dad, for the support and kindness you continue to show to me. To Heidi Klum for making me laugh when I really needed to and Howie Mandel for standing by my side. To my wing woman Geri Horner for understanding me and my Spice sisters Emma Bunton, Melanie Chisholm and Victoria Beckham for the happy memories. And to my three girls, Phoenix, Angel and Madison for being my life.

I would also like to thank my agent Claire Powell, my literary agent Charlie Brotherstone and everyone at Quadrille and Audible for making this book happen, especially my editor Susannah Otter, Robin Morgan-Bentley and Harriet Poland.

I am also so very, very grateful for the support of the people who were all part of this story, Simon Jones, Ben Todd, Janet Neale, Randy Stodghill, Alan Edwards, Andrea Brown, Danielle Brown, Phoenix Gulzar Brown, Charlotte Robinson, Chris Little, Kim Deck, Dean Keyworth, Nicola Collins, Teena Collins, Rosie Nixon and my dad Martin Wingrove Brown. I know you are still watching over me.

CONTENTS

—

MELANIE'S MESSAGE

—

This book is for all women who have ever been controlled, put down, cheated on, abused, shamed, lied to, used, treated like the eternal underdog and had their spirit and self-esteem completely snatched away.

It's about taking back your power, rediscovering yourself, putting joy, happiness and peace back into your life. And it's about the hardest journey a woman will ever make in her life – learning to love herself.

I know what it's like to be beaten down. I know what it's like to be punched, humiliated and isolated, and to feel there is no way out except suicide. The most frequent question women in violent relationships are asked is, 'Why did you stay?' The most common thing women have said to me over the past years is, 'But you're such a strong woman. How did this happen to you?'

By telling my story, I want to answer those questions – for myself – and, in some way, on behalf of all other women who find themselves in the vicious trap that I lived in for almost a decade. I also want to talk about how fame changes your life – in good ways and bad ways – and how, if you live in the fast lane, you have to deal with the crashes along the way and how, as a woman, I cope.

Mine is a life lived in headlines, from my crazy days in the Spice Girls to my lifestyle, my divorces and my court cases. It never ceases to amaze me how stories can be so near to yet so far from the truth. You have probably – based on these headlines – made your own minds up about me already, and I wouldn't blame you for it. But lies and mistruths kept me trapped for long enough. Now I want the truth to set me free. I am ready to say what really happened to me, what really happens to women like me and what will keep on happening if we don't stand up and say, 'Enough is enough.'

I kept silent for a decade in order to protect myself and my three beautiful girls. I had to declare, in front of an American judge, reasons why I needed legal safeguarding from the man I was married to for ten years. And even though I continued to smile for the cameras on stage, on screen and on social media, I was lost behind a wall that kept out my family, my friends and my soul.

Since my story became public, I've had so many women – from other female celebrities to nurses, receptionists, bankers, teachers – who have held my hand, hugged me and poured out their own problems. Every single story has touched my heart, and I'm thankful to all of those women who sought me out because even though I was still fragile, their words helped give me strength.

But there is so much I've never said. With the help of amazing friends and supporters, I've taken the very painful but healing step of confronting my past and trying to answer all those questions as brutally honestly as possible – picking at scabs, opening wounds, looking at the way I handle fame and slowly unlocking secrets I hid from the world. It's taken a lot of trust and a huge amount of tears, but – traumatic though it's been at times – it's the only way I can learn from what I've been through. I refuse to be shamed any more.

——

My story isn't simple. Parts of this book may really shock you, and there are parts which may make you laugh. I've not flinched from some very tough details – but it is my truth. It weaves together past and present; woman and child; fathers and husbands; motherhood and family. It is about weakness and strength, and it's about a woman who always knew that one day she would escape and be free.

I've written this book for myself, for other women and for my girls, because if we are honest, if we are kind, if we are compassionate and if we are just there for each other, we are unstoppable. We are goddesses.

1
GIRL POWERLESS
—

What drives a woman to want to take her own life? What makes a woman believe the only way out is a bottle of pills?

I can tell you the answer – Melanie Brown, Scary Spice – that gobby girl from Leeds who ran riot through the whole bloody world with the Spice Girls. The girl cheeky enough to pinch loo roll from Nelson Mandela's house (sorry to the late Mr Mandela; I absolutely loved you and was beyond privileged to meet you, but I also know you had a little chuckle about the loo roll) and cocky enough to crack jokes with HRH Prince Charles.

I was Girl Power. One fifth of that fantastic group of girls who were invincible, hilarious, fearless and bonded like glue – 'chicas to the front', taking the control from men and generally kicking butt, big time.

And now, almost two decades on, you still see me in the spotlight on massively successful television shows in Britain, America and Australia. Still being loud and proud, still waving the flag for Girl Power.

But here I am, thirty-nine years of age, staring in a mirror in the en-suite bathroom of my rented house in Kensington, London, holding an open bottle of aspirin from the stash I've stockpiled over the years, putting one pill after another into my mouth – watching myself as I swallow, tears rolling down my cheeks.

As each pill goes into my mouth, I ask myself, 'Are you sure?' And I take another one. Ten, twenty, fifty. A hundred. 'Are you sure?'

Everything and nothing is running through my mind. It's Thursday night. 11 December 2014. I've come back from dinner with my husband, Stephen. Tomorrow I'm going to 'The X Factor'. It will be the red-carpet launch for the final weekend in front of the press; there will be fans going wild for me, interviewers desperate to talk to me, Simon Cowell, Cheryl Fernandez Versini (as she was back then) and Louis Walsh; I'll be wearing a beautiful dress, my hair and makeup will be perfect, but if you want the absolute truth, I'm not thinking about any of this at all. I don't care about any of it. There's so much bullshit about being famous, being the fabulous Mel B. Right now, right here in this fancy, swanky bathroom of a multi-million-pound palace of an apartment, none of it means anything. I can't plaster that happy grin on my face anymore. I can't pretend I'm not living in some twisted, violent hell.

My life is a mess and I want out.

As I look in that huge bathroom mirror, it is not my face that is reflected in the expensive, flawless glass. It is not a large, cream, stylish bathroom with a giant bath and sleek metal racks filled with white, fluffy Egyptian cotton towels that I see behind me. Staring back at me is a fourteen-year-old, mixed-race girl called Melanie Janine Brown, from a bog-standard three-bedroom semi in Kirkstall, who felt so lonely, isolated and misunderstood that she took a whole bunch of Anadin Plus pills she'd nicked from the family cupboard.

When I tried to kill myself back then, I'd also watched myself in a mirror in my bedroom as I took the pills, putting them onto my tongue one by one, gazing at myself as I sobbed and swallowed.

A hundred and twenty. 'Are you sure?' A hundred and fifty. 'Are you sure?'

My life had changed unrecognizably in the decades in between. Here I was – rich and famous beyond that girl's wildest dreams – the kind of woman who was on magazine covers; on television; stepping out of beautiful houses or chauffeur-driven cars. I have had enough good wine in my time to know the difference, by smell alone, between a £100 bottle of Puligny-Montrachet and a £10 bottle of Mâcon-Villages. I've worn enough designer clothes to tell a Gucci dress from a Christian Dior dress by feel and fit alone. I'd worked my backside off to have a lifestyle that was a million miles away from the one I was born into.

From photographs posted on my Instagram pages, anyone – not just that desperate fourteen-year-old – would feel a pang of jealousy looking at my glamorous, gilded existence. But it was all a lie. A big, fat lie. My life was a sham. Behind the glitter of fame, I felt emotionally battered, estranged from my family. I felt ugly and detested by the very man who once promised to love and protect me, my husband and manager, Stephen. A man who after ten years of marriage now had a library of sex tapes that could – as we both well knew – ruin my career and destroy my family.

—

So there I was. Trapped in the vice of my own celebrity image. All smiles on the outside, misery and self-loathing on the inside, always telling the world how happy I was when really all I ever wanted was to scream for help. With each pill I swallowed, I was going back through the mirror to that same desperate place I'd been to as a teenager, as if I'd opened up some portal in time. I could see my very core as I was now and then – crushed, numb, unhappy and broken. Girl Powerless.

The only thing that made sense to me in that bathroom in Kensington was just to go. A hundred and eighty. 'Are you sure?' A hundred and ninety. 'Are you sure?'

I wrote frantic, disjointed notes for Phoenix, my eldest daughter, my soulmate – the girl who is little sister, friend and daughter to me. 'Leeds', 'Train', 'King's Cross'. She was the one person I knew I could

100 per cent rely on. My Phoenix. It was going to be up to her to get my other little girls, Angel and Madison, to Leeds where they could all live with my mum. In my head, in that moment, it was that simple. They could start a new life. They could be happy. They really would be better off without me. They would all rise from my ashes.

Two hundred. 'Now what's going to happen, Melanie?' STOP!

As soon as I'd swallowed that last pill, I knew I didn't want to go anywhere. My hands froze against my mouth and in the mirror I saw me, Melanie – a woman, a mother. Time spun on a second. Broken images and random, fractured thoughts went through my mind. I had done a cover shoot dressed as an angel for *Grazia* magazine and now I was going to die before it hit the shelves. I had seen someone I knew from dance school in Leeds the day before and I couldn't remember her name. What was it? The thoughts drifted away like leaves in gusts of wind, disappearing before I could catch them.

Then a voice howled through the silence, sending an electric shock through the messed-up jumble of my brain. 'MY GIRLS.' The scream came from my mouth. My two beautiful, innocent little daughters were asleep, yards away from the bathroom, and my Phoenix, who was away at a boarding school in the country, would be asleep too, thinking she was safe and sound. I jolted forward in a panic, clutching my throat, my forehead breaking out in beads of sweat. 'Melanie! What the fuck are you doing? Get a grip!' Swallowing bottles of pills was never going to be the answer. 'My girls, my girls,' I muttered to myself. I could never, ever leave my girls.

—

Looking back now, four years later, I know that overdose was a massive cry for help. A primal scream from a broken woman. Emotionally – and for all sorts of reasons that I will explain – I was at rock bottom. I'd allowed myself to disintegrate over those three months of filming

'The X Factor' in London. I was exhausted, worn down by seven years of what felt to me like constant emotional abuse, mind games, degradation, threats and sexual exploitation. I was drinking too much – wine, vodka, tequila – and had lost all self-respect. I was lost.

At that moment, I felt it was Stephen who was in control of every aspect of my life. I felt he owned me. My self-esteem was on the floor. I felt trapped. I felt helpless because I'd allowed this man into my life, and, little by little, insult by insult, indignity by indignity, deal by deal, sex tape by sex tape, I had allowed him to completely take over. He was the one that decided where I lived, whom I saw (unless I was working), what my money was spent on, who looked after our kids (not me but a selection of nannies or members of his family). It was up to him whether I was a piece of filth that day or a goddess or a whore.

In my head, I had to answer to Stephen for everything, account for every second of my day. It was for my own good, he would tell me and I would agree. Even when he was miles away in Los Angeles and I was in the middle of recording 'The X Factor' in the studio in Wembley I could feel him everywhere. He would call me to check in on me. What was I eating? What was I wearing? Who was I with? If I was late home from work (and I would often try and be as late as I possibly could) there would be 15 missed calls on my phone from him: 'Where are you? Call me now.' Even though Stephen was effectively banned from 'The X Factor' studios, (Simon Cowell could not stand him) he made his presence felt everywhere.

To me it seemed there was no escape. If I didn't answer his calls, he'd phone my driver, my security, my hairdresser Randy Stodghill, screaming: 'Where is she? Tell her to call me this minute.' And then I'd finally get back to Kensington, walk through the door of our luxurious apartment, and, even before I saw him, I would feel his energy crackling through the pale-hued space that was the size of half the street I had been born in. Madison – my youngest gorgeous baby girl – would run to the door: 'Mommy!' And as I buried my face in her tiny dark curls and felt her little hands clutching me tight, I would hear him.

'Madi, give Mommy a kiss. Then Mommy and Daddy need to talk. We need Mommy and Daddy time.'

'I want to see Angel,' I'd say, hauling Madison up with one arm as I walked into the sitting room, where my middle daughter sat watching cartoons on the giant-screen digital TV.

'You didn't answer my calls,' he'd start, calmly enough, but then that is always how it started, with the tiniest, barely noticeable hint of a threat behind the words.

'We were filming all day,' I'd answer casually. Was it worth walking over to the fridge to pour myself a glass of wine, I wondered. Might as well. I'm in for it anyway. A nice, chilled glass of white would take the edge off. Or maybe a glass of red. I'm much more of a red-wine woman. An intense, powerful red like Châteauneuf-du-Pape. Maybe there was something like that amid the bottles of wine in the kitchen.

He would know – we both knew – he had reason to be suspicious of me. He would look through my handbag, scroll through my phone, looking for evidence of bad behaviour. I'd let the insults roll over me. I'd avert my eyes because I hated looking at his mouth. His massive, pouting mouth that never stopped opening and shutting. I'd drink my wine, calculating in my head how much longer it would be before I could pour myself another glass to take off another edge.

He made me feel ugly. Like a waste of space. Like I was a terrible mother, a whore. Like I was lucky to be married to him because no-one else would put up with trash like me. Yes, I knew all this. So what would I do? Me, so-called Scary Spice? I would nod. Or laugh. Anything to shut him up. I would – like a controlled and emotionally abused wife – do anything to stop him kicking off. 'Do you want to fuck then?' I'd ask coldly. Anything to make it stop.

Anything. That's what I'd do. I'm going to be brutally honest here. And I'm not going to hide or lie like I constantly did back then. Good, bad or ugly, I'm going to peel back the layers and tell it like it was. You can judge me or you can try and understand me, understand what I was going through; what millions of other women go through when they are in toxic relationships that strip them of their self-respect, their souls, and drive them to a point where they believe they are either crazy or completely worthless. It's hard to think myself back to that woman that I became because she makes me cry when I think of her, she makes me sad and she makes me angry. I want to be a better woman. None of us are perfect and I'm the last person to pretend I am. But to become a better woman I have to understand exactly how I fell apart and how I let go of every single thing I hold dear to me.

2
NUMB
—

After years of clinging onto my soul and pretending everything was okay, in London I went into freefall. Coming back to the country I'd been born in made me see how messed up my life had become, how far away I was from everything I loved. I was so low that two weeks into filming 'The X Factor' I'd started using cocaine to get me through the run of the show, to get me through living with Stephen, which felt like neurotic claustrophobia, and – for deeper, darker reasons – to get me through the emotional gridlock of being so geographically close to my family in Leeds and my Spice 'sisters' in London. On so many, many levels I felt myself sinking.

I'm not proud of taking cocaine, but I can't pretend it didn't help me to have a line of that white powder when I got up in the morning. Sitting in my car a few minutes before I'd faced Stephen, I'd snorted a line. And he knew it. There are reasons people choose to self-medicate; usually it's because they aren't ready to face up to the reality they are living in. It can blur the voices around you, it can keep you in your own world, or it can keep you moving.

I want to talk about this connection between substance abuse and women who feel abused (buckle up, there's a lot more to come) because since finally walking away from Stephen I've discovered how commonplace this link is but how it's something we don't talk about. It's more shame we have brought on ourselves and our families, and we don't address it. We don't ask why. We carry on suffering with the problem itself and the guilt. We break one cycle but don't realize that we are still in its shadow. I don't even know myself if I would feel inclined to be so open had not so much of my private life been splashed all over the papers (and online) since my horrible mud-slinging court case against my ex-husband. Everything happens for a reason. I chose not to walk out but to speak out and tell it like it is.

And this is how it is. It's not clean, it's not pretty, but it's real. I've recently discovered through looking at information available from groups like the brilliant Women's Aid that women in any sort of abusive relationship are fifteen times more likely to abuse alcohol and nine times more likely to abuse drugs than women in stable relationships. That makes perfect sense to me. But then it would because I've been there. And I admit it.

Think about it. How do you deal with feeling ugly, unwanted and humiliated 24/7? How do you deal with feeling you are not loved and pretending to the world you are living the perfect happy-ever-after fantasy? I had found techniques to stop my mind from constantly spinning. I would just block – block thoughts, block emotions, block fears. And, as much as I could, I would block Stephen.

Once I was at work, on 'The X Factor', I felt safe. Stephen couldn't touch me and I could ignore his constant calls ('I've been filming', 'I couldn't get to the phone'). I could start to feel good about myself because I knew what I was doing. I didn't need anything and I didn't take anything. In Los Angeles when things got tough, I'd go through periods of drinking to blot out my emotions, and there were times – the blackest times – when I would turn to drugs. But in the country where I was born, I had to have something strong to help me cope. That 'something strong' was cocaine.

The great irony is that, if you'd seen me back then, you would have thought my life could not have been better. I was enjoying a triumphant transformation from former Spice Girl to the 'most popular judge' (according to the tabloid press) on 'The X Factor'. I loved being on the show, I loved the group of 'boys' I was mentoring, and even the hard-to-please fashion critics were raving about the way I looked – sleek, sophisticated and immaculately tailored (a great glam team can perform miracles). Invitations to prestigious parties poured in. Requests for interviews kept on coming. Social media whirled and – for the first time in a decade – everything, absolutely everything – was 100 per cent positive.

Even – Shock! Horror! – *The Guardian* liked me: 'Mel B: The Surprise Star of X Factor'. I was so stunned when I saw that headline above the interview I'd done that I asked my PR, Simon Jones, to get more copies. I got into Fountain Studios – on a small trading estate close to Wembley where 'The X Factor' was then filmed – ran into the other judges' dressing rooms and left a magazine on each of their tables. I know it's childish, but then that's me. I love to show off. And for a few hours I got to be proud of myself. An intelligent, witty man called Simon Hattenstone from a paper I'd only ever seen sticking out of a teacher's briefcase (my dad read *The Sun*) had met me and liked me. He didn't think I was annoying. He didn't think I was too much. He didn't think I was stupid. He thought I was 'funny', 'fanciable' and 'warm'. I wanted Simon, Cheryl and Louis to read his words.

Simon Cowell, my boss on 'The X Factor', would tell me after a show, 'Melanie, you are having a real moment. You've got to own it.' I remember sitting with Joe Stone, a writer for *Grazia* magazine, and him telling me how perfect my life seemed. I was nodding and thinking, I am in hell. Right at that moment I knew I was coming to a breaking point. Two days before, I'd taken my girls to a Sunday-morning film premiere and had had to leave after a few minutes. I took the girls home and then asked Simon Jones to come with me to a hotel next to our apartment in Kensington. He remembers me ordering tea and then hysterically bursting into tears. 'You have to help me, I'm desperate!' I cried. Simon is one of the most respected and experienced PRs in London. He is used to dealing with anything.

'What's going on Melanie?' he asked. I couldn't say the words. I knew he couldn't stand Stephen, and that he'd been witness to his rants and aggressive behaviour. But I couldn't let my shameful secret out. Melanie the mess. He sat with me as I wavered between sobs, smiles and silent shakes of my head, trying to make me feel better.

And then, two days later, just minutes before I was due to sit down with Joe – with a pair of Victoria's Secret angel wings fixed to my back for a happy, heavenly cover shoot – I was sitting upstairs in the make-up room hysterical, unable to breathe as the sobs wracked my body. A team of makeup artists and fashion assistants looked like they wanted the floor to swallow them up. I guess they probably assumed I was an absolute diva who hated the clothes and the makeup. I didn't care about any of it. It was my life I hated. It was my life that was coming apart at the seams.

'You need to tell me what is happening, Melanie.' Simon was by my side, asking everyone else to leave the room.

'I have to get away from Stephen. I want a divorce!' I sobbed. He nodded calmly. 'But he's got all these videos of me. Really bad videos. He could ruin me.' Simon was the first person I'd ever said these words to and I couldn't look him in the eye. He was calm, he was kind. 'I'm going to pull this shoot,' he said. 'We'll work this out.'

I shook my head. 'No,' I said. 'You can't. I have to do it.' I needed to pull myself together. I couldn't believe I'd actually said those words out loud. I had to stop falling apart and put everything right again.

And so there I was, half an hour later, with Joe from *Grazia* telling me how everything was wonderful, and how he was a long-term fan of the Spice Girls. My head was spinning. I barely registered what he was saying. I was opening my mouth and saying words to stop his questions as fast as I could. God knows what he thought of me; in fact I could see he thought I was being difficult. He even said someth ing to that effect as he ploughed on in the face of my unhelpful answers. 'Sorry, I've had a row with my husband,' I said abruptly.

I could say nothing more or I could say everything but not there and not then.

I wanted to get out of there, get out of everything. I could see Simon looking anxious, but I had become so used to pretending, so used to covering up, that I knew I wouldn't drop the ball. I wasn't going to cry anymore. I had retreated behind my hard wall of blocked emotions and empty words. When Joe left, Simon looked at me. Obviously he wanted to talk. I didn't. I shouldn't have said anything. No-one could do anything. Stephen could trump any PR or lawyer by simply leaking any one of the tapes from his sex-tape library. My family would be humiliated, and everything I'd worked for would be ruined. It was easier to stick to my 'happy life' lies. And it was easier, when I was desperately upset, to risk being hard and rude than to break down, sob and tell the truth.

—

Thing is, I could always convince myself I was okay as long as I had my kids with me and as long as I could work. In the days after I finally left Stephen, and even in the very worst, humiliating days of my court case when my reputation was being stripped from me headline by headline, what got me through were my kids and my work. I never wanted people to know anything, but news of my horrific marriage came out because in Los Angeles I felt I needed to file court papers to get a temporary restraining order on Stephen to protect myself and my girls. The judge granted the order, and the contents of that piece of paper – including some sordid details of our marriage – were immediately reported in the press all over the world (the law in the US states that restraining orders are made in open, public court).

The very next day I was sitting at the desk on 'America's Got Talent'. I had only recently returned from my father's deathbed in London and it was my first day back. I could see from the faces of the producers, the researchers and the cameramen that they didn't quite know what to say. The outrageous, funny Mel B they all thought they knew was actually a woman who'd had to go to court to get away from her husband, a woman who feared for her own safety. Before the cameras start rolling, there's hair and makeup, a meeting with the producers about that day's show. There's the sound guys fixing in the microphones, the lighting crew checking the lights – it's a good few hours before the actual show gets on the road. In this time, I was being inundated with silent looks of sadness and concern and little gentle pats on the shoulder, which only made me feel incredibly uncomfortable. 'Excuse me, Melanie. Is there anything I can get you?' This from one of the production guys who usually greeted me with a wolf whistle and cheeky comment like 'Legs looking good today!' People were talking to me softly, treating me as if I was about to break. I wanted to be treated like Scary Spice with a joke or a saucy smile.

You've got to say something, Melanie, I thought. I jumped to my feet. 'I want everyone to know that I'm fine. No-one has to look sad or ask if I'm okay. I don't want a pity party. I've left my husband and I'm bloody happy I've finally done it. Now I want to work. Boom!' I guess I could have been more thoughtful or eloquent and explained that my nightmare had ended and I was going to be okay. Or maybe 'Thank you for keeping me working because work has been my only safe place, which is why I'm so glad to still be here.' But I didn't want pity or to be treated differently. I didn't feel fragile. I finally felt strong and I wanted to move on. Simon Cowell got it. He made a joke. Something like 'And let's not forget this show is actually all about me.' Then he winked at me, and that cheeky wink meant more than a hundred sympathetic looks because it was exactly what I needed. He'll never know how much it meant to me.

Simon Cowell and I don't always get on. We have our little rows and spats (I've been known to throw water in his face and have had occasion to call him an ass-hole), but ultimately we connect because, as different as we are, we are cut from the same cloth. He's a middle-class Jewish boy from Hertfordshire and I'm a mixed-race girl from the wrong side of Leeds. But he loves to work, I love to work, and of all the things in our lives, work is the one thing that makes sense. On a stage, in front of an audience or even a camera – whatever is going on in my life – I feel liberated. Simon is exactly the same. He's never happier than when he's working. And if there's a problem at work (he decides he hates the lighting, or something on the set bothers him, or a particular twist in the show fails to come off the way he wants it to), he will keep working on it until he has solved it because he gets the biggest kick out of doing what he does to the best of his ability.

I feel nothing but privileged doing what I do. And what you see on the telly or the stage is the real Melanie Brown. The very best of me. I am in my element. I literally throw myself into doing as good a job as I can whether it's as a dancer, a singer, a judge, a TV host or on Broadway. I always want to prove myself, always want to show I can do anything you throw at me. I never want to let anyone down. That year at 'The X Factor' the producers sometimes had to stop me going to the studio all the time because I never wanted to leave. I was the only judge who said exactly what they thought with no notes written down for me. Even Simon joked, 'Go home, Melanie. You're showing us all up!' (And this from a man who regularly works till 3 a.m.).

—

Most of the time, getting up and working, and then spending time with my daughters, was enough to keep me going. But a few weeks into filming, I could feel I was starting to sink. I could feel the dark cloud of depression descending. I didn't want all the crap in my life to get in the way of the job I wanted to do, and knew I was doing really well. So, as insane as it may sound, my quick-fix answer was cocaine. The drug that fuelled '90s Britpop and that has been a bigger fixture in the record industry than Gibson guitars or iTunes. It took me less than a minute to get my hands on a regular supply – such is the power of celebrity. I started using a couple of lines before I went into work.

I had a routine. I'd wake up in the morning and snort two lines. Then I would pray: 'God, I'm sorry for taking cocaine, but please, God, help me get through this day.' I was ashamed of what I was doing, but I felt I had to have it. I told myself God would understand and forgive me because He could see through all the glitter and the crap. He could see me. The mess. And cocaine could help that mess. Just for now. It numbed my pain, it lifted me up enough to be ready to fire on all cylinders and forget everything but the show. Just for now. I promise.

Once I was at work on 'The X Factor', I didn't need anything and I didn't take anything. I'd crack jokes with Simon and the other judges, get to know my boys and have a laugh with the crew. But as soon as I left the building, it was like in 'Cinderella', where everything turns back to shit and rats and pumpkins. The black emotions I was holding off crashed right down on top of me like fat, heavy bricks. The cocaine would come back out of my bag and up into my nose. One line, another line, and yes, another and another. Just for now. I was, as Stephen delighted in telling me, 'a fucking mess'.

The truth was, I was kidding myself that I had found a magic formula for dealing with my life. The cocaine only made my depression worse, and I was permanently anxious and on edge. I was not in a good place mentally and emotionally, and at home in Kensington I was not in a good place physically. Stephen's preference was to have the curtains tightly closed at all times, to keep us from prying eyes. We were living in permanent darkness with no natural daylight, and I'm someone who loves – and needs – lots of light and air.

I don't need flowers, but I love flowers. I have to have flowers in my house now, not because they are beautiful but to remind me that I welcome the outside world in all its colour and beauty into my home. They make me feel happy. Stephen didn't like them because they go off, they drop petals, they make a mess, and they are unhygienic.

My mind began to play strange tricks on me. I began to fear the outside world. I had these weird, paranoid ideas in my head, telling me that everyone around me was selling stories about me. I felt I couldn't trust anyone at work and was suspicious of everyone I met. Stephen did nothing to disabuse me of these ideas. He was disdainful of my work: he'd refuse to watch the recorded shows on television, or he would talk loudly all the way through them while the girls and I were trying to watch. 'It's so boring,' he'd moan, turning up his rap music so none of us could hear.

Party invitations would sit unanswered because – apart from going to work – I felt I shouldn't leave the apartment without his approval. I didn't feel in a fit state. I worried that I would be a liability, that I was an idiot. I thought having his approval was for my own good. I had lost my grip on reality.

—

You start to believe that it is you who is the crazy one because all the time you feel you might be insane, you've got it all wrong, you don't know what you are doing, you don't know who to trust, who to like. You're the one who is responsible for being unhappy, for making him angry. You are the idiot, the slut, the bitch. It wasn't Stephen who upset Phoenix when she came home from school at the weekend and stayed in her room, it was you because she hated being around you. She told him that.

'You're an embarrassment to her,' he'd say. You'd believe it. The hug she gave you when she left to go back to school had felt too quick.

Cheryl hadn't responded to your text. You forgot that he checked your phone. You forgot that he deleted messages whenever he wanted to. You allowed yourself to be isolated, allowed him to make the rules. You didn't realize that you were stuck in some toxic game of control and that all that mind-bending manipulation had a purpose.

Psychologists refer to a technique to assert absolute control called 'gaslighting'. Is that what was happening to me? Many therapists believe it often results in nervous breakdowns and suicide attempts. Sometimes I would laugh at Stephen when he criticized me. I would laugh so I wouldn't cry. Then he'd leave the room and I'd find myself tidying cupboards, straightening sheets with tears streaming down my 'ugly' face. Other times I'd sit with my diary and write pages and pages of notes, and then hide my diary so he couldn't rip up my words or throw away my book.

3
CRAZY

—

I remember once sitting in that flat in Kensington, looking at a cheese sandwich and wondering to myself whether it was poisoned. Come on, Melanie, you've got to be crazy to think like that. That thought was even worse. Was I actually going mad? As a kid I used to build wobbly towers out of Black Grandad's dominoes on Black Grandma's swirly living-room carpet, and try to wait till they fell over (I was rarely patient; I used to knock them if they weren't quick enough). But there was – when I was patient enough – that one moment when you could see the wobble start, before the dramatic collapse when everything fell to pieces. That was how I felt most of the time, and I'd think the only way to deal with my situation was to have a glass of vodka or wine, or both, and then take more cocaine.

The cocaine only made my mental state worse because – as a lot of people know – cocaine makes you even more paranoid. I was probably taking five or six lines a day before and after work. Stephen knew what I was up to. 'How many lines have you done today? Tell me. I know you've been snorting that shit!' he'd yell. I wouldn't react to him. I'd shut the bedroom door and just sit there. If he dragged me out into the sitting room, I would stumble and slur my words. 'What's going on with you, Melanie?' he would rant. He would go through my things, and if he found a packet of powder in my bag, the rage would ramp up twenty notches: 'Are you insane? This will get you fired! Think about your image.' I was a sad pathetic person. I was out of control.

Stephen loved 'proof'. He'd pull out his phone and video me while asking me questions: 'Melanie, have you taken cocaine? Look at you, you are off your head.' He'd wait till I was at my worst and then once – in fact it was the day before I took the overdose – he pushed me in front of his computer and Skyped our family therapist, Dr Charles Sophy, telling him that I needed to be institutionalized. As well as being our therapist, Dr Sophy is the Medical Director for the County of Los Angeles Department of Children and Family Services, so he is in a position to have anyone at risk sectioned. 'Look at her,' Stephen would say. 'She's off her face. She's a disgrace, she needs serious help.' I did. Just not the sort of help Stephen meant.

As extreme as things were with Stephen, my messed-up state of mind wasn't entirely down to our relationship. My reasons for doing 'The X Factor' had been complicated and conflicted. Part of me hadn't wanted to do the show because it meant coming back to England, and part of me had wanted to do it for exactly those reasons. Being in England meant being right in the face of my family. Since marrying Stephen in 2007, my relationship with my mum, dad and younger sister Danielle had become completely toxic.

It's only since leaving Stephen that I've been able to reconnect with my family, to talk, to cry and to begin to heal that rift. It's only since leaving him that I've begun to realize that the problem I saw then as entirely my own issue was actually the result of being isolated from my friends and family. I didn't understand back then – because I didn't see any of it – that the best way to gain control over someone is to cut them off from the people they have known and trusted all their lives and cause maximum conflict with their loved ones.

After you come out of these situations, people all nod knowledgeably when you talk about being isolated, when you talk about subjects like gaslighting. The term was even used by lots of political commentators to describe the way Donald Trump (with whom, back in 2013, I co-hosted Miss Universe in Moscow and spent most of the evening trying to avoid him) denies stories and tells 'half-truths' to project his own version of events. I never knew about this stuff. I wish I had. I wish I had been in a position to nod in understanding rather than have to go through it to even know about these words and syndromes.

—

I remember, in fact, sitting in my bedroom in the rented house in Coldwater Canyon, Los Angeles, that my three daughters and I moved into when we left Stephen. A friend handed me a list of fifteen things to look out for as warning signs that a relationship might be controlling or abusive. I read it in shock. Step 3 was 'isolation'. I also felt I could relate to many of the others. This list is among the final pages of this book. I want you to look at it and show it to your friends. I want it to be read out to girls – and boys – at school. I don't want anyone else to have a story like mine.

The entire circle of people I trusted and relied on most in the world was decimated within a year and a half. My parents, my friends – even my gorgeous, smart personal assistant Janet Neale, who worked for me for five years when I moved out to LA – hated Stephen from the get-go. After a series of what my mum now describes as 'the most abusive, disgusting and terrifying' phone calls, he had successfully cut my parents out of our lives, making me feel like the best thing for me was to have no contact: no calls, no emails, nothing.

Then, when Phoenix was nine, my mum and dad contacted her dad, Jimmy Gulzar, to try to help him get custody. Child services were called in, and I had to watch as my kids were stripped and checked over. That broke my heart. I couldn't understand why my mum hadn't simply talked to me. Asked me to explain how I was steering my way through this mess. I would have flown her over to see how my kids were being protected, how my whole life revolved around keeping them happy. 'Because she doesn't care, she hates you,' Stephen would sneer. 'She prefers your lowlife ex-husband to you.' It became another battle, a legal battle to fight for my kids, me and him against them – the lines drawn. Me and Stephen against my family.

It is only now that I realize how deluded I was. Since leaving Stephen, this has been one of the most heart-breaking realizations of my journey. Children are not protected from the behaviour of their parents. Ever. My mum and dad knew that. They tried to do something about it, which at the time seemed the ultimate betrayal. They were stopped by my lawyers, and they were kept out of my life by my husband. I blamed them, they blamed me. I know now that none of my family could see beyond the wall of Stephen. My email addresses kept changing, we moved house every year, all my old employees and friends had fallen by the wayside. In their minds, I'd become as much of a monster as him – at least that's what I thought back then.

For all these reasons, part of me wanted them to see me on 'The X Factor', to see that I was still the same Melanie – 'It's me, look, Melanie' – and that my kids (my parents had never even met Madison and had last seen Angel as a baby and Phoenix as a nine-year-old) were gorgeous and happy, as they smiled alongside me from the covers of magazines like *Hello!* I was still the goofy girl they knew, the one who would say anything that came into her head, except now I was doing it on the telly. 'Melanie, don't forget your roots,' my dad would often say to me. I think of that now as I sit on the yellow sofa in my bedroom in Coldwater Canyon, which is all very over-the-top with a sky painted on the ceiling (it was decorated like this when I moved in and I've grown to like it). My roots were never forgotten; they just got buried under the weight of what I was living through.

Strangely enough, the first night I moved into this house I heard an owl. I first heard an owl in Leeds when I was fifteen, and I swear I would hear them every now and again up until I married Stephen. I think of the owl as my spirit animal (there are three owls on the coat of arms for the city of Leeds), and that owl in Coldwater Canyon has hooted at me every night since I moved away from Stephen and into this house. I also feel my dad's spirit here with me. I feel it so strongly that sometimes it makes me happy and sometimes it makes me cry because I miss him so much.

I always wanted my dad to be proud of me. 'Look at me, Dad. This is what I can do. And see how people love it' – those thoughts have always been in some subliminal part of my brain, whether I've been dancing with the Spice Girls or hosting 'Lip Sync Battle UK' or even performing a tap dance on an improvised stage in the Mandela Centre in Leeds. It's the thought that goes through the mind of so many people who make their living on the stage. The bottom line is we want to be loved. By everyone. But most of all by our mums and dads, and to show them that even if we didn't come top of the class at school, or live up to their idea of the perfect child, we'd done well for ourselves.

Back in 2014 when I was doing 'The X Factor', it had been so long since I'd heard my parents tell me they loved me or I'd been able to say it to them. It had all gone so wrong; being back in England made that so much more real. Part of me wanted them to see how so many other people actually liked me, so why couldn't they? All these mixed-up feelings I'd tried to keep at bay in LA were right in front of me in London.

—

It was in the midst of filming the London auditions that the production office at 'The X Factor' got a call from my sister, Danielle. They gave me her number and I called it straight away. 'I wanted you to know that Dad isn't doing well,' she said. I was completely silent, not knowing what to say, not knowing what she was going to say next. And then I heard the words: 'Melanie, he's dying. You need to come and see him.' I didn't answer or say anything coherent. A jumble of disconnected words flew out of my mouth, mainly, 'No, no, no.'

For the previous few years, Dad had been treated for multiple myeloma cancer. I knew that, but my dad was a strong guy. I never believed cancer could really get him. He was tough like me, a survivor; knock him down and he'd get up. I could feel the fight in him because it's the same fight that is in me. Every now and again when I could, I would call his doctors in Leeds to check on him, but they would always tell me he was coping well. Sometimes – because my relations with my family had got so bad – I wasn't allowed to call and speak to the doctors. There was a pass-code for family and it took me months to find out what it was. It was 'Phoenix'. The fact that Dad had used my daughter's name as his code meant a huge deal to me. It meant there was still hope, still a bond. Still family. I needed to fix things before it was too late. And I needed to do it when Stephen was in LA so he couldn't try to stop me or come with me and ruin things. In a massive panic, I left the auditions and drove up to Leeds.

After four hours of driving, I arrived outside Dad's house. The house in Kirkstall that I'd grown up in, the same one he refused to leave when I bought my parents a beautiful house in an upmarket area of Horsforth. I sat in my car outside the house for a few minutes. I looked a complete mess because I had been crying all the way up the motorway, going through speeches in my head, imagining the worst scenes awaiting me. Outside the house there were no other cars. Just mine. I looked at this pile of bricks and mortar as familiar to me as my own features, and through the curtains I saw a shadowy figure. It was my dad. He peered through the curtains, he saw me, and then he disappeared and I saw the front door open. I was shaking as I got out of the car; my emotions were all over the place. I felt so happy that I was going to see him but distraught at what I was going to be faced with.

I walked to the door. Dad was standing in the hall. In his hand was a can of Special Brew, which he lifted to his mouth and gulped at as I walked in. 'Special Brew. What the hell …' went through my head. It was the last thing I expected to see. I'd been picturing him at death's door, weak and fragile, not knocking back a can of beer. The first words that came out of my mouth after years of not speaking, after years of lying awake at night imagining the day we would be reconciled, were, 'Dad. What the hell are you doing drinking?' I blurted them out because the thought was pinging round my head in shock. As I heard them fall from my lips, I knew I'd blown it. I should have hugged him and kept my mouth shut. I knew him well enough to know how riled he'd be, how he'd take it as me coming in and criticizing him.

The atmosphere – after years of no communication – was tense enough. Now it was like I had chucked a lit match into a room filled with petrol. My dad had not forgiven me because five years previously I'd made a documentary in Leeds. I'd been filming a few streets away from him and hadn't gone to see him once. Now he wanted to know why. I garbled something but it wasn't right. I didn't know what to say. 'Because I'm a fucking idiot,' I should have said. 'I love you,' I should have said. 'And I'm sorry.' In the end it was all the wrong words.

My dad started shouting at me. 'Melanie! Mind your own business! Go home. I don't want you here.' He kept ranting, saying that I'd forgotten who I was and that he never wanted to see me again. I couldn't take those words back or turn back the clock, and it just went from bad to worse. He literally pushed me out of his house – the house where, after he died in March 2017, my sister, Danielle, found his dozens of scrapbooks with almost every magazine article I'd ever done, pictures of all my children, even cuttings from posh women's magazines like *Grazia* and *Glamour* that I can't imagine him standing in a newsagent's and buying. There were even – on the kitchen wall – scribbled messages from me, Geri, Emma, Mel C and Vic when I'd dragged them up in the early days of the Spice Girls to meet my dad. He'd repainted his kitchen, but he'd painted around those messy scrawls. I cried all the way back to London. Everything I really cared about was a mess, and I didn't know how to make it better.

—

All of these emotions had been swirling around me for months, but now in this Kensington bathroom I had to get control of myself. I couldn't let myself go under. I had to believe things could get better. I couldn't do it to my girls, my family or all those people who actually believed in me. I looked in the mirror and said, 'No.' Suicide was not the answer. I had to make my life count. I had to get to a hospital. I had to get those pills out of my stomach before anything happened.

It was like being shocked out of a trance. Actually, I felt weirdly calm, as if I'd finally taken control of myself and I was going to be all right. I thought I could hear Stephen on the other side of the door, in the bedroom. I looked at myself in the mirror. I looked weird. I was wearing pyjamas and no makeup, and I was kneading my hands together trying to compose myself as much as possible. In a very clear, calm voice that sounded to me like a teacher talking to a child, I said, 'Stephen, I've done something stupid and I need you to help me. I've taken a massive overdose of pills.'

My head was spinning. All I thought was that I needed to get out of the room but for some reason the door was jammed. I can't clearly remember what happened next but I remember throwing myself at the door, crashing my full weight (at the time I weighed around 110 lbs) against it. I felt like a trapped animal. I was so confused. Why wasn't it opening? Why couldn't I get out? I knew I needed to get my stomach pumped and I could picture myself in a hospital bed. Safe. But I wasn't safe, I was stuck in this bathroom flailing around in complete confusion. My mind wasn't working properly, I didn't know if words were coming out of my mouth or whether I was hearing voices in my head. I couldn't feel my hands, my arms and my grip on reality was going. I was telling myself to shout to get help and not to shout because I didn't want to wake up Angel and Madison who were asleep in their beds a few hundred yards away. 'Maybe this is it', I told myself. 'Maybe I'm never going to get out of here.'

Those bruises on my face and shoulder everyone saw on television at the 'X Factor' final three days later – most of them were caused by those moments trapped in that doorway. I can't remember the pain but I can still remember the fear, the panic and the absolute confusion in my head.

Then everything started to go black and I collapsed to my knees. I could feel the life in me starting to drain away. I kept trying to get up and I could hear my own voice sounding strange and blurry. I remember scrabbling for my phone and talking to people, but I couldn't remember who – feeling myself not thinking straight, not remembering the number for emergency services. 'Is it 911?' went round and round in my head.

I heard another man's voice in the other room. (I later found out that it was Chris Little, my security guy for the London run of 'The X Factor'.)

And then nothing, silence. I lay semi-conscious on the bathroom floor and, with tears streaming down my face, drifting in and out of consciousness, waited to die.

—

It was only three years later that I found out the full events of that night. As I can only remember the haziest details, I'm going to let Randy, my hairdresser at the time, tell it in his own words …

RANDY'S STORY

It was about 1 a.m. on Friday morning. I was asleep in bed in my hotel in Kensington.

My mobile went. I picked it up and heard Melanie's voice saying, 'Randy, Chris,' (her security guy), and then the line went dead. She sounded very strange. I called her back, but she didn't pick up. Straightaway I called Chris, who was already on his way over to her apartment.

Half an hour later, she called me again. She was sounding really blurry. She said, 'Randy, I took a bunch of pills. I need it to stop.' I knew she was talking about Stephen even though – as close as we were – she never actually talked about how bad it was with him.

Then she told me she was going to lie down with her kids till she died. She wasn't making much sense. I could hear Chris in the background. I could hear the word *ambulance*. But again the line went flat.

I ran over to her place. When I rang the buzzer downstairs, Stephen appeared. He was cool as a cucumber. He was smiling as he opened the door, like he couldn't believe there was any reason for me to be standing there on his doorstep in the middle of the night.

I thought something was wrong. But I knew Chris was there and he'd look out for Melanie. Stephen was super-calm, so I thought I'd go home and see her in a few hours. There was no way he was going to let me push past him so I left.

At 7.30 a.m. I went back to the apartment. Melanie buzzed me in, which was a relief. But when I walked in and saw her, I was shocked beyond belief. She was slumped like a broken doll in a pile of clothes in the middle of the hall. The kids and the nanny had all left for school. Stephen was in the bedroom with the door shut.

I grabbed her under her arms and dragged her into Phoenix's bedroom. She was groaning, telling me she'd taken an overdose, and that all the pills were still inside her. Everything she was saying was jumbled, but I knew it was bad. I had to get her out of there as fast as possible without alerting Stephen that I thought anything was wrong.

I pushed Melanie into the shower and she keeled over. I dragged her out, wrapped her in a towel, picked her up and lay her on the bed. Then Stephen walked in and looked at her. She was curled up in the foetal position, moaning to herself. Then the most bizarre thing happened. Stephen put on this sweet voice – not the way I normally heard him speak – and said, 'Cuddle me, babe,' got on the bed and started spooning her from behind as if this was the most normal situation in the world and his wife wasn't looking half-dead. I went cold as I watched him kiss the back of her head.

It was mad, but now I was on a countdown to get Melanie out of the house, in a car and on her way to a hospital. There were photographers outside, so apart from getting past Stephen, we had to get past them without causing a media storm. I had to keep everything calm.

I picked out a black, floor-length Versace dress, pulled Melanie into it, found her mobile phone in the bathroom, and then took her into the kitchen and sat her on a stool. When the makeup girl arrived (I'd tried to call her to stop her coming but couldn't get through), she looked at me and said, 'I hope she hasn't taken an overdose.' I shook my head and told her that Melanie was just feeling very unwell.

I got a fur coat, put it on her and half-dragged her out of the apartment. When we got outside, I said, 'Melanie, there are photographers here.' Miraculously, she jolted upright and managed to walk to the car. Once inside it, she lost consciousness.

I told the driver to take us straight to the hospital and I was shaking

Melanie awake, talking to her all the time. Chris, Mel's security, had called a private hospital – the Clementine Churchill in Harrow, London – so we could keep the situation as quiet as possible. Once we got there, the doctor asked her how many pills she'd taken. She lay there in her Versace dress and fur coat and said, 'Two hundred,' like some Hollywood movie star.

It was completely insane. The doctor looked stunned and said she'd have to be put in an ambulance and go straight to A&E. It was too critical an emergency for them to handle.

I got into the ambulance with her. I knew then that she could have died because the doctors had said 200 pills was a matter of life or death. She was lying there, groaning and crying. Even in the middle of this, she wanted me to put a blanket over her face when she was taken out of the ambulance so she wouldn't be recognized.

In the hospital – Northwick Park NHS – you could see these doctors looking completely shocked when they saw her – Mel B, covered in bruises and delirious from all those pills. Unbelievably, she then started making calls to Simon Cowell, in between having tubes stuck down her throat and vomiting up her insides. She was telling him that she was sorry, but she didn't think she could make it into work, and the nurses were running around getting ready to do a total blood transfusion because of the damage she'd caused by having those pills inside her for so long.

The only thing I knew for sure was that I wasn't going to leave her side in that hospital.

—

It's weird, the bits you remember. I remember hearing the words 'Get up. You have to go to work.' I remember Randy being there and the strange, charged atmosphere in the apartment as he got me ready. It was all quiet.

Even through my disconnected, drugged-up fog, I knew no-one would say anything out loud. Up until that point, I'd never said anything to anyone – apart from that one desperate outburst to Simon Jones. I'd told Simon because I'd got to know him well. He is the sort of man who doesn't judge, who isn't shocked (he represents some of the biggest celebrities on British television) and who is incredibly kind, clever and practical.

Women living with abuse are used to creating a conspiracy of silence. With emotional abuse you often don't even realize you are being abused: it is a sneaking cycle, and, by the time you do realize, you have lost your confidence to such a degree that all you feel is that you are the mess. And abuse thrives in silence like a cancer. Everyone guesses what's going on, but if you don't say anything, no-one can know for sure. No-one likes being around someone screaming abuse at their partner or seeing them put down again and again, but no-one says anything because they are embarrassed, for themselves, for you, for witnessing something no-one should ever see.

I remember getting to the hospital and calling Simon Cowell (there have always been a lot of Simons in my life!). I remember he didn't sound horrified, just calm like he knew that's what I needed from him. Not more drama. He said very quietly, 'I didn't think it was this bad, Melanie. Take your time. Come back when you are ready. Tell me if there's anything you need.'

I also remember the nurse having to stab me so many times in my arms because my veins are so bad and they were trying desperately to get the IVs in. She gently told me that she needed to focus on getting me stable (Good luck with that! I thought). I was screaming and screaming because I wasn't going to be silent anymore. I could feel my panic. I could hear my noise. I could see the looks of concern around me from kind strangers in medical scrubs and uniforms. It felt both very real and completely surreal. Everyone knows now, I thought.

I must have lost consciousness again. When I woke up, I was surrounded by doctors and nurses, and Randy was there too. Again I was flashing back to me at fourteen. Then I'd come round to find my teachers standing and talking at the end of my hospital bed. The only words I remembered hearing back then – as I'd been rushed into an ambulance by my mum and the paramedics – was my dad screaming, 'Get her out of the house. She's insane. Don't let her come back until she's normal.'

Normal. Who the hell is normal? What the hell does *normal* even mean? If I was 'normal', maybe I would never have left home halfway through my GCSEs to get a job dancing at a summer show in Blackpool. I wouldn't have auditioned for anything I could find (including *The Sound Of Music* at Leeds Grand Theatre, even after my mum tried to tell me they'd never give me a part because I was the 'wrong colour' for a member of the very Aryan Von Trapp family living in Nazi-threatened Austria. My response was, 'You never know, though.'). And I wouldn't have got on a National Express bus to London, to audition for an ad my mum spotted in *The Stage*. 'RU 18–23 with the ability to sing and dance? RU streetwise, outgoing, ambitious, dedicated?' Hell yes. That was me.

'Normal' didn't figure. Being 'normal' would never have got me to become a Spice Girl. If I was 'normal', maybe I'd have married my first boyfriend (he was also called Stephen) and stayed in Leeds, and none of this, good and bad, would have ever happened.

4
SORRY

—

'Mom. What the hell?' Phoenix was standing by my bed. Furious, shaking, full of rage. Of all the memories from all those hours, it is the one that still floors me. There are things I can't remember, things I have blanked out and then things I remember so clearly it's like a knife through my heart.

Broken. My tough, loyal, beautiful girl crying and asking me why in hell was I going to leave her and her two little sisters. 'Why?' is the only word she said between her sobs. 'Why, Mum? Why? Why?' It was the saddest moment of my life. It will always live with me. All I ever want is for her to know how sorry I am, how lost I was and how I will never, ever abandon her again.

What does a mother say to a daughter? How do you explain, how do you apologize, how do you make them realize that it was nothing to do with them, that your mind was so far gone you weren't thinking straight? No mirror I ever looked in reflected me back like Phoenix did in that moment. I saw myself through her eyes and I knew I had to get myself together. I had to get her and my girls out. I had to be the woman and the mother she deserved.

I don't think I actually said any of those words. I don't even think those words had formed in my head. I kept telling her over and over again, 'I'm sorry.'

Sorry. It's a word that never quite cuts it, no matter how loud you say it (and you know how loud I can be). It's too small. But it's the only one I had. When I think about it now, all these years later, I can't quite believe my daughter had to face seeing me like that. It's something I have to live with and something I will keep on saying sorry for.

Sorry. Sorry. Sorry.

The mask I thought I'd so carefully constructed had fallen and shattered in front of my daughter. Who was I kidding? My daughter had never been fooled by any mask. But she had been fooled into believing I was strong enough to cope. 'It'll be okay,' I always said when she caught me crying in my room. 'We'll be okay. I'm going to sort it out.' Well, it wasn't, and I hadn't. And now my daughter was shattered into pieces in front of me.

I genuinely believed I had always tried so hard to protect my kids from the rows, from the fights. 'Let's take this upstairs,' I'd say as calmly as I could when the shouting started, and I would see the children's eyes go wide or, more worryingly, their little, innocent faces freeze.

When a relationship is out of control, you are a fool to think it just affects the two of you. It's like hurling a rock into a lake – the ripples go on forever. And the emotional fallout affects your kids, your family, your friends, your colleagues – even the waiter who serves you in a restaurant and the man who looks at you in a hotel. If tensions are running high, that waiter will have his evening ruined and his nerves shredded, and that poor unfortunate man might end up in hospital. I am speaking from experience.

If you're in it, you don't see it. Horrible events happen time after time and you see no connection other than 'I can't believe this is happening.' Violent things. There is, there always is, trouble simmering between the two of you, but you remember it wasn't always like this. Back in the early days, you'd go out and you'd both laugh and he would tell you, 'You look great.' And maybe you want to get some of those moments back because somewhere inside you wish that everything would change and he would tell you he was sorry and that he loved you and then you could fix things, make them work … And you could be happy.

—

So one night you are in a beautiful, sophisticated place where the two of you are very lucky to be, such as The May Fair Hotel in London in October 2010. 'Let's have a nice night, have a drink at the bar,' you say. You sit in the luxurious leather chairs and you have cocktails. This is so sophisticated, you think, because you are still a girl from a council estate in Leeds and this is a stunning five-star hotel dating back to the 1920s where royalty have stayed, as well as the likes of Rod Stewart, Michael Jackson, Aerosmith and the Rolling Stones. There's the quiet buzz you get in posh places like that: people enjoying themselves, behaving themselves, wearing their best outfits, trying not to wince at the prices of the drinks.

A group of guys walks past and looks at you. So what. You're a Spice Girl; you've grown up with people pointing, staring, asking for autographs. You know what you should do is smile, because you know it also makes people happy. It's so easy. A quick nod and a smile. You wouldn't be sitting here if it wasn't for other people buying your records, watching you on television. It's a smile. They feel acknowledged and they move on.

Except they don't, they carry on looking, laughing. And you can't do that little smile or nod because you worry that it is going to cause a problem with him. You don't want that. But the men are still there. You know what is going to happen. Your head is bowed and your hands are sweating because you can hear across the small, polished wooden table his breath coming faster and faster. 'Don't do anything, please,' you whisper to yourself, thinking faster and faster about what to do. But nothing is coming out of your brain. And then it happens. Bang! Screaming, shouting. Your husband is up, and then he is on the floor brawling with the two men. One gets up, but the other man is still on the floor, and he is being punched again and again. Blood is pouring from the man's head, and two other men are shouting, pulling him away.

No, this is not happening – this thought is flashing like a siren in your brain. It is your worst nightmare. There's a rushing sound in your head, and you want the ground to swallow you up. You can't look up because you will see all those other people in the bar who were enjoying their drinks – you know what the look on their faces will be now. And you know they will be thinking, 'Oh my God, isn't that Mel B?' And you can't get the sound of the punches out of your head, and a horrible noise which sounded like it could be the flat crunch of a broken bone. You wonder if that man has a wife, a girlfriend, a child, and you have to stop yourself thinking about it because you are going to start crying.

You don't want anyone to know you live like this. You see someone take a photograph. Stephen's sweatshirt has been ripped from his massive, barrel of a chest and he is up, panting and pacing in the bar as staff (you can see one barman looking terrified) ask you to leave. The man with the blood pouring from his head is taken to hospital and now you know he is going to make you call your lawyers and those lawyers are going to have to stop charges being brought (they did).

I felt I had no choice but to defend Stephen. In a press statement, I claimed that he had been rushing to defend my honour. I can't say what happened in our room later that night, but in the early hours of the morning I rang a friend in north London. I hadn't spoken to her for years as she was one of the many who had been dropped when Stephen had come along. She was never one to mince her words. I remember gushing to her years earlier about this guy I'd met, how great he was, and her asking me a couple of questions. Then, bluntly, she had said to me, 'Belafonte. But he's no relation to Harry Belafonte. Why would he pick that name? Melanie, you can't take this guy seriously.' A serious businesswoman, she had seen through the LA bullshit in a second. I hadn't listened.

Now she was listening to me. I was conscious that I was making no sense, just crying hysterically down the phone. 'Melanie. Stop,' she said. 'Get in a cab and come to me.' I snuck out of our hotel room. I was too mortified after what had happened to ask anyone on the door to get me a taxi, so I ran outside onto the street and hailed a black cab. When I arrived, my friend said nothing. She gave me a clean nightdress and put me into bed, next to her. Her poor husband slept on the couch downstairs.

When I woke up, the house was empty because they had both left for work. I sat for a moment, soaking up the quiet domesticity of their home, with kids' books and toys scattered around the living room. It looked so peaceful, so happy. I could see little notes scrawled on the fridge, 'Milk and eggs' and 'Remember, I'm out Thursday'. We didn't have notes like that. I couldn't remember the last time I'd bought milk. I looked at my phone. 'Where are you?' 'Call the lawyers' flashed up, amid the dozens of messages from Stephen.

I wanted to stay in that quiet house, but I knew that eventually I would have to leave. Stephen would find me. It felt like he always knew where I was, and I didn't want my friend's serene family nest to be sullied by our family drama. I let myself out. It was a long time before I spoke to her again. After all, what do you say? 'I know you hate him and I really scared you, but … ' It wasn't exactly a surprise to her.

'I hoped you would be there when I got back,' she told me eight years later. 'But I think I knew you wouldn't be. I felt he had an absolute grip on you.'

My abusive relationship with Stephen was like a drop of black dye in water, colouring everything. Spoiling everything.

—

We lived in several different houses in Los Angeles – five in total – when we were married, and nearly every one of them was arranged over several levels. We would always be on the top floor, while the children would always be on the basement level, with at least one floor in between. Why? So they didn't hear the vile, vile words coming out of both our mouths.

Our therapist Dr Sophy later told me that he observed that I had two modes of dealing with Stephen: 'Mostly you would say very little and just nod, and that worried me. But sometimes you would go right back at him and challenge him, and that actually terrified me. I always wondered where it would end.' I picked up a lot of his tricks and his way of speaking – with full on relentless aggression – especially if I was drinking.

'No-one likes you and you know it,' I'd shout after his worst rants. 'They think you are scum.' I could see him flinch, so I'd carry on telling him what I thought until his mouth turned into a machine gun firing insults like bullets. Those times were open warfare. But I thought if we were in our room, the children wouldn't witness it. I was keeping our dirty secret from them, from the world, from everyone.

But Phoenix would hear me crying. She tells me now that she would stand at the bottom of the stairs that led up to my bedroom and listen to me fighting. Then she would wait for Stephen to leave and she would listen to me crying. She wouldn't move, just listen in silence, twisting herself into knots, not knowing what to do, who to tell. I was her mother, her famous mother, who was on the telly – this strong woman admired by other women, whose guard never came down. Only she had a glimpse – in those moments – of how desperately miserable I was.

In my hospital room in Harrow there was no more pretence. Things were so bad I'd tried to kill myself. Phoenix could join the dots; she could see those threads of desperation and misery, but she was too young, too helpless, too damaged by constant rows with her stepfather to know what to do. And I was too broken.

I – the mother who was meant to protect her – promised her I was going to make it right. That as tough as it was to be in this situation, for me and her to be like this, it was reality and we had to deal with it. I hated that she had to see it, but it was going to make us both learn. Years of words never spoken between us tumbled out in that room –

many of them incoherent, many of them drowned out by her cries. I told her I would never leave her, that I never wanted her to make the choices I'd made, to be with a man like Stephen, to take cocaine, to become weak and powerless. I told her I loved her. I hoped she was listening to me.

Even now, I can't really think back to that moment. It wasn't like something out of a movie with meaningful speeches and perfectly choreographed embraces. It was a mess. Phoenix didn't want to hear it. She'd heard enough. She'd seen enough. She was a kid, she had no control. Her mother had brought this man into her life. And now she'd found out that I had tried to check out by throwing a bunch of pills down my throat, leaving her and her sisters with him?

'Just go away,' she yelled. 'I don't want to be here. I can't listen to you.' I remember her tears, my tears, her screams and accusations as she went running out of the room, and me ripping the IVs out of my arms with blood spurting everywhere so I could go and find her, hold her. 'What are you doing, what are you doing?' she was screaming at me, terrified by the blood, terrified her mother had lost the plot completely.

It was – and still is – unbearable to me. But as painful as it was, looking at my daughter – distraught, devastated, angry – was the moment I knew the fight back had to start.

5
WONDER WOMAN

—

I'd like to say that suddenly I was completely transformed – like Wonder Woman – filled with immediate strength and power. That I leapt from my bed with confidence and a fully formed plan.

I didn't. And if you want to know how I felt back then, it was the scandal of the moment. The mother who had seen her daughter fall apart in front of her eyes. The woman with everything and nothing who had tried to kill herself. I felt ashamed, humiliated, petrified, guilty and isolated. You want to know what I did? I cried. Cried and cried. Buckets of tears.

There's a lesson we all learn. Huge, dramatic things happen in your life and the world does not stop. It carries on. I had my children to deal with, a decision to make about my marriage, and calls coming in from Geri, Emma, Vic and Mel C, asking, 'Are you okay?' My mother who had received a panicked call from Stephen was also trying to track me down. 'It was the first time he'd spoken to me in seven years without screaming abuse. He told me he would agree for me to be back in your life. I knew if he was saying that, then there was something seriously wrong. So I was even more terrified than usual,' she told me a few months ago.

Meanwhile, the 'X Factor' juggernaut was in full throttle with the finals looming. Simon Jones went over and above his duty as a PR. He sat by my bed in intensive care every single day. He fended off endless abusive calls from Stephen. 'I'm blaming you for this,' Stephen screamed down the phone at him. Obviously my husband was taking none of the blame. And on a daily basis Simon Cowell was sending people to see me or talk to me, to check that I was going to be okay.

A few days after I took my overdose at the age of fourteen, I was back in Intake High School in my regulation navy blue V-neck jumper and being bollocked for not finishing my maths homework. Like I didn't have a good reason! At home, it was Dad's oxtail soup for dinner, 'Coronation Street' on the telly, and my mum rushing about and complaining about her job as a shop assistant at the high-street store C&A, which – like so many of the great old department stores – no longer exists. 'We've got this new girl who made a right mess of the bras,' she'd tell me. 'I had to spend two hours putting it right.' The stomach pump, the terrified faces, the drama of the ambulance all faded to nothing.

Things happen and life moves on.

——

When Geri left the Spice Girls in 1988, in the middle of a European tour, we had no idea why. We had no idea where she was; none of us knew what the hell was going on. But we carried on – we did 'The National Lottery' show and simply pretended that she was ill and then went on to do two shows in Norway. I remember thinking every time I turned around she'd appear behind me, stomping in her platform boots, geeing the crowd up as she waved her hands in the air, or doing something funny and cheeky like flashing her knickers as she left the stage. But she didn't. I used to lie in bed unable to sleep, sad and confused, trying to work out why the hell she'd left us and why she'd never told me. The two of us were so close. From the first moment I saw her, Geri was always my girl.

She'd left shortly before my birthday on 29 May. She said goodbye after we got off a plane at Heathrow. Emma said later that she thought it was weird that Geri had said goodbye because none of us ever said that to each other. We worked nonstop, we were together 24/7, so we never said goodbye. Even when we landed back in Britain, we all scattered to our separate homes, but we'd be seeing each other first thing in the morning because we had a show to do – 'The National Lottery'.

Except we didn't. Geri didn't turn up; she didn't do the show; she didn't answer her phone. Then there was no contact for nearly a week until our lawyer, Andrew Thomson, called us to say she wasn't coming back. That really hurt – all four of us were devastated. We couldn't get hold of her. She didn't call us. All our messages went unanswered. 'Geri, where the fuck are you?' I ended up screaming down the phone after endless voicemails were ignored. I wrote her a letter. We asked her mum to get her to call us. Nothing.

I understand it now. She was having massive problems. Her eating disorder – which she has since very bravely and openly discussed – was out of control. This was something I was completely oblivious to; it made me feel so awful when I finally found out. She was depressed, she was anxious, and she was keeping it all secret – and the pressure was too much. She couldn't cope anymore, and, as much as she loved us, she couldn't face telling us what was going on. She retreated and cut herself off.

It was what Geri needed to do. I was so upset. Then I got so angry it took me years to get over it. 'Why didn't she tell me?' were the words that kept going round and round in my head. 'Why didn't she say?' The funny thing is, I get it now. Completely. I know that place she was in, and I know I don't want any woman to ever feel she is alone. We make ourselves feel ashamed of so many things, and the silence and the secrecy just add to our burdens.

It's hard – when you are proud, when you are frightened, when there are expectations on you to not rock the boat – but we need to be able to say, 'I'm in trouble. I need help.'

Like me in my hospital room in the full whirlwind of 'The X Factor', we remaining Spice Girls didn't have time think about Geri. We didn't have time to stop and to ask ourselves whether she might have a problem (thank God, the stigma of mental-health issues is so reduced these days and so much more acceptable to talk about) because her quitting kicked off a hundred urgent meetings we had to deal with instantly. Our fans were distraught, the press was going crazy. We had to scrap a live album. A recording of 'Never Give Up On The Good Times' (the irony does make me laugh now, even if it didn't at the time) had to be ditched and an American tour somehow salvaged.

Our personal drama and the loss of my mad, scatty, beautiful wing girl had serious financial implications. Geri told me years later that Prince Charles wrote her a letter saying the band would never be the same without her. More importantly for our management team, the share price of our record company, EMI, dropped by 10p as a direct result of Geri leaving the Spice Girls.

—

That's serious stuff. My job is in show business. It's two words. *Show* and *business*. 'It's show business, not friends' business,' as an agent I know always says. You can't keep on crying or break down, even if you want to. You can't pause for breath. The show must go on. Or you must get out.

My responsibility is to keep the 'show' going so that the money men, the managers and the producers can keep the 'business' going. It's the way it works, and I completely understand that's the deal. Whoever you are, whatever you do, the world doesn't stop. If you have to work as a welder like my dad, or in a department store like my mum, you need to turn up, clock in and keep on going as the world keeps on turning.

So in between those tears, in between the chilling realisation of a hundred different emotions no longer buried behind a cloud of cocaine or denial, in between my anxieties over my children, I had to deal with the reality of the show – my job on 'The X Factor' and my position as a woman in the public eye. The situation with 'The X Factor' was quickly sorted because it had to be – the show's semi-finals were going to be shown live in two days' time. Simon Jones explained to the then-executive producer, Richard Holloway that I wasn't well and that Tulisa Contostavlos would cover for me on the Saturday night and be on stand-by for the Sunday-night final.

As rumours were flying left, right and centre about me, Simon initially fended off questions by saying that it was a private medical matter: the law prevents newspapers from printing medical information. So I had some breathing space. I know for a fact that various journalists were aware of the truth, but I also knew no-one would be able to print anything without absolute confirmation. Laura Armstrong from *The Sun* contacted Simon. Clearly she had very good sources, even down to the fact that I was being treated for a stomach ulcer, which was the one thing we agreed to allow her to run as the ulcer was one of the (many) concerns the doctors had.

I have never and will never moan about how difficult it is being a celebrity, how hard it is to keep things private and how upsetting it is when journalists write bad or false things about you. It's part of the job. Their job. My job. Part of the show. I've had terrible things written about me and I've had lovely things written about me. I've tried never to let either change me. I've always tried to be myself, know my own truth (good and bad) and be as honest as I can be.

So was it honest for me to blame everything on a stomach ulcer? No, it wasn't. But the aim was to protect the show, to protect me and to not destabilize the four finalists on the show (including my lovely, gentle Andrea Faustini) who were battling to win fame and fortune. Right at that moment, no-one knew exactly what had happened because

I hadn't actually explained everything to anyone. I was in so much pain and on so much medication, I was incapable of remembering everything that had happened, and I was still not ready to really talk about my problems.

There were certain extremely sharp journalists, such as Will Payne and Dan Wootton from *The Sun*, who knew there was much more going on than a stomach ulcer. They had contacts everywhere, and rumours about my overdose were leaking like the blood that was seeping from my IV cuts (ripping tubes out of your arms is never a good idea). Simon was in full fire-fighting mode, with his mobile beeping every minute. He kept assuring me that everything would be okay and that I would be protected. Oddly, I almost didn't care. Now some people knew what was going on, I felt – amid all the other emotions – a bit of relief.

Fame and fortune do not – I can assure you – guarantee a happy-ever-after ending. During that period there were many moments when I would have swapped places with anyone. I did want the world to stop. It continued to spin. I wanted my daughters Angel and Madison with me in the hospital. I wanted to turn back time and hold them close. They'd been told – by Phoenix and by Randy – that 'Mummy has a bad tummy'. Another story, but only to protect them.

Stephen had been calling me constantly, but I blocked him. Chris would not take his calls either, and Simon Jones refused to tell him where I was, despite his increasingly aggressive threats. It felt incredible to know he couldn't get near me. I wanted Chris to bring the girls to me. But when he went to get them, they had disappeared from the Kensington apartment. It was only after several frantic calls to Stephen's personal assistant that I was told that they had gone to Germany to stay with family friends. What the hell? Distraught, I insisted they return to Britain. After more phone calls, I got a text saying they were on their way back.

'Melanie, your blood pressure is still going up. You need to rest,' said one of my lovely, motherly nurses. That was never going to happen. Despite all the drugs I was being given, I was wired. The doctors kept telling me that I was in the High Dependency Unit and was seriously ill. I needed to get well. I was used to being in pain, I was used to running on empty, so I barely noticed any difference. I'd been living for years with my fight-or-flight reflexes on permanent alert. It's exhausting. It's another one of the many, many reasons I got used to drinking so heavily

But I couldn't think about switching off now. When the nurses left the room, I was on the phone constantly – to Stephen's assistant, to the 'X Factor' producers, to Phoenix, to Simon Cowell's team, to my poor contestant, Andrea, who got voted off in the semi-final on the Saturday night I missed.

I felt sad that I hadn't been there for Andrea. I would look out of the window near my bed and tell myself things might be okay. But I couldn't stop a nervous, creeping feeling in my stomach that I had made an even bigger mess, and that the strands of my life I was pulling at were unravelling fast like loose bits of wool.

If you think I was surrounded by friends, relatives, other concerned celebrities and flowers, you would be wrong. Thanks to my relationship with Stephen, I was pretty much on my own apart from my security, my hairdresser and Simon my publicist. They were my ring of steel, all of them on my payroll. Every one of the Spice Girls tried to contact me through my driver – who had driven us all in our Girl Power days. I couldn't speak to them. I wasn't ready, and I was too ashamed. Only a week earlier, I'd made a huge fuss about a massive diamond wedding ring Stephen had got me from Leon Diamond in New York. It had cost about £20,000. 'He upgrades my wedding ring every year,' I'd boasted to Cheryl. 'Isn't he the best?' I'd grinned as I showed it off to Simon Hattenstone from *The Guardian*. 'He's the love of my life.' What a pathetic liar. My money had paid for the ring, and to me it was a constantly sparkling sign of my own misery.

My family had also managed to track me down, but they were the last people I wanted to see. After the hugs and the tears, it would have been 'You shouldn't have ever married him, Melanie. What have you done?' I didn't want to hear that. I couldn't face anyone. I couldn't face the questions, the grief, the disappointment, the pressure to explain something you can't explain. I totally understood why when Geri had left, all those years before, she had wanted to disappear. Animals hide to lick their wounds. So do we. If you are someone like me, you can hide better because you have people answering phones for you, you have a network in place, a system to make it easier.

I remained trapped behind a wall of guilt, shame and worthlessness. I'd been hit in the past, but bruises fade. If you feel emotionally abused – whether it's a partner, a boss or even a parent – you can't see any scars, but they go way deeper, right down to your very sense of self. I felt empty, worthless. I'd loved Stephen. I wanted him to love me. There must be a reason why these men never loved me – and that reason must be me, I told myself.

Those feelings of worthlessness don't disappear. They stick with you like a filthy stain you can't get rid of. You can be absolutely fine, happy, and then you feel it knock you off balance, clouding everything. I would look in the mirror and see an 'ugly old tramp'. You think of your kids and then you think of some of the things you have done. Disgusting things.

And it's strange what goes unsaid. What is seen and not seen. Chris told me later that he had never witnessed any man speak to a woman the way Stephen talked to me. 'Ugly', 'Slut', 'Fat', 'Stupid', 'Bitch', 'Worthless', 'Drunk', 'Pathetic', 'Monkey', 'Derelict'. They'd become just words said so many times to me that I would absorb them like a sponge. His behaviour towards me affected everyone. Chris – an experienced and élite security operator – took it upon himself to try to protect me, emotionally as well as physically. It wasn't his job, but he felt compelled to look out for me. In front of him, Stephen would say those words with a smile on his face. He'd act exasperated or make a joke about how useless I was. Chris wasn't fooled. No-one was. Not Chris, nor Simon Cowell, Sharon Osbourne, Heidi Klum, Geri, Vic, Emma or Mel C, nor even the runners or the drivers.

'Why do you let him speak to you like that?' Chris had asked me one day before the drama of my overdose. I was embarrassed he'd asked me. No-one ever asked. I didn't answer. He didn't ask again. I didn't like to think a man was treating me like dirt. I would argue back sometimes, and in front of other people I would try to laugh it off. 'He comes from New Jersey,' I'd say, trying not to acknowledge that my friends looked horrified by his language and aggressive tone of voice. I'd add my usual outrageous Mel B-persona comment. 'And he's great in bed. He's even more insatiable than I am. Our sex life is amazing.' That always shut everybody up. And I needed to make everyone shut up because I didn't want to give the answer: 'He hates me because I'm nothing.'

6
FROG
—

Stephen would say if you wanted to kill a frog, you heated the water very slowly and then the frog would never realize that it was being boiled.

I was a frog. It happened very slowly. Stephen knew, when I met him in 2007, that all I wanted after the humiliating mess of my breakup with Eddie Murphy was for someone to love me, someone to want to marry me and be a father to my girls.

I had been truly, madly, deeply in love with Eddie. Then, after planning our wedding and me getting pregnant (something I believed Eddie wanted very much), I had been spectacularly dumped after leaving him for a few days to think about our relationship. Eddie had remarked to a journalist that we were no longer together and had cast doubt on whether he was the father of our child (there was never any doubt in my mind, and Eddie is now a huge part of our daughter Angel's life). I was devastated for so many reasons. I loved Eddie and I lost him. I am, deep down, a romantic, and – you may be surprised to know – I am also a traditionalist. It killed me that my daughter would not have a father.

Along came Stephen, full of compliments and declarations of love. As my mum would say, I wanted to be seen as 'respectable' after being publicly slated in the wake of Eddie. And like the genie in his favourite movie, *The Wishmaker*, Stephen gave me all my wishes, with promises of love, solidity and loyalty. Then he married me. And then – like the genie in *The Wishmaker*, which is in fact a horror movie – he owned me and could do what he liked with me.

I liked that he was so possessive about me. 'Where are you going? Who are you with? Call me when you arrive. Call me when you leave.' It made me feel wanted and owned. 'He can't bear to be without me,' I'd laugh to my friend when, twenty minutes after I'd arrived to meet her, I'd get a text. I'd race back to him, so excited that this man wanted me so much. My first husband Jimmy hadn't, and not even Eddie could convince me – in bed – like Stephen did, that I was the most desired woman in the world.

After we got married, I felt that Stephen was uncomfortable about me hanging around with straight men. 'He's so jealous,' I would preen, and slowly dropped my male friends. Then I felt I had to call to say exactly where I was and how long I would be.

Though I hadn't had a nanny with Phoenix, we ended up getting nannies for the kids. I was working nonstop so I could see it made sense. Sometimes things would happen. I'd get worried about one of the kids being upset and text the person who was with them to find out what was going on. Stephen would go ballistic and want the nanny out immediately. I have never put a barrier between me and the people who work for me. He made me feel I should. 'You're too soft. You don't see they think you're an idiot and they all take advantage of you,' he said.

I accepted that, when I was working on 'The X Factor', in a two-hour period he would call my phone 50 times, asking where I was, what I was doing, telling me when I had to be back, accusing me of sleeping with Simon Cowell (obviously, I wasn't), accusing Chris of covering up my affair with Simon (he didn't, as I wasn't). I also accepted that he checked all my emails and answered them, deleted them – same with my phone messages, Twitter and Instagram pages. He controlled all my bank accounts, my work schedule.

'You have to leave him,' Chris told me in the hospital. Everyone was saying it. The producers on 'The X Factor' told me the same thing, as did Simon Cowell. I agreed. I nodded my head yes. Simon Jones, who had a hint of how much more complicated everything was going to be, told me he was ready to help me through a divorce. 'It will be OK, I promise,' he said. All I could really think about was Phoenix. Angel. Madison. It had to stop. I had to leave Stephen. And I had to make him know I was serious.

—

There are very many things I don't understand. I can't quote lines from Shakespeare. I can't put together flat-pack furniture (I've tried and had to run across to some workmen in the garden of the house opposite and ask them please to give me a hand) or explain quantum physics (I've never even bothered). But I do understand show business.

In my job you suddenly have a platform to make a statement and people will listen. You can speak up for a cause. You can recommend a hair product. And you can also make a huge statement without ever saying anything. Nowadays we can all do it. We can put up a picture on Instagram that says how we feel. We can send an emoji with a smile, a laugh or tears. Social media is a sort of stage for everyone. I decided I was going to use a very different stage to send a message to Stephen to say it was all over. The biggest one in Britain. The one part of my life he was never allowed access to. The 'X Factor' stage.

It wasn't exactly simple. My doctor looked at me as if I was completely crazy when I mentioned in the very early hours of Sunday morning that I would be on 'The X Factor' later that day. 'That is not happening, Melanie,' he said. 'I don't think you realize how serious your condition is. You are in intensive care; among other things, there is serious damage to your liver and kidneys.' He checked the levels in the IVs running into my arms – I swear he must have thought I was on too many painkillers to be even considering getting out of bed.

'OK,' I said. As my doctor walked out of the room, I texted my stylist, 'Send me pix of all the dresses you've got me for the final tonight.'

Simon Jones arrived in the afternoon and was immediately collared by the doctor. 'Under no circumstances can she leave this hospital,' he told Simon, who called Richard Holloway to pass on the doctor's order; Tulisa was told she was standing in again. Simon knew I was up to something: I had Randy doing my hair, moving tubes out of the way as he did so, and my makeup artist was in the room with her pots, pencils and brushes. 'You can't go,' said Simon. 'You have to listen to the doctor. Please. This is about your health.'

'I'm not going, Simon,' I told him, and then added, 'But YOU better get down there. It's the final show.' The door closed behind him and I swung into action.

'I'm completely okay,' I told Randy and Chris. 'I don't want a fuss. Let's see what we can do.' I got up and walked slowly around my bed, wincing in pain. Everyone held their breath; they all knew I was beyond talking sense to. It was agony to move, but this was one of the most important decisions of my life. I had to do it. 'I'm discharging myself,' I said to the nurse, who practically burst into tears when she saw I was out of bed.

'You can't,' she said.

'I can.' I argued back. My doctor tried to change my mind, but even he knew it was useless. If I want to do something, I will do it regardless. Ask my mother. The doctor sighed. I promised him I would come straight back after the show. Then he took me to one side. 'I don't know why you are doing this,' he said. 'I know you must be in agony.'

'I've been in agony for so long it doesn't even register,' I said. I was more concerned with having some makeup put on my face. I didn't want anyone on the show to see what a bad state I was in. I didn't want questions or looks of concern. I wanted to focus. 'I'm fine … I'm fine.' In fact I looked terrible. I had bruises round my eyes, my cheek was swollen and sore, and I had massive dark welts on my arms from the constant stabbing at my weak, narrow veins with the IV drips.

I got in the car. Chris texted the producers: 'She's coming. She's going to do the show.' Twenty minutes later I was rushed in through the backstage doors. When I arrived in my dressing room, Simon Jones walked in. He looked deeply anxious. 'Don't fuss,' I said. 'I'm okay. I'm a lot stronger than you think.'

I understood that it was important that neither the media nor the 'X Factor' audience knew what had happened to me. Neither Cheryl nor Louis had been told anything – as far as I knew – other than the suspected stomach-ulcer story. But as the makeup artist carefully applied layer after layer of foundation to my face and body to cover the bruises, I felt myself getting more and more angry. Madison and Angel had flown back from Germany, but I'd have to wait a few more hours to see them. I clung onto that anger because it was going to give me strength.

'I've got three perfect dresses with sleeves,' said my stylist, nervously eyeing the welts and purple marks on my arms which were clearly showing through the thick body foundation.

'No,' I said. 'I've picked the dress already. No sleeves.' I knew the bruises were still visible as I put on a beautiful, long white silk dress, semi-sheer at the top then hugging every curve of my body. It had to be a white dress. I didn't exactly look my best in the mirror, but I didn't look like that broken woman crying in her hospital bed. I wasn't saying anything, but I wasn't hiding either. I was giving the British press confirmation of all the rumours that had swirled for years about the state I was in. I would stand proud in this stunning white dress, with the marks of my agony all over me. I asked for my hair to be pulled right back from my face; I needed to be seen. I needed all those bruises to be seen.

I do not do anything by halves. My message to the world and to my husband was going to be VERY CLEAR. I wanted people out there watching to be my witnesses. I took off my vast, square-cut diamond wedding ring. A ring I had worn on 'The X Factor' a few weeks before to show the world what a solid couple Stephen and I were.

The next hour was a blur of adrenalin and throwing myself into the drama of the show. I had my mic pack-fixed into my dress by a technician who could not have been more gentle. 'Let me know if I'm hurting you,' he whispered as I stood at the side of the stage avoiding the stunned look on Cheryl's face. Simon winked. Louis covered up whatever shock he was feeling. (I knew he would know what had happened because Louis Walsh knows everything that is going on. He is the most brilliant and – usually – the most hilarious gossip, but I also know he's always had my back.) 'I won't let you go,' he said as he grabbed my hand and stood behind the stage set at the top of the stairs for the walk out in front of the audience.

I actually laughed to myself. All I was waiting for was the moment to open my hands – minus the wedding ring – to the cameras. My heart was thumping as a camera swivelled towards me. I let go of Louis' hand and lifted my left hand into the air, directly in the centre of the camera focus, knowing the whole TV audience, the press and, most important of all, Stephen would see my ring-less finger. 'Fuck you big time,' I thought.

—

What I remember next is walking towards the judges' panel and then realizing – because of all the bruises down my spine and legs, and because of the agony of my internal injuries – that it was going to really hurt to sit down. I winced and couldn't stop myself from gasping in pain as I eased myself into my seat very slowly. I heard Cheryl gasp, 'Oh my God!' Her hands flew up to her eyes. It had taken her a few minutes to realize what was going on, but I could see the penny had dropped.

The two female judges on the show had made massive mistakes in their real-life choices. Our relationships were the subjects of a lot of gossip. Neither of us acknowledged it. Especially not to each other. We'd both pretend everything was great – because that's what you do in the business of show. But I couldn't let myself start thinking about that. I had to be strong. And I was. This was something I knew how to do. I was in my comfort zone, in my own power.

As the show played out, I focused entirely on the battle between Ben Haenow and Fleur East. They were both fabulous, talented and committed. They were both out there singing because they wanted a whole new life to start. I was with them all the way. I felt incredibly emotional because all our lives were going to change. I thanked the doctors and nurses for looking after me (thank you again). I joked with Simon and Louis, and tried not to ignore Cheryl's looks of concern every time the camera was off us. 'I'm okay. I'm okay.' As ever, on that stage – any stage – I felt fully myself. Untouchable. Melanie Brown. Wonder Woman.

7
GUNS
—

I get offstage, smiling at everyone, happy for Ben (who won), happy for Fleur, who showcased everything she could do with that genius song by Mark Ronson and Bruno Mars, 'Uptown Funk', and happy that the razzmatazz of the final was distracting everyone from talking to me. I'm happy I didn't collapse. I'm happy I've done it. I've sent my message to Stephen; there is no going back. I'm going to leave him, get a divorce. I am going to be free. I'd been promising Phoenix this for years. It would be me and my girls from now on. I'm on a high. Even the pain pumping constantly through my body makes me feel alive.

In my dressing room, the first thing I do is grab my phone.

My heart stops. Wonder Woman melts. I'm Melanie Brown. My baby is gone – with Stephen, on a plane to LA. I feel like I've been kicked in the stomach. I have to think. I want my baby girl back. I need to get out of here. I ask my runner to tell the producers I can't do 'The Xtra Factor', the hour-long show with Sarah Jane Crawford where everyone discusses the highs and lows of the night's performances. I don't think they were even expecting me; the producers were just grateful they didn't have to have me taken off in an ambulance during the show. My dress is peeled off me and I'm back in sweat pants and a hoodie, clutching my phone as Chris rushes me back to the hospital. 'I couldn't watch you,' one of the nurses tells me. 'It would have made me cry.'

Over the next hour, I speak to everyone and rewind the last few hours of real life. Phoenix had been with Stephen at the apartment in Kensington. He had been packing his bags to go back to America, and packing a bag for Madison to go with them. Phoenix remembers shaking as Stephen raged around the flat. She knew Madison was supposed to come to me but she couldn't do anything to stop him taking her to the airport and back to LA. Phoenix was only 14 years old. 'She's my kid,' he told her. 'She is coming with me.'

As soon as I stepped out in front of the cameras, social media was inundated with speculation about what had happened. My mum and sister waded in on the attack and the story spiralled. 'Really worried for you after seeing this!! not sure what went on now, heard it was a stomach ulcer now domesic [sic] violence x Laura Sorrie @laurasorrie14'. This was just an example of the flood of messages out there in the Twittersphere.

I stayed silent. Once he landed, from the safety of LA, far away from my home turf, my then-husband tweeted, 'I don't usually respond to Twitter msgs but I will respond to comments of hitting my wife which I think are quite disgusting untrue!'

A few minutes later he tweeted again: 'Mel was very ill a bunch of doctors helped her get better if fans can't just relax B4 being negative they r not real fans of @OfficialMelB.'

Yeah. Right!

But I had no time to look at the storm I'd started. He had my baby girl. My sweet, sweet Madi – the one and only beautiful thing we had made together. She was the baby I'd been desperate to have because I thought it would make us a real family and I thought his heart would melt with his own child and I wanted to be a mother again. Madison is a special child. She was – and is – my little baby angel. I felt my heart being ripped out of me. In between calls to Phoenix, to my security and to his assistant, I was howling like an animal for my girl.

I didn't pay attention to any of the messages flying around, not from my family, not from anyone. I couldn't. Phoenix worked out the flight they were on and then Chris – who like a lot of the best security men is an ex-copper – finally made me call the police. I'd wanted to ring them the day I was admitted to hospital, but what was I going to say? That I'd taken an overdose? That my relationship with my husband made me feel suicidal? That I was frightened of him? But this was beyond everything – beyond me, beyond any media cover story, beyond any pain of mine. I dialled 999. 'Police, please.'

—

At 2 a.m. on 15 December 2014, while newspapers had gone to press with pictures of my bruised face on the front pages, and Ben Haenow, Simon, Louis, Cheryl and the 'X Factor' crew were still knocking back celebratory champagne, I was sitting on my hospital bed as Police Constable Cunningham asked my age, ethnicity (on a police form I am 'Code 3. MI – Mixed White and Black Caribbean') and I tried to explain that my husband had taken my child.

PC Cunningham stood for the Law. He was kind, he was concerned, he was – I could see – shocked at what I was saying. And shocked to see that this woman who had just been on the telly was hooked back up to IV tubes with bruises – now wiped clear of makeup – standing out like fat, raw stains on my arms and face. But there is no actual breaking of the law if a father – in this case an American citizen who has parental responsibility – takes his child – also an American citizen – out of the country without the knowledge or consent of the mother. It is not abduction. It is a domestic dispute.

PC Cunningham was not stupid. He took in the bruises, he put together some of the garbled half-sentences, gauged my fear and anxiety. He started asking me questions about my relationship with Stephen. Patient, logical, police-trained, step-by-step questions. I was part-hysterical, part-terrified as I tried to answer them. I could see him struggling as he tried to take in what I was saying. He would have thought I was all over the place – and I was – but this was the first time in seven years I was talking about Stephen. There was so much to say and so much not to say.

I told him about the overdose, how scared I was, how isolated I was from my friends and family. That I was going to divorce Stephen. That I could no longer cope. That I needed my baby back. I wanted my baby back.

There was other stuff I didn't say, that was too much. I was already registering that look people get on their faces when I talk – it's a sort of mix of pity, concern, disbelief and revulsion. Voices drop, heads cock to the side. I saw that look so many times. Sometimes it would make me want to scream. I never wanted anyone to pity me. I am, after all, that cheeky, stompy, fearless kid who stands for Girl Power.

—

On the street where I grew up in Hyde Park, Leeds, there was a women's refuge. 'Battered Wives' we used to call them. I'd walk past and see them sometimes on their own and sometimes with their kids. I knew they weren't like other women, my mum, my aunts, Mrs Wood who ran my dance school. I didn't see any bruises and I didn't really know what 'battered' meant. I thought of fish-and-chips and sausages in batter at Bryan's Fish and Chip shop near the Cottage Road Cinema in Leeds. Battered to me, as a child, had nice associations. Lots of salt, vinegar and scraps (the fried 'bits' of batter that dropped off the fish into the hot fat. Scraps are a Yorkshire treat.)

What I saw in those women, what made them seem so different to the women I knew, was this sad, distracted, lost look. They sometimes stood in pairs smoking, but they never seemed to speak to each other. I never saw them hooting with laughter like my mum and her sisters and my mum's best mate, Bernie. Those faces, those women, that haunted sadness came back to me now. I felt I was just like them.

The term used by family therapists is 'coercive behaviour', which became a crime in the UK in December 2015. It may be a new crime, but it is not a new situation; controlling relationships have gone on for centuries. Men – and women – manipulating their partners (or their children or their staff), damaging their self-esteem, leaving scars way deeper than bruises and driving people to the edge. I have, more recently, spoken to members of the British police force who have told me how seriously it is taken. It is a situation we need to look at very carefully because people involved are often unaware it is happening to them. It's hard to recognize it's happening, it's hard to speak about it, and it's very hard to prove.

It has taken till 2018 to make the first successful conviction (an eighteen-month prison sentence), and I would like to congratulate the midwife who spotted what was going on with a young mother in her care, and Surrey Police who listened and helped that conviction happen. Bizarrely it turns out it is often the apparently stronger woman who is more likely to be abused. According to statistics, women earning more than 67 per cent of the total household income are seven times more likely to experience psychological and physical abuse. But statistics don't always explain what it feels like to be perceived by the world as one thing and to see yourself only through the eyes of your abuser.

When I saw the Harvard-educated, former magazine editor, Leslie Morgan Steiner, on YouTube giving a TED Talk about her experience of her four-year violent marriage, I wept because I recognized everything she talked about. In the eyes of the world – at the time of her abusive relationship – she seemed like a woman who had it all, a woman to be admired. But according to her talk she was living on a daily basis with secrets, shame, pain and silence. Just like me.

'Melanie, I want you to watch this,' a friend said a couple of months after I'd left Stephen. I looked at what it was – Leslie Morgan Steiner's video – and I didn't want to watch it. I was in a good place. And it wasn't quite like my story. Nothing was quite like my story (or so I thought). Why on earth would I want to be reminded? 'Yes, yes,' I said. I didn't click on the YouTube link. I was too busy. When I wasn't in court or sitting in meetings with lawyers talking about my ex-husband, or reading horrible stories about me and my ex-husband in the tabloids, I wanted to switch off. Focus on good things.

Charlotte Robinson, my oldest friend from Leeds, had come over from my hometown to my new place in Coldwater Canyon, Beverly Hills, and introduced me to Cutting Shapes, where you dance like a madwoman with your feet moving constantly like Michael Flatley in *Riverdance*. I'd got everyone into it, all Phoenix's friends. As the vile headlines blazed through the Internet, Charlotte and her teenage daughter, Tillie, along with my daughter and her friends would pile into my big yellow bedroom in my rented house and we'd dance. I'd found these light-up trainers online, speakers that glowed in different colours. I was ordering shoes for everyone. I had reset my mind to think happy.

My friend wouldn't let up about the YouTube link, though. 'Have you watched it yet?' she'd text every other day. I'd ignore her, or say no. She didn't stop. She sent it again. Two weeks later, I sat on my large, four-poster bed with the yellow silk headboard in my cotton pyjamas and clicked on the link. I'd watch it for a few minutes and then tell her I'd seen it to shut her up.

———

Leslie Morgan Steiner looked like someone I'd met in a fancy office in London, Sydney or Los Angeles. Some elegant, intelligent magazine editor – the kind I'd have felt a bit intimidated by back in the Spice Girls days (not that they would ever have guessed) because she looked like one of those very smart, well-educated women who knew lots of long words and how to be feminine, understated and powerful all at the same time – a trick I'm always trying to pull off (even though I'm not good at 'understated').

During the day, Steiner wrote witty, clever articles in the offices of a Manhattan magazine, and in the evening she would go back to her Ivy League, Wall Street trader husband who she claimed would hold a gun against her head and threaten to kill her. But she loved him. He said he'd had a terrible childhood, an abusive father and step-father. He was sexy, he pursued her, he made her feel special and she thought she could fix him by loving him and being happy. He kept three guns – one under his pillow at night. He told her he needed to feel protected but she knew it was really a message for her.

I watched the video, stunned. How did this happen to someone so smart, I wondered, because I always think this about myself: I made bad choices with men because deep down, underneath everything I've ever achieved, I was never that smart at school. I was dyslexic, dyspraxic (except it was never diagnosed then; my English teacher used to say to my mum: 'If she could write how she talks, she'd be all right. But her essays are all over the place.') I had ADHD and I believed I was, as Stephen told me so many, many times, 'thick as pig shit'.

I watched the video again. And again. I cried. I felt sorry for Leslie. I felt proud of Leslie. I saw myself in Leslie, and I felt so many of my own pre-judgements about 'types of women' disappearing. I thought, I want to do something like this. And I do. This is my mission.

I thought about that gun Leslie felt was pointed at her head. I pointed a gun at Stephen many times. On his orders. He knew I would be too terrified to ever shoot. I could still feel the smooth, surprising weight of it in my hands, the scary, snub barrel, the bullets always cold, hard and very slightly oily.

Stephen kept a gun in our bedroom. He knew I hated guns, he knew I was frightened of them. I didn't want guns in our house. I didn't want guns anywhere near me.

Family and close friends are generally the ones who know you well enough and are brave enough to ask the questions and force you to tell the truth. My mother and my sister never stopped telling the world Stephen was bad news, but even they didn't know exactly what was going on because they had been locked out. They were – according to Stephen – the Enemy. We had our own world. We had to protect it. With guns if necessary. He had shown me how to use one. 'Melanie, go and get the gun.'

But there, in my hospital room in England in front of PC Cunningham, I was answering questions from a police form that didn't mention guns or coercive behaviour or murky, sordid sex and videotapes. He saw a mixed-race White-and-Black-Caribbean entertainer called Melanie Brown, aged thirty-nine, born in Leeds and based in Los Angeles, who needed to get away from her husband who had gone from Kensington, London back to their home in Los Angeles with their two-year-old daughter called M-A-D-I-S-O-N.

I kept telling PC Cunningham that they needed to put out a warrant for abduction, but he kept, very patiently, explaining to me it wasn't likely to be approved.

The morning rolled into more interviews with the police. Most of them were with policemen, but there was one policewoman who made me feel I could really talk, not just about particular incidents but also about the other stuff that made me feel helpless, lost, crazy – the way Stephen treated me, the way he spoke to me. Like I say, emotional abuse and coercive control weren't even something the police could do anything about then. And it's hard to explain how you feel violated by words and by your husband being cold, dismissive and controlling. But all of the police – especially this woman – were smart and switched on. They knew something very bad was going on. They needed me to spell it out.

I told her the vile things Stephen would say to me. But even as I said the words out loud, panic started rising within me. I still had no idea where Madi was, and the focus was shifting away from finding her. I'd opened my silly gob, and more and more officers were getting involved. I didn't want this to be about me. I wanted it to be about getting Madi back, but now all the questions were about me and Stephen.

After the police left, I began to feel sick. They had talked about bringing together different agencies involved in domestic violence (to create a MARAC, or Multi-Agency Risk Assessment Conference). I knew I couldn't handle anything like that. I'd lost any control, and what if I never saw Madison again? They didn't seem to get that that was the only thing I was worried about.

I couldn't think straight any longer. The hospital room seemed too small; I wanted to get away. Panicking, I switched into flight mode. I needed to see Angel and Phoenix, who were less than a mile away from me at The Grove hotel . I wanted to know how much longer I had to stay in hospital. I cried as I spoke to my girls for as long as possible. I told Angel I had a bad tummy ache, but all she wanted to do was cuddle up and watch movies with me.

I also thought I had made a mistake talking to the police about Stephen. All I needed was Madison back. No more interviews about him and me, no more questions. I called the PC I'd spoken to earlier in the day and said I wanted to report Madison as a missing child. 'And that's the only report I want to make.'

The divorce lawyers would deal with Stephen. This nightmare would end.

8
MORTIFICATION

—

My life turns on a dime. It always has. In the Spice Girls, one minute we were all cramming into a public phone box on a street near our shared house in Boyne Hill Road, Maidenhead, pushing coins into the slot as Geri bullshitted her way into meeting with a music manager whose number we had tracked down. (If Geri hadn't been a Spice Girl, she would have been one of the most successful saleswomen in Britain. Forget ice! She could sell a lawnmower to an Eskimo.) The next minute, we were in the best seats on a Virgin flight to America. We'd sit there ordering champagne, rooting through the first-class goodie bag ('Look, there's a toothbrush in it and a silver pen') wondering how on earth we'd got there.

In that hospital room in Harrow, my plans slammed into a wall in a matter of one day. On Monday, 15 December 2014, all I knew was that I was going to get Madi back – by whatever means – and then I would leave Stephen.

Simon Cowell sent various members of his team down to help me, and Simon Jones began to speak discreetly to lawyers. I asked him to help me because, without him, I knew I would never be able to make it through unscathed. Numbers for divorce lawyers were given to me, and I made plans with my security for them to be there while I went through a separation. I knew I would need proper protection. The newspapers were having a field day, pulling up information on Stephen's murky past.

Ben Todd, Senior Vice President of Syco Records and Syco TV, sat me down and tried to help me sort out my finances. 'Do you know your bank codes and bank accounts?' he asked. I shook my head. Stephen did all that. Ben explained that the fee for 'The X Factor' would be going into my bank. I finally found details of an old British bank account I'd had years before. They must have thought I was a total idiot.

A lady from Freemantle (the company that produces 'The X Factor') was contacted and eventually we got the codes to the bank account where my fees were to be deposited. It was Monday. By the time we cracked the codes, we discovered the money had been paid in on the Tuesday (when I was in hospital) and had been removed again from that account. Ben looked at me with a mix of concern and sympathy. The money I earnt had gone without trace. And I had no way of finding out where that money had gone. It is something I am still trying to do years later and I still do not have the answers.

In the press I was being treated with absolute kid gloves. My face did not move from the front pages of the British tabloids for thirteen days straight as 'Bruised Mel Without Her Wedding Ring' became the most speculated-about celebrity issue of the day. I was grateful for the concern but didn't want to read anything. I knew the mistakes I had made and I'd got into the habit of blocking things out rather than face them. I had a few medical issues that still concerned my doctors – they were worried about the long-term effect of the pills on my liver, kidneys and stomach lining. I'd also missed an operation to reverse damage to my left eye; a previous bout of laser surgery had left me almost blind. The police were constantly in touch because they wanted to follow up 'issues of concern' from my previous statements.

For the next seven days, positive plans were made, important people were spoken to, curious journalists were avoided, and I was moved (eventually) into the blissful calm of The Grove hotel.

For the first time in years, I fely safe. I ordered Sunday roast, insisting on Yorkshire pudding and gravy to remind me of home. I got Christmas puzzles and games for the girls. And I began to think, 'Our life is going to change.'

And then something happened. It was something no-one – not Simon Jones, not Simon Cowell, not Chris, not my family – saw coming at all.

—

All week I had been researching the best divorce lawyers, telling Phoenix we were going to get Madi back and find a new home. Everyone was on my side. I felt confident that I'd get Madi back imminently, and I was going to make peace with my family. I was already picturing myself in a new life. I could see myself back in Leeds sitting around the kitchen table at my dad's house where I grew up with my mum and my sister and my three girls. I could see them coming out with me to LA to find a place of my own. I could see my dad laughing about how Madison was a mini-me. It made me smile.

But on Monday, 22 December, I made an announcement. 'I'm going to drop all charges and go back to Stephen,' I told everyone. 'But don't worry. I have to do this for all sorts of reasons which I will explain and then I'm going to come up with a plan to finally leave him.'

Actually, that's not true. I did want to tell everyone, but how could I stand there and say those words to all the people who had seen what I'd gone through? All the people who had been in and out of my hotel room, talking to me, advising me, supporting me. I had no plan. I said nothing. I felt like a traitor to them, to myself, to all other women. But I had no choice.

I got on a flight home to America. Stephen wanted me to go to him straightaway, but I didn't. I couldn't. I felt outsmarted, mortified, foolish. This whole dramatic episode had crumbled to nothing.

Christmas was staring me in the face. A time to celebrate. But not in the way I had planned. I couldn't spend the two days with him, so I checked into a hotel with Angel and Phoenix. Dr Sophy had persuaded Stephen to allow Madi to speak to me every day on FaceTime. I saw her sweet little smile and soft brown eyes on my phone screen and all I felt is that I had let down my little girl. I can't remember much, I felt so low.

The next day we drove to meet Stephen at a house in Malibu that he had hired for the day. It was one week after the episode at the Kensington apartment. When he saw me, Stephen's words of greeting were, 'You fool.'

Journalists wrote that they despaired of me. The tabloids continued with their speculation about what was going on in the marriage and why I had gone back to him. 'Because, in spite of everything, she loves him and wants to make her marriage work.' Wrong. That was never the reason.

—

It's only now that I can explain. I had no choice but to go back to Stephen. That weekend in London, at The Grove hotel, Dr Sophy – the man I trusted with my life – flew from Los Angeles to see me. Stephen had asked him to come to talk to me. Dr Sophy assured me that Madi was fine and he had made a deal with Stephen that he put her on the phone every day to speak to me on FaceTime. Stephen had given Dr Sophy his version of events – how crazy I had been in London, how he hadn't been able to see me and Dr Sophy obviously knew something very bad had gone down.

I told Dr Sophy about the overdose. About how I'd got so desperate that I wanted to kill myself because I couldn't see any other way out. He'd already guessed. He'd seen me slurring and crying on Skype the day before I'd taken the overdose, with Stephen shrieking,

'Look at her! She's a fucking mess.' Over the six years he'd been our therapist, Dr Sophy had witnessed the tension between Stephen and I time and time again even though, despite him asking, I would never tell him what was going on. I knew – even though he had never said it out loud – that Dr Sophy thought it was in my best interests to leave Stephen. I told him that I had just been discharged from hospital. I saw him take in my bruises, still very visible on my face and body, but I was smiling. 'I'm going to get a divorce and just stay here,' I announced. 'I know you've always thought I should.' I waited for him to smile, to hug me, to tell me this was the news he'd been waiting for. He didn't. He shook his head. 'You have to go back to LA, Melanie,' he said in his calm, collected therapist's manner. 'It's not the right time. It would be the worst thing you could do.'

I was stunned. This was the one man who must have guessed what I'd been going through these past six years. He was the one who protected me from Stephen when Stephen ranted at me or threatened – as he did over the years – to get me committed. It was always Dr Sophy I would turn to even though I could never tell him everything that was happening in my life. He'd even had a taste of it himself when Stephen had turned his rants on him after I had left the room after one of our therapy sessions. I would hear him yelling at Dr Sophy that he was useless, that he would get him struck off, that he only cared about being a celebrity himself. And now he was sitting there in my safe, happy hotel room telling me I needed to go back to LA and face him, shaking his head over and over again. What the hell was going on? I snapped and screamed at him, 'Stephen has got to you. You don't believe me. Why can't I stay here?'

Very carefully, very seriously, Dr Sophy explained to me that if I left Stephen now, I would risk losing Madison and possibly lose full custody of all three of my children. I had taken an overdose and Stephen could make that public. Stephen could then say I was not mentally stable enough to care for my children, that he'd had to take

Madison home to America because he didn't trust me to have her in my care. Dr Sophy talked to me for hours as I sat in shock with tears rolling down my face, saying, 'No, no, no.' He explained softly, again and again, how different my situation could be made to look. How it was good that I had made this decision, but that now I had to take things slowly, do it properly, and that he would help support me and get me through it. But it was going to take time.

'How long?' I asked blankly. Dr Sophy shrugged his shoulders. I felt my world falling apart. I could see that what he was saying was true. He was – still is – Medical Director for the County of Los Angeles Department of Children and Family Services. He knew what he was talking about. He had also been brought in by Stephen as a witness to my worst moments in those Skype sessions, where he had been so shocked to see me with my hair all over the place, slurring my words and out of control.

Dr Sophy tells me now that he was horrified to see me like that and that he tried to call me back several times. When I didn't answer, he tried to call 999 from America because he was so concerned. In all the years he had been treating me, he had never seen me in that state. To him I didn't just look skinny, wasted and wrecked. I frightened him because I looked like I had lost myself. He had kept trying to call me when the news leaked out that I was in hospital, but I hadn't returned his calls. Stephen had contacted him as soon as he got back to LA because he knew I would listen to him. He had told Dr Sophy that if I tried to leave him he would take the children. Dr Sophy needed me to listen to the consequences I could face. And what he was saying was terrifying. In my life I have taken many, many risks. But there was no way I was going to risk losing my children.

My only option – much to the horror of everyone around me – was to cut off contact with a lot of the people who had stood by me and helped me so much. I left London without saying a word to anyone.

One month later, Will Payne of *The Sun* newspaper ran a story about the Kensington apartment incident. The police had confirmed the story but refused to comment. Stephen went berserk, blaming me and everyone who was with me at the time. In a panic, I contacted Simon Jones. He was at the theatre when I finally managed to get a hold of him. I was so frantic and so terrified that I insisted he leave the theatre immediately and get the story pulled. 'It's not true, it's not true,' I yelled hysterically with Stephen standing beside me. 'It was all a mistake. You need to stop that story, get the lawyers onto it.' God knows what Simon thought, and I felt terrible lying to him, but I knew Stephen needed me to deny the story and I felt responsible. The whole incident needed to be wiped from the records. It took seven more months before the police closed their investigation.

The trap had just got bigger.

9
DAD

—

MARTIN WINGROVE BROWN
28 MAY 1953 – 4 MARCH 2017

If you met my dad, you would love him. Everyone did. From every single one of the Spice Girls to the rough, tough families on the back-to-back council estate in Hyde Park, where my mum and dad moved in the 1970s after they had me, and where he, as a first-generation immigrant from an island in the Caribbean, stood out against the landscape of white working-class Yorkshiremen like a piece of coal in the snow. At his funeral more than six hundred grown men – and countless hundreds of women including Emma Bunton – wept at the sight of his coffin. He was sixty-two years old.

My dad, Martin Wingrove Brown, was funny; he was cool and he was smart. He was the life and soul of the party, and the sort of man you felt you could rely on for the rest of your days. He seemed sure of his place in life and was never fazed by meeting some of the most famous people in the world. 'Hello, I'm Martin,' he'd say in exactly the same way, with exactly the same smile, whether it was Paul McCartney or the milkman.

I have never loved a man like I loved my dad. I used to watch him out of my bedroom window going off to work on his bike. It took him forty minutes to get there and forty minutes to get back – and he did that journey every day for thirty-five years. He worked as a welder at Yorkshire Imperial Metals. It's brutal work, long hours, and when

I was a kid, he'd do double shifts (sixteen-hour days) for years so we could all go on holiday camping in Abersoch for two weeks, or have a Barbie house for Christmas.

I didn't know how he could do it. I used to cry sometimes when I watched him with my nose pressed against my bedroom window, getting on that bloody bike at the crack of dawn on a freezing-cold, grey day in November, January, March – take your pick. Even at the age of seven I'd think, as I watched the wind and the rain crack at his navy anorak, 'Why does my dad have to do this every day? There has to be a better life.'

Not a day goes by when I don't think of Dad. His laugh. The Heinz oxtail soup he'd use as gravy – he was a terrible cook, not that you could ever tell him. The music he blasted out on a Friday or Saturday night – everything from Aswad and Fleetwood Mac to the Eurythmics – and his beloved soul classics by Sam Cooke, Otis Redding and Al Green. The way he would say so seriously, 'Remember who you are, Melanie. Where you came from.' And the way he would shake his head or laugh. A cheery, deep laugh.

I miss him so much it hurts. Sometimes I wake up in the night and I am crying. Because he's gone. Because so many years went by without us speaking. Because there are so many things I want to say to him. My dad. The first man I loved and the first man who broke my heart.

—

The parent is the bow and the child is the arrow. The child is shot out into the world but is covered in fingerprints from the past. All my life I have looked for a man like my father. And I have confused his good and bad qualities, his strengths and weaknesses, and defaulted to the oldest scars my heart knows.

I see control and emotional withdrawal in a guy and some part of my brain goes, 'There, Melanie, there is a real man. A strong man.'

A man will criticize me and deep down my brain will react: 'This man really sees you. You know this man. You understand him. You need to make this man love you.' As a Spice Girl I went around the world shouting from the rooftops, 'Don't take any shit from a man!' and telling other girls to stand up for themselves.

I went out with some great, kind, inspiring guys, from the actor Max Beasley to my Icelandic soulmate Fjölnir Thorgeirsson, but I married or had children with Jimmy, with Eddie and with Stephen, all in their own ways difficult men who on some primal level carried with them darker shadows of my father. It is a pattern I have to recognize and one I have to break by trying to understand my father more.

I am – like so many British people – part-immigrant. I have my mum's British blood in my veins and my dad's Caribbean blood, carried over the seas to the docks of Southampton along with so many others who came over in the 1950s on ships like HMS *Windrush*. I'm proud of that. Being an immigrant is all about struggle, survival and having a dream of a better life. It's in my blood, passed down by my grandparents. It's part of their past and my past, and it has propelled us all forward into a different future.

And, as I have said, my dad often told me, 'Remember who you are, and where you came from.'

10
NEVIS

—

In 2017 my great friend Gary and I took a break by some stunning natural hot mineral springs in the desert to rest and meditate. I saw a shaman who really made me feel I was making sense of my past and future. In Native American culture, they believe that you are not just the product of your parents and a collection of DNA. They believe that your bones and blood echo with the ghosts of your ancestors. Their stories are within you. So I'm going to tell you something of my history.

My dad was born on a tiny island called Nevis in the Caribbean, part of the stunning arc of islands that is the West Indies. It is thirty-six square miles and only seven miles across, and was discovered by Christopher Columbus (although Arawaks and Caribs had been living there for a thousand years before that). In the seventeenth century, Nevis was known for its fabulous wealth, glamour and wild parties – all of it paid for by the finest sugar in the world. The sugarcane grew on its grassy slopes and plains. Sugar, back then, was known as Caribbean Gold.

The history of Nevis is the history of slavery – although for the British it is also known because the young Horatio Nelson was first stationed there as a young sea captain. The sugar plantations, owned and run by the British, needed lots of workers. Nevis – which is 2 miles from St Kitts – became the depot for the Leeward Islands slave trade. More than eleven thousand slaves passed through each year. Two-fifths of the slaves brought from Africa – the ones who didn't die on the voyage – died on the plantations. The ones who survived were the strongest and toughest, and these were my ancestors. My family has risen to do Nevis proud – my cousins include Carlisle Powell, a minister in the government, and his son Kieran, who is a massively successful cricketer on the West Indies team.

But our blood is in the earth of that land and our history is one of chains, hard labour and humiliation. Slaves were treated worse than dogs. If slaves did something to upset their white masters, they would be whipped. In the main square near my great-grandma's old house in Gingerland, you can still see a large, wooden post with chains hanging off it. That is where slaves were tied up and whipped.

The eighteenth century brought battles between the French and the British, the collapse of the sugar industry and starvation of many Nevisians. In 1834 the abolishment of all slaves from the British Empire meant freedom for almost nine thousand slaves working on the island. Some of the land was given to the slaves but battered by hurricanes, and, with the sugar trade in ruins, Nevis went from being one of the richest islands to one of the poorest.

When my dad was born, there were few good roads, no phones and no electricity. Two electricity generators were introduced to the capital, Charleston, in 1954, the year after his birth. When my dad was two years old, his mum and dad (known to me and my little sister, Danielle, as Black Grandma and Black Grandad) decided they could have a better standard of living if they left Nevis to earn a living in England. It was 1955 – the year after HMS *Windrush* brought migrants from the Caribbean to England. My grandparents were part of the Windrush generation.

—

Dad and his older sister, Kathleen, stayed in Nevis with my great-grandmother Celian, who is – at 106 years old – the oldest inhabitant on the island. Celian – known to everyone as Mrs Martin – is a local legend for her wisdom and her flamboyant outfits. She has one leg and a glass eye, but she still rocks bright satin dresses in yellows, pinks and white (and you think I'm the outrageously dressed one!). She also refuses to go in a wheelchair and is generally carried.

I can't imagine what it must have been like for my grandparents Ersdale (or 'James' as he became known in England) and Iris, coming from hot, sunny Nevis to cold, rainy England. Dad's parents first tried to make a go of it in Ipswich, where they had some relatives. Then, after a difficult six months, they moved 200 miles north to Leeds because Grandma was a trained tailor and Leeds was the heart of the textile industry. Their lives were hard. Black people were not easily accepted in Yorkshire in the 1950s; signs in the windows of rental flats read, 'No animals, no Irish, no blacks'. People would cross the road when my grandparents walked by. All they wanted was to work hard and have a better life for their kids. It took seven years for them to carve out a life for themselves. They got steady jobs in the textile houses, with Black Grandad working as a plasterer and cab driver. They bought a house in Chapeltown, one of the poorest areas of Leeds – home to prostitutes, drug dealers and a large Afro-Caribbean community. When my dad was nine and Kathleen was twelve, their parents sent for them to join them.

My dad was completely traumatized by having to leave Nevis. There were few luxuries to be had, but he loved the island – and his very religious grandmother who would insist they all started and ended their days on their knees in prayer – with a passion, and he didn't want to go. The day he and Kathleen were due to get the boat, he ran off and hid for hours.

My dad didn't talk much about his early life. 'Tell me about Nevis,' I'd ask him as a kid.

'Tell me what you learned at school today,' he'd answer. I knew he had lived on a small farm with goats and chickens and that he spent his days roaming the island with his mates, playing cricket on the beach, doing chores and going to the village school. His life was idyllic for a young boy, and while my great-grandmother was strict, he was the absolute apple of her eye. She used to sing to him every night. After he left to go to England, he never saw her again for thirty years.

When the Spice Girls took off, one of the first things I did was pay for us all to go back to Nevis because I wanted my dad to be reunited with the woman who had raised him, my great-grandma. By then, Black Grandma and Black Grandad had moved back to Gingerland, a place where everyone sits out on their porches in the evenings and chats to neighbours as they pass by and keeps an eye on everyone in the village. To me, after a frantic year with the Spice Girls, it was bliss. Black Grandma kept pigs and her garden was full of mangoes, which you could pick right off the trees and eat. Delicious. It made me laugh that she had plastic covers on her sofa just like she did on her sofa in Leeds when I was a kid.

Meeting Great-grandma felt completely surreal. On Nevis she is treated with absolute respect like a queen. I felt a real connection to her because you can feel this incredible, wise spirit. She made me feel proud to be her great-granddaughter. 'You are beautiful,' she said when she saw me. But then she peered at me for a little longer and noticed my tattoos and piercings. 'Get me some water,' she shouted. A bowl full of water was brought to her which she threw all over me. As I gasped with shock she leaned towards me and said, 'Marking your body lets evil in. I've washed it out for you.' Thank you, Great-grandma. That was one hell of an introduction.

She was, however, not very accepting of my mother. 'It's not my fault Wingrove married white,' she said when she saw her. My mum – who'd had a lifetime of dealing with racism both ways – made a joke of it. Since we'd been in Nevis, she'd lost no opportunity to lie out in the sun and was extremely proud of her tan. 'I'm not that white now,' she laughed. At the time, I was dating a lovely guy, an engraver called Ritchie Meyer, who was also white. Great-grandma didn't even acknowledge him. I felt tempted to say something as I can't bear anyone being insulted because of the colour of their skin, but my great-grandma was old enough to be closer to older, deeper wounds of slavery. 'Some things you have to leave alone and understand,' my mum advised.

I am proud of my history, proud of who I am, but even for me going to Nevis made me conscious of how hard it must have been for my dad and my grandparents. A few months before, I'd been to a luxury holiday resort in Antigua about 50 miles away from Nevis. I'd taken Mum, Dad and Danielle, and Geri had also gone out with a friend. You couldn't help but notice that me, Danielle and my dad were the only black guests at the resort. All the other black (and brown) people were staff. Danielle and I spent most of our time with them.

I did, however, make a lasting impression on all those guests. When everyone was celebrating New Year's Eve in all their finery, I insisted we do the conga around the pool. As cheers went up at the end, I pushed every single person into the pool and then jumped in with them. Being soaking wet in your best gear is a very levelling experience. It didn't matter what colour we were, we were all drenched in the same water.

—

In the late '90s it wasn't uncommon to be the only person of colour – bar the staff – in the expensive restaurants, first-class cabins and five-star hotels we frequented. As a Spice Girl I was often the only black person in the room at business meetings in the music industry. 'Cool Britannia' was a pretty white era. The girls always used to say, 'We don't see you as a colour, we see you as Melanie.' It bothered me that they had no idea of what it was like to have my skin. London has always been more cosmopolitan. I once took Geri to an underground blues club in Chapeltown that was massively popular with the local black kids. In the middle of dancing, I stopped her and said, 'Look around the place. Do you see any white faces?' She shook her head. 'Now do you realize what it is like to be me?'

Dad hated England as a kid. Black Grandma told me that. He arrived in snow, and, after first thinking it was amazing, he looked behind him, saw his own footprints and screamed, 'Someone is chasing me!' He was petrified. Black Grandma was incredibly strict and there were no fields to escape into. The tough life she had endured had made her very unemotional and hard. I always loved her because she would let me try on her old dresses in her attic and carefully remove her good china from a cabinet to clean – it made me feel special that I was trusted to do it. She even once caught me bouncing on her bed (completely forbidden), but instead of shouting at me she laughed and said, 'You're crazy.' I knew my dad was terrified of her. I took advantage of that because I found it fascinating that my dad was so different with her than with anyone else.

As soon as we got to her house – with its 'good sofas' covered with squeaky plastic and her prized ornaments on display – I'd tell her a list of my dad's 'wrongdoings', anything from 'He was mean to me' to 'He shouted at Mum and said a bad word.' I knew what was going to happen next, which was the thrilling bit for me. She would call Dad into the kitchen – 'I say, Wingrove, I need a word' – and let rip at him in her accent that was pure Caribbean mixed with Yorkshire dialect. He would stand there saying nothing, his head bowed. I never once heard him contradict or talk back to Black Grandma. And he expected that same submission from his young British daughters, me and Danielle.

West Indian women can be very tough on their kids, especially when it comes to education. My dad left school at fifteen and Black Grandad pulled strings to get him an apprenticeship with an engineering company. It was a good position, and – if he was taken on fulltime – the firm he was with would take him to Canada. A golden ticket. A chance to change his life.

But something happened and there was a family row and my dad ended up leaving home, quitting his job and going to live with his auntie. He didn't speak to his mother for a couple of years. I used to pester him to tell me about it: 'What happened, Dad? Tell me what happened.' He would never tell me, nor would Black Grandma, or my lovely, dapper Black Grandad, or Dad's sister, Kathleen, or his younger sister, Beverly, who was born in Leeds a few years after my dad arrived.

I found out recently what it was all about. I wish I'd known decades ago because it was something my dad must have felt ashamed of but something that actually makes me feel closer to him. All those wasted years.

—

My dad had actually been dropped after his apprenticeship because he was constantly going out on wild nights with his mates. It was 1968, and my dad was busy throwing himself into the Swinging Sixties scene of twenty-four-hour parties and endless rock concerts. He'd go out wearing black eyeliner and later (in the '70s) flares and platform boots, with his hair in a massive 'fro (sounds familiar?). He'd turn up later and later for work, looking wrecked, or even miss a day's work completely. So he got fired. The family was shamed, and Black Grandma – who still to this day gets up at 6 a.m. to feed her pigs and start her chores – was outraged. He had let the family down. He had let himself down. And he had let his golden chance for a new start in a new country slip through his fingers.

I can see now why he'd never want me – or Danielle – to know that. He spent his life making sure we were in by 10 p.m., policing the people we hung out with and breathing down our necks about our schoolwork because he believed education was the golden ticket for us, even though neither of us was exactly cut out for a life in academia.

He must have so regretted not sticking at his engineering traineeship when he was dodging sparks of flame and breaking his back doing shifts as a welder. No wonder he hung on every word our teachers said on parents' evenings. No wonder he used to scream at me for missing homework. No wonder he worried he had two daughters who were chips off the old block.

Strangely enough, it was me who brought Dad's family back together again. In a roundabout and not exactly easy way. I was – from the start – a bombshell.

11
THE REBELS
—

My mum, Andrea Dixon, met my dad when she was seventeen at a party on Christmas Eve in Chapeltown. He was nineteen. She knew him because – having also left school at fifteen – she did all sorts of jobs, including working two nights a week at the front desk in a nightclub at the Bellevue Centre, where my dad played championship table tennis. Obviously she fancied the flared pants off him because my dad was gorgeous. And my mum – blonde, blue-eyed and giggly – was pretty hot herself.

They were, in their own way, complete trailblazers – or rebels. My mum thinks we all have the 'rebel gene'. Her dad, White Grandad, was in the military police and then became an engineer. He was pretty strict with his five daughters and two sons (I am part of a VERY large family).

My mum hated school but loved to go out partying. As she says, 'It made me laugh later to think that Martin would be climbing out of the window to get out of his house to go out to clubs because his mum tried to keep him locked in. And I'd be climbing into my house in the early hours of the morning to get back in before everyone woke up for breakfast, because my dad would lock the doors at 11 p.m.. We were both the rebels of our own families.' It was 1972 and there were no black people in Seacroft, where she lived. But my mum – and all her four sisters – thought my dad was wonderful. I love the fact that this working-class girl from Leeds didn't see colour in a time where racism was completely accepted. She didn't see a black man. Instead, she saw a man – a cool, charismatic dude. She'd had her eye on him for a while. And he'd had his eye on her. And then, finally, they got together under the mistletoe.

Now, White Grandma and White Grandad – my mum's parents – didn't quite think my dad was wonderful.

The first time he went over for dinner, White Grandma (who, like Black Grandma, was a seamstress) spoke to him VERY SLOWLY, as if he didn't understand English. She explained what all the food was on his plate, as if he had never tried roast potatoes and chicken before, or used a knife and fork. White Grandad was stunned when Dad opened his mouth and addressed them in a broad Yorkshire accent. 'Bloody hell, you speak just like me,' said White Grandad, as if he was expecting some African tribal greeting. Still, they were dead against the relationship. But my mum – God bless her – refused to ditch my dad just because he was black. Within three months she had moved into his bedsit in nearby Headingly.

For two years they lived together, despite the opposition from Mum's side. Dad's parents weren't speaking to him, which meant they never saw them either. On their first Christmas together, Dad wasn't invited back to the Dixon family Christmas. So Mum stayed with him and they ate scrambled eggs and baked beans, and stayed in bed all day. The following Christmas, she found out she was pregnant with me (must have been the result of all those days in bed), and my mum made my dad call Black Grandma. 'It's time you made up with your family,' said my mum. 'We're going to be a family and we have to have the support of both our families.' He made the call, which was awkward and embarrassing for all of them: 'Hi, I know I haven't spoken to you for three years … But my girlfriend is pregnant … And I'd like you to meet her.' They came round to see her, and Black Grandma sat my mum down. Black Grandma told her it was going to be too hard for them to stay together. 'It won't work, and the baby won't fit in,' she said. 'And the baby won't be black or white. It's not right.' My dad said nothing.

My mum had heard exactly the same from her family. She didn't care, though. Mum and Dad were happy. 'We are going to make it work,' she said confidently.

—

My mum went into labour on my dad's twenty-second birthday. I was born after sixteen hours and fifty-nine minutes of labour, a forceps delivery as I was 7 pounds and got stuck because my mum is tiny. I caused a lot of pain on my way out into the world – sorry, Mother. That our birthdays were a day apart always bonded me to my dad (just in the way my daughter Angel's birth on her dad Eddie Murphy's birthday has given her a special bond with him). Black Grandad – dressed up as always in one of his beautiful suits with a colourful shirt and matching tie – was one of the first people to come and see me, and White Grandad – who had never visited any of his other eight grandchildren in hospital – also came.

I looked at the world through one eye (I refused to open my other eye for a week), and both sides of the family fell in love with this baby with a huge mop of thick, black ringlets and realized they were all in it together. I didn't come out brown. Initially I was very pale, and my White Grandad's first remark was, 'Oh! She's white. Just like us.' A month later, my skin went dark and I was neither black nor white. A few months after my arrival, my parents got married – her in a tight pale blue dress and platform heels, and him in flares. No wonder I was born with a very different dress sense.

The day of the wedding was also the day that the black and the white sides of the family met for the first time. My mum and dad arrived together, but they were so late, everyone else was already there, sitting on opposite sides at Leeds Register Office. They hadn't spoken a word to each other.

'Mum, come over and meet Iris and James,' my mum said, hastily.

'Is that them?' White Grandma said, eyeing up the ONLY black people in the whole building. 'I thought it might be, but I wasn't sure.' My mum could barely contain her laughter. But surprisingly, Black Grandma and White Grandma became the best of friends.

—

I can't begin to imagine how difficult it was for my mum and dad being a mixed-race couple back then. Even though both families finally accepted their relationship after I was born, time and attitudes have changed so much. But in 1975, the National Front was rife in Leeds and many other parts of Britain. People would look away if a black man or woman was being abused or thumped. Skinheads, with their swastikas, shaved heads, Doc Martins and racist chants, were part of everyday life. 'Just use your common sense, Melanie,' my mum would tell me, which was her code to let me know not to attract attention to myself in front of guys like that. Common sense meant not standing up to racists, and, even as a kid, I had a screaming sense of the words 'Why not? What's wrong with me?'

I didn't vocalise that till I was older because all around me there was this 'don't rock the boat' attitude. When I was a baby and my mum and dad went on a bus, my mum would whisper, 'Martin, hold Melanie.' Then she would hand me over to my dad because she thought no-one would attack a man holding a baby. They were often shouted at on a night out (they didn't shout back). And they never went out in the city centre after a football match. This was called using your common sense.

But you would never hear my dad complain, or even talk about the colour of skin. That was what everyone else did. If I got chased home from school or got called a 'Paki', he would not go to the teachers to complain. 'Melanie, you have to learn to fight your own battles,' he would say, as I came belting into the house after being chased a full fifteen minutes all the way back from school with the cat-calls still ringing in my ears. I was called all sorts of names, from 'Red Skin' to 'Half-breed' to 'Half-caste' and the N-word.

There were times in the playground, or out playing in my street, when I would see kids pause for a bit before they started shouting insults at me – because they couldn't work out what I was. 'Oi, you … Are you a Paki, or what?' It was as confusing for me. I wasn't black or white. The black girls often made it clearer than the white girls that I wasn't part of their gang. I was in a no-man's-land – or more like a no-child's-land – of being mixed race; not one, not the other. 'I'm brown,' I'd sometimes shout. Usually I'd say nothing. I did not belong anywhere.

When we moved to Kirkstall, my dad couldn't join the local working men's club, which was two minutes up the road. He tried a couple of times but then just stopped. It was obvious why. There were no black members. He didn't make a fuss. Nor did my mum. But I never forgot. When 'Wannabe' went to number 1 in July 1996, I marched into that place, straight up to the manager and said, 'When I get enough money I'm going to buy this place and ALL my family will be drinking at this bar.' I didn't actually buy it, but I made my point.

Dad never talked about what he went through as a black man growing up. I never knew how much his experiences affected the way he was towards me and Danielle. Six months after I was born, there was a riot in Chapeltown on Bonfire Night after a black youth put a brick through a police-car window, causing the driver to swerve and hit a tree. All hell let loose, with three hundred black teenagers fighting running battles with the police. That was ten minutes away from where we lived and the area my dad had grown up in. I only know about this because I read about it, and I read about it because I wanted to know more about what his young life was like.

I came across a submission to a Parliamentary Select Committee by Chapeltown's United Caribbean Association, written in 1972.

It paints a picture of life that would have been an everyday reality for my dad:

> *Harassment, intimidation and wrongful arrest go on all the time in Chapeltown; black teenagers returning from Youth Centres to their homes in groups are jostled by the police, and when the youths protest, police reinforcements with dogs are always ready just round corners. Police boot and fist youths into compelling them to give wrong statements, but the right one that the police requires. We believe that policemen have every black person under suspicion of some sort and for that reason every black immigrant here in Leeds mistrusts the police, because we think that their attitudes are to start trouble, not prevent it.*

I never heard anything like that from my dad. He didn't talk about his childhood or his teenage years. My dad didn't do emotional. He wasn't emotional with his mum and he wasn't emotional with his children. After I married Stephen, my dad didn't call me up begging me to leave him. He didn't fly across the world, wanting to fix everything that had gone wrong.

He shut down. He'd play his music, drink his beer at the Merry Monk pub, sit talking to his mates. He was Martin Brown. He didn't feed into drama. Yet he lived most of his life with three dramatic women (my mum can out-drama-queen me any day). In the few phone calls we had in the last ten years of his life, he would not get into anything. 'Talk to your mother' was what he would say to me if I rang him in tears from my home in LA where my life was falling apart. 'Sort things out with her first. I don't want to hear it.'

Dad just wanted me to do well at school, get good grades and shine at sport. Whatever low-grade job he did outside his house, within it he was the boss. He didn't want to know about the arguments I had with my mum or sister, or if I had a problem with a friend at school.

'Listen to me, Dad,' I'd yell at his back as he got on with cooking the tea. 'You're not a nice person,' I'd shout and leave the room.

But if I'd had an issue with a teacher he was right in my face, wanting every detail, asking, 'What have you done now, Melanie?' He'd never be on my side. He'd be furious with me. 'You have to keep quiet and do your work, Melanie,' he would say. 'All I care about is you getting good marks.' I was dyslexic. I had ADHD. That was never going to happen. In contrast, my mum would let me and Danielle get away with murder. She loved having fun with her kids, covering up for me if I went out late to a disco, talking about boys, gossiping with her sisters and best friend, Bernie.

My dad was insistent on respect, manners and hard work. There were rules for everything – washing the dishes in a certain order, helping with the vegetables, how long you could be on the phone, how much water you could have in your bath, where you could eat (NEVER in the lounge or in your bedroom). He knew exactly how long it took to get from the bus stop to home, and if me or Danielle took any longer than fifteen minutes he'd be raging, wanting to know where we had been. Danielle was once grounded for three months for playing truant from school for a day with her mates. Danielle and I memorized all his double shifts or his nights out with his mates because it meant we could get away with going to a club or hanging out late with boys. Mum – who had grown up with two brothers and four pretty lively sisters – never landed us in it.

There were times we got my dad's timetable wrong. On one of those nights, my mum made us spaghetti Bolognese, which we all took into the lounge on trays, giggling as we settled down to watch the telly for our illegal night of NOT EATING AT THE TABLE. We had not, however, memorized the Leeds United football schedule, and my mum had no idea there was a match on the telly that night. If there was a match on, my dad would swap his shift. So there we were, plates on laps, watching 'Top of the Pops', when we suddenly heard the front door bang. 'You and Danielle were up like lightning,' my mum recalls. 'You both threw your plates onto my tray and ran out of the room. I couldn't move because I was covered in Bolognese and laughing my head off. Your dad did see the funny side – eventually.'

My mum's still like that today. I'll be shouting at Phoenix to do her work and my mum will be letting her go out to her mates. It does make me laugh that my role has been completely reversed. And I never let my kids eat in their room or the front room. 'YOU HAVE TO EAT AT THE TABLE' is still shouted (by me) in our house.

When I was younger, my relationship with my dad was different. I was his pride and joy, and on weekends we were rarely apart. 'That's Martin's Melanie,' I'd hear people say. I'd go down and play football with him and his mates. I'd sit on his knee for hours having cuddles. I'd help him in the kitchen because in our house my dad did all the grocery shopping and all the cooking and my mum did all the DIY. Funnily enough, most of the men I've ended up with have also always done the cooking, but unlike my dad they cooked really well. Jimmy was great in the kitchen and Stephen could make any dish. And then Eddie – well, Eddie had his own private chef.

When I was at primary school (Kirkstall Road Primary) and it was the week before sports day, my dad would take me down to the playing fields. We'd both get dressed up in sports gear and my dad would have me running, jumping, kicking footballs. He'd time me with his watch as I ran. 'Come on, Melanie. You're going to win this!' he'd yell. It was us against the world, my dad focused entirely on me. He wanted me to succeed. And I did. Every year, I would sweep the board clean. I was as competitive as he was, but I cared far less about winning my medals than I did about seeing a great big smile on his face.

But all games had to be played his way. He loved a party with Mum's four sisters – Sheila, June, Di and Pamela – and various neighbours, and friends from football and his work. He would drink his cans of Special Brew and he would want everyone to be happy. And then he would want it all to stop. And when he wanted it to stop, it had to stop. It was always his party, not anyone else's party.

When I got older, I never had my friends to a party in our house. Friends had to wait behind the gate till they got the OK (from my dad) to come in. If it was just Mum, anyone was welcome. It was lucky my dad worked so many shifts because me, my mum and Danielle always loved having a laugh with as many people as could fit in our kitchen. When he watched TV, me and Danielle had to be quiet. The television was his. 'I pay the licence, I choose,' he'd say when we wanted to watch something everyone at school was on about, like 'The A-Team'. He loved sport and his soaps – 'Coronation Street' and 'EastEnders' – and you had to be completely silent when they were on. But the show he loved most was 'Dynasty'. When that was on, if you made so much as a squeak, you were out of the room and in your bedroom for the rest of the night.

—

Yes, he absolutely loved 'Dynasty'. So did I. It was my first glimpse of real Hollywood glamour spilling its golden gloss from our 24-inch colour telly onto the tiny living room of our three-bedroom council house. These people lived in mansions with pools, swooshed around in silk lingerie in the middle of the day and got on planes like we got on buses.

I actually met Joan Collins at the thirtieth birthday party for *Hello!* magazine in London in May 2018. I don't go to many events, but I was in London and I wanted to take my daughter Phoenix to a grown-up London party. We stayed for an hour or so, and my feet were killing me in sky-high yellow heels. Also, Phoenix could barely stand because she'd borrowed a pair of my suede thigh-length Balmain boots, which looked fantastic but were two sizes too small. 'Mom, we need to leave, I'm literally dying,' she groaned.

But then I saw Joan and that was it. I'd never met her before and she had no clue how much she meant to me or my dad, so I dragged my daughter through the party crowd, waited till Joan had a moment and then asked her if I could have a photograph. I swear that woman is even more glamorous in real life than she even was on 'Dynasty'. All I was thinking was, Dad, this is for you.

Never in a million years did I imagine that I'd actually experience a life like the glamorous 'Dynasty' life that we watched on our TV. Neither did my dad. But when I did finally get on a private plane, my dad wasn't impressed. He loved seeing me onstage, at Wembley Stadium, and he loved seeing me on the telly. But he wasn't so keen on me being what he would call 'flash'. 'Don't waste your money, Melanie,' he would say. He rode the same bike all his life till he was too ill to ride it. He never used any of the beautiful leather wallets I bought him. On the handlebar of that bike was a Morrison's bag with his money in it. That was all he would use.

When I bought him and my mum a fabulous stone house in Horsforth, Leeds, my dad refused for months to move out of our little old house in Kirkstall. By the time he did eventually move out, my mum had enjoyed three months of watching whatever she wanted on the telly and having her friends round whenever she wanted. She realized life was so much better without his never-ending rules and they decided they should split up. I got it. By then, I was living away from home, had my own life and realized they needed to have theirs. So I understood their decision and was not traumatized. At home it had been his way or the highway. Now, the highway looked more appealing. Sometimes people are better apart, and that was definitely the case for my mum and dad.

—

When I think back to my childhood, I realize that as I got older, my dad grew colder. I reached an age when I was no longer his little mate. I was growing up fast, developing into a young woman as I hit puberty.

And I talked back. Sometimes. Boys looked me up and down in the street and my dad would silently fume. 'That skirt is too short,' he'd say, and push me into the house. 'And ignore those lads. Don't think I didn't see you smiling at them.'

He retreated behind a wall of more rules, more complaints, more criticisms and more punishments. My mum has since told me that he was worried she was too soft and that I was headstrong. He thought I'd end up running around with boys, dropping out of school, so his way – Black Grandma's way – was to shut down and pile on the pressure.

'I'll see you on Friday,' he would say to me on a Tuesday morning as I was running down the stairs to school. It meant I'd done something wrong and I was going to get either a slap or the belt. Often I had no idea what it was and I wouldn't know till the Friday. The anticipation of the punishment was worse than the belting itself. I'd lie awake at night with my stomach churning wondering what I'd done now. It could be anything from being seen wearing lipstick to getting a C in maths at school when he insisted I should get As and Bs for everything.

And then Friday would come around and I'd find if I was getting five straps with his belt for a minor misdemeanour or twenty for something serious (failing a test or he'd found out I'd sneaked out to a club). I would lie across the bed and will myself not to cry as the belt cracked across my legs and backside. 'Is that it?' I'd say when he'd finished, walk out of the room, then bolt straight into my bedroom and sob silently into my pillow.

12
THE COIN
—

Love and hate are two sides of the same coin. When I was fourteen, I often hated my dad because he seemed to hate me. His mum had pushed him away with her strictness and now he was doing exactly the same to me.

If family friends came over to our house, I'd be sent upstairs. I'd always been allowed to join in before, so I wondered why I had to go to my room.

'Because I say so.'

If I asked a question, my dad would tell me he was too tired to answer or I was too stupid to bother with. I was grounded constantly for not doing well enough at school, not wearing the right clothes, not eating my breakfast, saying something inappropriate. I felt he was constantly annoyed and disappointed in me. I had no idea what had gone wrong with me and my dad, but it was making me desperately miserable – so miserable I ended up taking that overdose.

The teenage years are the years when you most need an open emotional dialogue with your parents. My dad had not had one with his mother, and now I didn't have one with my dad. Maybe he learned to do exactly the same thing she had – get stricter and become more distant. And, when something difficult happened, shut down.

In the same way no-one ever spoke of what happened to him and Grandma, no-one spoke about my overdose. I know he felt guilty – and so did my mum – but none of us ever discussed it properly as a family. My dad saw it as something mad that I had done and would never do again because of all the trouble and embarrassment I'd caused. Teachers had been dragged into it; my aunties knew about it. The 'whole bloody street' had seen me carried into an ambulance. I'd shown everyone up, and the best thing was to stop talking about it and pretend it never happened.

Bizarrely, I did the same. After a few confused weeks of wondering why on earth no-one was saying anything, I also blocked it out. I didn't even remember it happening for almost two more decades. Like my dad and my grandma, I inherited that ability to seal off painful emotions and block them out of my mind entirely. I still do that. I compartmentalize because it is my coping mechanism. But locking things away never helps anyone; it just comes out later in life or festers away. I think it's so important for teenagers to be able to talk about their problems, open up to people they trust, whether it's a teacher, a family friend or a counsellor. You have to sort out issues as they arise or you leave them to get bigger and bigger.

My dad – like all of us – also had a dark side. He was a terrible flirt (as was Black Grandad) and I'd occasionally catch him laughing and joking with other women. I'd threaten to tell my mum, but I never did.

I once saw a nasty episode when we were living in Kirkstall. I came down the stairs in the early hours of the morning, and my mum had blood running down her face. He'd gone to hit her and she'd fallen and hit her head on the edge of the fireplace. They'd had a row because she'd been out with her mates and then come in drunk three hours after she was meant to be home (his curfew). He'd sat up, waiting to have a go at her. My mum always tells me it was just a really bad accident, and that she was the one who fell over because she was drunk. But I didn't see any of that. I saw my mum covered in blood, my dad angry and then the blue lights of an ambulance.

My mum made my dad leave the house after that. He moved into a flat but would come over every evening to see me and Danielle. After the third month, my mum took me to the doctor because I'd started stammering. She called my dad on the phone, said, 'Come home, Martin. I don't think Melanie can take it anymore.' He was back that evening. My stammer disappeared, but my memory of that night didn't. 'Tell her you love her,' I would tell him before he took me and Danielle down to the park, something he would do every evening (largely to wear me out by running and jumping). I would make him hold her hand. *Love* was a word that he never liked to use. I'd make him say it. 'Tell me you love me, Dad.'

'I looooove you, Melanie,' he'd say, with an exaggerated sigh.

—

When my parents eventually divorced, a few months short of their thirtieth anniversary, they still spoke every day on the phone.

Ironically, they split up over that house I bought them. My dad refused to move in until he was ready. My mum spent three months on her own there and realized she was a lot happier. I understood. They were different people and they needed their own spaces.

I also knew – even when they both had different partners – that actually, they still loved each other and they would be there for each other till the end. My mum went to every single one of my dad's doctor's appointments in the last six years of his life, and she was there when my dad drew his last breath. That says everything about their relationship. My mum never held back her love. It was always there. Like mine. I don't think my dad could deal with the unconditional, dramatic, all-consuming love I needed. And I think I always knew that, because he had never experienced anything like it. For my dad, love was a different story.

When I was fifteen, Black Grandma and Black Grandad emigrated back to Nevis. The night before they left, my dad was supposed to go and help them pack up all their belongings. But he went off to football and turned up late when most of the packing had been done. Black Grandma was raging. The next day, we all went off to the coach station with them to wave them off. She said goodbye to all of us except my dad. He stood there with his head down – his usual posture when he was in trouble with his mum. Everyone was a bit scared of Black Grandma, but I never was and I couldn't let her leave like this. As she grabbed hold of the rail to pull herself onto the coach, I pulled her down by the arm, saying, 'You have to say goodbye to your son. You can't leave and not give him a hug. You might never see him again.'

She was shocked but she hugged my dad. It was an awkward hug, but it was a hug. Nearly twenty-seven years later, I brought her back to England to give him one last hug. When he was on his deathbed in hospital, I arranged for her to be flown first class to see him. She sat on that flight bolt upright all the way with a frown on her face, refused all food and drink from the air hostesses. But she saw her son before he died.

That was the sort of unspoken, tough love my dad knew best. I have it in me too. It's there. My gift from Black Grandma. I can shut myself down emotionally even though it breaks my heart. The fact I didn't have a relationship with my dad in the last years of his life is something I will have to live with, something I have to learn from and something I will make sure will never happen with any of my children.

I think about my dad so much now. I understand so much with my dad was motivated by fear. When I was a teenager he was frightened for me. Frightened that he had produced this loud, emotional, in-your-face girl who loved to dance and go out and didn't want to go to university or get a job in an office. I think he felt – like a lot of men I've been involved with have felt – that I needed to be controlled and kept in my place. In his case, I think he felt it was the only way to keep me safe. He worried I'd get pregnant or get into drugs or 'get in with the wrong crowd'. He didn't believe that I would ever do anything with my life.

'Stop dancing,' he'd tell me. 'Just give it up,' he'd say every time I talked about an audition or the chance of a job somewhere. My dad thought you could only be successful if you were sensible and studious. And he got me as his daughter.

When I was sixteen and dancing in Blackpool, he came to see me at the Horseshoe Bar with Danielle and my mum. I was in my element, wearing some sequinned sheer catsuit and a G-string, and with feathers in my hair and pushed out like a tail above my bottom. 'Push your G-strings up your bums,' we were reminded every night by the choreographer. 'We want to see bum cheeks.' My family sat in the front row, which was so close to the stage you were practically waving your backside in peoples' faces as they sat there, chomping their dinner (it was an eat-in experience so as you danced, there would be people shouting, 'Oi luv, you forgot the extra portion of chips …').

I was so excited as I pranced out in my dancer's finery. I didn't notice, but my sister later told me that my dad's eyebrows shot up so high they practically shot off the top of his head. 'They're going to think I'm amazing,' I was thinking as I kicked my legs higher than ever and shook my booty like Tina Turner (this was well before Beyoncé). My dad could only take about fifteen minutes before he raced towards the exit. I didn't even notice because I was so swept up in showing off my moves.

'Did you love it?' I asked him afterwards (they'd all waited for me to get changed and meet them outside).

'It was very good, Melanie,' he said, clearly mortified that his teenage daughter was showing off pretty much everything to the audience. It makes me laugh to think about it now. And it makes me cry. All I ever wanted was to make him proud.

13
DANCING QUEEN

—

I will let you into a secret. When I am sitting on that judges' panel in 'America's Got Talent' or 'Australian X Factor', I know I am so bloody lucky. I have a career I never expected as a brown kid from a council estate where my boasting claim to fame was that my dance teacher, Jean Pearce, once did choreography for 'Junior Showtime', a TV show where a singing group called The Nolans were discovered.

'What exactly do you want to do with your life, Melanie?' my mum would ask me when I was about fifteen. 'Be a dancer on a cruise ship,' I'd say. That was the height of my ambition. That or getting a part in an Andrew Lloyd Webber show. I would dream that he would somehow see me in a show and wait backstage to tell me he was going to make me a star.

My mum would have been happy for me to get a regular dancing job. 'I think you'd be great in "Miss Saigon",' she would tell me. 'You could be one of those prostitutes; they have loads of them in that show,' she'd say. That was the height of her expectations for me. Secretly, though, I always felt something big was going to happen to me.

So here I am sitting next to Heidi Klum – one of the world's biggest supermodels – who is now a properly good mate and who, like me, has no filter. I am whispering, 'Which one do you fancy?' every time a group of guys walks in, and she will whisper back something totally inappropriate. We are always forgetting that everyone in the gallery hears everything we say. She cracks me up – like my best friend, Charlotte, who I used to mess about with during local dance competitions in Leeds and all around the north of England. We would be supposed to be sitting perfectly composed as the dance judges deliberated, but we'd be pulling faces at each other, loudly dropping our number cards ('And this is Melanie Brown, number 8, performing Nancy Sinatra's "These Boots Are Made for Walking"') and generally not taking ourselves too seriously.

During breaks, I make Heidi dance with me in my dressing room. She's so serious and German on the one hand … and, on the other, so completely mad and crazy (she's also a Gemini like me) that it never fails to make me laugh to watch her dance.

I know how lucky I am. If the Spice Girls hadn't happened, I could have been that dancer on cruises showing my children a battered album with all the photos of myself winning competitions when I was younger. I see something of myself in so many of the kids – and adults – who walk through the doors of those television talent shows. I'll catch that spark of total drive, a girl who spends every single night in her bedroom singing Whitney Houston songs for hours; someone who has really put thought and effort into their outfit; someone with a personality too big for their body; someone who just wants to be noticed and told, 'Yes. You do have something special.' That was me. All of them.

When I found my passion, I was precisely seven years old. The woman next door to us had a daughter called Sharon who was two years older than me and had just started dance classes. 'Shall I take your Melanie with us?' she asked one day.

'Yes,' said my mum, before the question was barely out of the neighbour's mouth. Everyone knew I was this hyperactive bundle who was sent up the road to various aunts and friends of the family with a request from my mum to 'have her for a bit' because Brownies, swimming club and skipping in the garden didn't even put a dent in my endless reserves of energy. The walls of the terrace houses in Westfield Road, Hyde Park, were paper-thin so Sharon and her mum would have heard my nonstop rampages jumping round the house and my mum's regular cries of 'Can you sit still for just a few minutes, Melanie?' People called me 'The Wind' because I moved so fast I created draughts everywhere.

So off I went with Sharon to a dance class in the basement of this house, a ten-minute bus ride from home. It had no central heating. If you wanted to keep warm in the winter, you had to keep moving. The Jean Pearce School of Dance was run by a very formidable, driven woman called Mrs Wood – Jean Pearce was her stage name. She had no time for anyone who couldn't pick up a step in a matter of seconds, and a routine in a matter of minutes. The classes – tap, ballet, jazz and modern – ran at breakneck speed. Finally, I'd found someone who insisted everyone went at my pace instead of shouting, 'Slow down for a minute, Melanie.'

'Quick, quick, quick, and move again and again. Turn, back and faster, faster – you with the hair move to the front.' That was me! At the front in my very first lesson! I hung on every word, moved like magic as she threw out step after step because there was no way I was losing my place at the front. Every inch of my body felt charged with a passion I'd never known. I could do this. It wasn't like maths or spelling at school. This was easy. This was fun, and there were loads of girls next to me who even I could see weren't getting it right. And they were even wearing proper dance leotards. I wasn't. I was in a T-shirt and jeans. What was wrong with them? Just listen to the beat, move your feet like she says, and dance. I felt that cold, down-at-heel house was the place I'd been looking for all my life.

In the space of less than an hour, Jean Pearce was my hero. She was – to me – just like Lydia Grant, the dance teacher from 'Fame'. 'You want fame? Well, fame costs, and this is where you start paying … in sweat.' She was showbiz. She had a son called Billy Pearce who was big news on the Northern comedy-club circuit. She took no prisoners. If you made a wrong step she would slap you hard on the legs. Years later, I used her leg-slapping technique on Geri every time she made a mistake in our Spice Girl routines. 'Ow, Melanie, that hurt,' she'd yell. 'Fame costs,' I'd laugh back. 'Get used to it.'

—

'Mum, I need to go to Jean Pearce,' I shouted as soon as Sharon dropped me back home.

'Who's Jean Pearce?' asked my mum. She soon realized Jean Pearce was about to loom very large in our lives. I would not shut up about her. The following week, I was officially enrolled. I discovered Miss Pearce did more than one class a week.

Two weeks later it was, 'Mum, I need to do jazz,' then 'I need to do modern,' along with 'You have to get me ballet shoes, tap shoes, a character skirt, a blue leotard, a pink one …'

My mum put up a mirror and fixed a shower bar to my wall so I could practise in my room, which I did every night for hours. And later when I started to do shows, it was 'Mum, you have to make me a cowboy outfit with a massive Stetson.' And my mum, who could barely sew a button on when I started dance, was within a matter of years the best costume maker – and borrower – this side of Yorkshire. I will never forget a black-and-red sequinned top she made me that I continued to wear for years – largely to clubs and parties.

And because neither she nor my dad could really afford to send me to dance lessons, my mum – who worked as a sales assistant in C&A – took on endless part-time jobs, from the chip shop to cleaning loos in an old people's home, in order for me to dance. Not only did she realize I'd found something that took up every minute of my day; I think she saw straightaway I was good at it. She believed in me. 'That was great, Melanie,' she'd laugh when I showed her a little practice number. 'Martin, watch our Melanie, she's really good at this dancing.'

But the real moment I realized I knew what I wanted to be doing for the rest of my life was on one of my first shows for Jean Pearce in Leeds. I was dolled up to the nines, red dots in the inner corners of my eyes (so the people at the back could see them) and lashings of black mascara. Before I went on, I was shaking, sweating and sick with nerves. 'I can't do it. I've forgotten the steps,' I whispered to Charlotte, in the backstage area. She shrugged and pulled a silly face to make me laugh. I went onstage and danced perfectly. I didn't miss a step; it was as if my body just knew what it was doing. The audience clapped and I saw a hundred smiling faces all focused on me – cheering. It was the biggest buzz I'd felt in my life. Better than winning the egg-and-spoon or sprint at Sports Day, better than jumping on the beds in my cousin Joanna's house (we weren't allowed to jump on the beds at home). As I walked offstage, I knew this was IT. This was my destiny. I need to start practising a really good autograph, I thought, because I'm going to be a world-famous dancer.

There is, however, a difference between what went on for me as a struggling performer and what happens on those TV shows. Between the ages of nine and fifteen, I'd entered hundreds of competitions, done so many auditions and performed in venues up and down the country, from Manchester to Skegness, 100 miles away. The stagefright completely stopped because I got so used to that giddy feeling you get just before you go out to perform. And if I didn't win or didn't get picked, I never cried. Neither did Charlotte or my other dance friend, Carly. We'd laugh it off and think, Better luck next time. We knew it wasn't easy and that we were going to hear more nos than yeses. But if you wanted to do it, you had to keep carrying on. Like I said, I even auditioned to be one of the girls in *The Sound of Music* at Leeds Grand Theatre. There was no way in hell a mixed-race girl was ever going to get that job, but I was completely oblivious. Another audition. Another rejection. Get up. Move on.

I used to lie in my bedroom looking at my posters of Michael Jackson and Neneh Cherry and dream of dancing in PROPER shows like Charlotte's older sister, Leisa (we were beside ourselves with excitement when she got a part in 'Singin' in the Rain' with Tommy Steele), or performing in the West End like a few of the older girls from Jean Pearce had gone on to do.

My dad wanted me to go to university or work in an office. I did try. I had two jobs in telesales at *Auto Trader* magazine and then later at *Motor Mart* in Leeds. I lasted three months in the first job and then a couple of months the second time. I was always in trouble for being late, being loud and wearing too short skirts. Most of the time I was pretending I was acting a part like Melanie Griffiths in *Working Girl* – except I didn't do much work. On the other hand, I loved my job in a jeans shop in Schofield Centre, dancing around to the Humpty Hump dance song and telling girls what style would suit them best. I'd lied about my age (you had to be fifteen to work there and I was fourteen), and I'd ponce around in cut-off shorts and tight tops, practising my Friday-night moves, thinking I was the bee's knees. That shop was my stage and the customers were my audience. Skirts could never be short enough there, and I could escape into my own fantasy world of being a famous dancer.

I got my first proper paid professional job when I was sixteen, working as a dancer in the Horseshoe Bar in Blackpool, which is a very old, quite scruffy seaside town in Lancashire. But Blackpool – famous for its electric lights and entertainment shows – still has a gritty, old-school glamour to it. So many household names – particularly comedians and dancers – cut their teeth there. 'Strictly Come Dancing' – the UK version of 'Dancing with the Stars' – is filmed from the Tower Ballroom there for two weeks every year, and every single celebrity wants to be there because it's so special. Dating back to 1894, it's stunningly beautiful with gold-painted balconies, ornate ceilings and beautiful chandeliers. It's unbelievable.

The Horseshoe Bar doesn't quite have the same class. It's more gaudy with a black stage and bright red curtains, but to me back then it seemed so glamorous it made my heart beat fast. I was fifteen when I auditioned for the summer-season dance. I begged my mum to let me go; we didn't tell my dad because it would mean missing some of my GCSEs as they clashed with the rehearsal dates. But I didn't care. I wanted to be on that stage, dolled up in lace and feathers, and dancing like a superstar.

Even now, years on, I still have the showgirl in me. That sheer, bejewelled blue catsuit by Rocky Gathercole that I wore for the first live auditions on 'America's Got Talent' is pure outrageous showgirl. It was the summer of 2017 and I was going through my horrific court case with Stephen at the time. Emotionally I was all over the place, so in many ways it was the last thing you would have expected me to wear. But putting it on made me feel in touch with myself, my inner showgirl, and it made me happy. So I wore it. As bizarre as it may seem, those brash fake jewels helped lift me up. Even more bizarrely, it brought my past and present right back together. One of the AGT team came running up to me saying, 'Everyone on social media is talking about you and Mystique.' I was totally thrown because Mystique was the name of the dance troop in Blackpool that I danced with. I was thinking, 'How does everyone know that?' It turned out they were actually saying I looked like Mystique the Marvel superhero who is all blue and wears catsuits. (It was one of those Bart Simpson 'D'oh' moments – I have a lot of those.) Mystique is a highly skilled strategist, she's a fighter and a great actress, so I'm happy to have channelled her along with my Blackpool past.

My mum was in shock when I got the job in Blackpool. 'Oh God, Melanie, what are we going to tell your dad?' she said. 'Tell him I'm going,' I said. 'And he can't stop me.' I was on a massive high. I was the youngest dancer they had ever employed. The woman who ran the dancers was so impressed with me that she got someone else to stand in for me while I finished my GCSE exams (I still missed a few) and someone to stand in for me in September because I had a place at the Northern School of Contemporary Dance and I'd promised I'd be there on the first day.

I left home a couple of days after my sixteenth birthday. My dad looked a bit sad when I finally left because I think he knew he was responsible for me being so desperate to get away. He didn't say anything to me, of course. Just 'Your room's still here, Melanie.' And I grinned and thought, 'This is it. I'm off.' I couldn't get away fast enough.

My mum packed her little blue Polo with all the things I wanted to take with me (mainly clothes, makeup and hair products) and I didn't look back. I moved into a holiday flat, ate hotdogs and burgers from the beachfront, and stacked my cupboard with crisps, chocolate and biscuits. In those days I could eat what I wanted. The dancers got weighed every week, and you had your wages docked if you put weight on – it was my first introduction to the tyranny of body image in this business. Lots of the dancers had eating disorders, but I was fortunate enough to have a very fast metabolism so I didn't ever succumb to starving myself or going on mad diets. I used to see girls bursting into tears if the scales tipped them a few pounds over. It would be years before I realized how deep the psychological scars can be for women who grow up being body-shamed like this. Even that expression 'body shaming' is something that didn't exist back then.

———

In the early days of the Spice Girls, Geri confided to me that she had an eating disorder. When we all lived together in Maidenhead, I barely saw her eat, but I didn't think about it. Apart from me and Emma (my partner in crime in midnight snacks and fried breakfasts), all the girls were quite quirky eaters. Melanie ate mushed-up vegetables, and Vic only ever ate breadsticks and dips. I didn't think twice about it, and it was only years later after Mel C and Geri started to speak out about their eating disorders and the pain they went through that I really began to think deeply about it.

We all have insecurities. Most of them come from things that are said to you in your childhood or teenage years when you are coming to terms with your own identity. For me it was the colour of my skin and the fact I didn't do well in school that made their indelible marks on me. There was nothing I could do about the colour of my skin. I was born with it. But I was also born with a naturally slim and curvy body that I never had to even think about. I'd hear my mum moaning about putting weight. 'I'm going to start a diet on Monday,' she'd say on a Friday night as she was tucking into a bag of crisps. It would actually drive me nuts. 'Mum, if you want to lose weight, just eat less,' I'd yell. I never thought it was anything other than that simple.

When we were all picked by Chris and Bob Herbert of Heart Management to be in a girl band, we had to meet a guy called Chic Murphy, who was the money-man behind Heart, and he had to decide that we were worth the gamble. The semi-detached house in Maidenhead (with a vast wet patch on the kitchen floor that we all learned to avoid even drunk in the dark) where we lived for a year was one of his houses. He lived nearby in a massive house with a pool. Right in the middle of the tiled bottom of the pool was a giant red 'C' for 'Chic'. 'How cool is that?' I shrieked to Geri.

It was the first time I'd ever been to a place like that. Even though Vic didn't bat an eyelid (her family were much wealthier than the rest of ours), I wanted a whole tour of the place and stood oooh'ing and aaah'ing as I took in the peach-coloured walls and all the marble in the bathroom and the massive room with televisions everywhere. There was even a huge Benidorm-style bar where we'd all spend the afternoon inventing cocktails to drink. On the one hand Chic was really lovely, funny and generous but he was also incredibly controlling with a totally out-dated attitude to women that could be very damaging to young girls.

Chic was a cockney – he even used cockney rhyming slang – and he was one of those men who had no problems telling us exactly what he thought. He'd do these old Temptations dance routines in front of us and tell us that's what we should be doing. Then one afternoon as we all sat by the pool he started telling Melanie and Vic that they should lose weight. 'You could fucking lose a few fucking pounds, couldn't ya? What's wrong with ya? You'd better fucking start watching what you're fucking eating.' We all sat there in shock. And that's really strange considering how feisty we all are. But it also shows how easily girls can be put down and deliberately made to feel insecure. If I could teleport myself back to that time, I would have stood up and pushed Chic in the pool.

It is partly because of what I saw my friends go through that I have never turned my body into my enemy – even after my metabolism finally slowed down once I hit thirty (it happens to us all) and even when my husband was on my case about it. Right now I am pretty much the size I was in my twenties – call it the divorce diet – but this isn't because I believe thinner is better. I have loved my body in all its stages. I adored being pregnant and seeing my body get bigger and bigger, I loved my post-pregnancy curves, and I never covered up or cried when my body got bigger.

If I wanted to diet – or get fitter – or I wanted to shut Stephen up and show him how easy it was for me to change my body, I would start exercising and watch what I ate or stick to my Jenny Craig food once I became the ambassador of that brilliant, practical, no-fuss Australian brand in 2011. I am – I know – very lucky not to have emotional issues tied into food and weight from childhood so it remains very simple for me. At the moment, when I want to improve my fitness I do six hundred stomach crunches a day. My abs and stomach are rock-hard. I have always been practical about my body. If you hate something, then change it – which is probably why I have no problems with cosmetic surgery. But I have always understood why for so many women, things are not this simple. Living with my skin colour has never been simple.

In Blackpool I was one of the few people of colour for miles around. There were days when certain crowds would turn up in bus tours and I knew it would be best for me to stay in. It doesn't make you feel great about yourself. And there is nothing you can do about the skin you were born with. I always knew I had to be careful.

I did, however, go completely mad for a while. Away from home for the first time in my life, away from my dad's incessant rules and regulations, I discovered gay clubs thanks to a couple of the male dancers in the group and threw myself into the life of a performer. In the upstairs dressing room, you had your own little space to put out makeup and sort out your costume. I felt so grown up and loved the bustle of the other performers and entertainers barging in and out of the dressing area – it was a bit like being with my mum's sisters and all my cousins.

When I think back now, there were some aspects which were pretty hard for that sixteen-year-old version of me, however ballsy I thought I was. Onstage and in rehearsals I was in my element. I'd been trained to pick up routines in minutes and loved everything about the performances, from the mad costumes to the cheering audience and the joking around that went on backstage. But I did get pretty homesick. I missed my friends, I missed my family, I missed home cooking and my boyfriend. I'd started dating Stephen Mulrain, a reserve for Leeds United who I'd met on a night out in an R&B club called Galleria I used to go to with Charlotte (we'd have to wait till my dad had gone on his night shift). I was madly in love with Stephen. Really sadly his life took a few wrong turns a few years after we split and he had an accident which stopped him playing football. But when I knew him, he was funny, he was completely devoted to me, and his mum was hysterical. She taught me how to wind and grind to reggae and made the best rice, peas and chicken or curried goat and macaroni cheese.

People say you have to be tough to survive a life in show business. It's true. You do. There is no getting away from it. You are often separated from your loved ones; you have to work long hours, make sacrifices like not being there for every Christmas and birthday; and you have to get on with all sorts of people. Now this is like a lot of other jobs, but in show business you have to get used to being judged all the time, criticized and put down, and you have to keep yourself focused on the fact that you love what you do. People say you have to be selfish, which is right in a way because you keep having to put your dreams first. You can never lose sight of what you want.

In Blackpool, I learned these lessons fast. I was the new girl in town. I was loud, I could dance, and I got a lot of attention from a few of the choreographers who offered me work on other shows. I did annoying things, like I'd bust out a couple of different moves in the show every now and again, which went down like a lead balloon with the other dancers because I wasn't totally sticking to the routines. I was the only mixed-race dancer on the stage – which felt a bit intimidating given certain members of the audience. In the dressing room there would be bitchy comments and rolled eyes. There would be a hole in my costume that I'd not made, and as I'd be putting on my dance shoes I'd see the straps had been cut. What do you do? You're sixteen. You've never been away from home before. Well, the only honest answer is you suck it up. You don't let anyone see it bothers you. If you cry (and I did, quite a few times), you do it in your room. And you get on with it because that's life. That's show business. You push yourself and you get pushed. And you keep a needle and thread on you at all times. (I still do.)

When I did 'Dancing with the Stars' three months after my daughter Angel was born – seven months after I'd had the horrific split from her dad, Eddie Murphy – I was not in good shape and it had been years since my dancing days. But my fabulous dance partner, Maksim Chmerkovskiy, straightaway recognized the old dancer in me and there was no way he'd cut me any slack.

'I think you do splits now in this dance, Melanie,' he'd say before we went out onstage.

I'd say, 'No way, Maksim. I can't.' We'd go out in front of people in a routine we'd practised and he'd add these moves, pushing me down into splits three, four times in a row, and unbelievably there I was doing the splits. When you look at my face on YouTube, behind the plastered-on smile you can see the shock in my face as it happens. All dancers have muscle memory and their bodies will always have that flexibility even if it has been buried for years. Maksim – tough as he is because tough is what you have to be – was teaching me that lesson.

But the most important lesson in my business is: Never lose your friends or your family because they will keep you sane, keep you happy and keep you grounded. They will also forgive you for being selfish – for not being there at your cousin's christening – because they know how much your dreams mean to you.

I'm talking from experience because two decades later I lost mine and my life fell apart. I am still in the process of mending bridges, and I will never let that happen again. My mum comes out to stay with me for months at a time in Los Angeles and my friend Charlotte comes out with her daughter, Tillie Armartey, whose birth I remember but whose growing up I missed out on because I was busy travelling the world and working. But it doesn't matter anymore. We are back together. We all have a laugh and leap around my bedroom doing dance moves from the days we did our competitions together. That to me is pure joy.

But back in Blackpool I was determined that I was going to succeed in show business. I didn't always get things right, and I had so many times when I thought I'd blown it, or I didn't know what to do or where to go next. But I refused to make a Plan B. This is something I think a lot of people who 'make it' have in common.

I'll never forget meeting Geri for the first time during the preliminary auditions for the group that was – in those initial stages – called Touch. Her voice was even louder than mine and she had a manic energy about her which really pushed us as a band. For her it HAD to work because she'd had one more year than me of things not working out, and instead of making her give up, it made her more determined to push this group of girls as far as she could and to take us as seriously as possible. We'd go out in matching outfits (I'd wear a short orange playsuit and she'd wear a blue one and we'd both wear long white socks) to some nightclub in Maidenhead at the weekend when the other girls had gone back home to see their friends or family.

We hadn't yet done anything except spend weeks singing together in rehearsal rooms in front of Bob and Chris Herbert. No-one had heard of us, and out of the five, there were just the two of us in the nightclub. Geri, however, would march right up to the DJ booth, grab the microphone and in this loud, husky voice would announce, 'Ladies and gentlemen, Touch is in the house,' as if we were the biggest band in the world. At the time, it made me laugh out loud. But it's a real example of how you really have to believe in yourselves to make others believe in you. Kim Kardashian has acted like a superstar ever since she was just one of Paris Hilton's best friends. When Simon Cowell was a post-room boy at EMI, he dressed like David Cassidy – the heartthrob of the day – and made sure everyone noticed him. I've sat at dinner with Rita Ora, and she is so flirty and confident, you walk away thinking she is the sexiest woman you've ever met. She did actually flash her boobs to everyone at the table, but she can completely get away with it because you know she knows exactly what she's doing. She's in charge of who she is.

—

At sixteen, I was impatient for the life I wanted to start. After my stint in Blackpool, I enrolled at the Northern School of Contemporary Dance, but my first year went very badly. I got bored because, as a dancer, I felt I was going backwards. I was in classes with people who had never even been in pointe shoes in ballet. I was broke and ended up teaching aerobics at the Mandela Centre in Leeds, which had been Black Grandad's top place for a night out for a bit of flirting and some shots of neat rum. I loved teaching aerobics. I was good at it. My class was full of well-upholstered black mamas and young guys who'd come to ogle this girl in a skimpy leotard. Initially the guys would watch me through the window till I stuck paper over the glass and marched outside and said, 'If you want to watch, you have to pay and come inside.' They'd all line up at the front, and as soon as the music started I'd march to the back and teach from there. No flies on me. The women didn't frighten me either. 'Now it's time to move those arses,' I'd shout, and we'd all begin.

I did eventually get kicked out of college for bad attitude and attendance. 'You're too loud and other girls can kick their legs higher than you,' the principal told me as I stood in her office trying to look as if I wasn't bothered. Another dead end. My mum entered me for a beauty contest, Miss Leeds Weekly News. I was furious with her, then decided to do it and won. I had a Renault Clio for a year so I had to learn to drive to make the most of it. Within a few months, Charlotte and I were driving it to the infamous Hacienda Club in Manchester, one of the wildest, greatest nightclubs run by the legendary Tony Wilson. We were outrageous. I definitely didn't live up to the image of 'doing good work and representing the best of Leeds' as we'd stumble out blinking into the streets at 4 a.m. to go home. Charlotte was always trying to scrub the lettering off the Renault Clio where it said 'Miss Leeds Weekly News', but I was gutted when I had to hand that car back.

My other jobs included teaching underprivileged kids from Newcastle how to dance and put on a show in an Austrian holiday resort (I loved that job); doing extra work on British TV shows from 'Coronation Street' to 'A Touch of Frost'; podium dancing (we got free non-alcoholic drinks); dancing on Keith and Orville's 'Quack Chat Show' and 'The Bonnie Langford Show' on television; going back to Blackpool to dance in the Billy Pearce 'Rock with Laughter' show. I had acting lessons and singing lessons. I nearly got a job on 'Miss Saigon' and narrowly missed being cast for 'Starlight Express'. Instead I danced for the troops in the Falklands, Bosnia and Northern Ireland, and appeared as a dancer in a pantomime in Lewisham, south London, starring Saracen from the hit TV show of the time, 'Gladiators'. I was given one line to say in the show, but I ended up getting sacked because – surprise, surprise – of a man. I'd met a guy called Julian in my second season at Blackpool and called in sick to the panto, got spotted out in town and grassed up. I was told I'd never work as a dancer again.

So I went back home to Leeds. I was eighteen, borrowing fivers from my mum and hunting for jobs through *The Stage* magazine, which was the bible at the time for anyone wanting to work in the West End or in show business. I went for one audition after another. Most of my money (or my mum's money) went on coach tickets down to London. 'Don't look at anyone or talk to anyone when you get to London,' she would warn me. 'And don't get your money out in front of anyone.' (Paying for a McDonalds involved me going into the loos to count out my money first and then holding it tight in my fist.) I'd sleep or look out of the window on that three-hour journey from Leeds to London and daydream about getting my break. I felt like the very tips of my fingernails were scraping at this world I wanted to be part of, but I hadn't got a grip of it yet.

'Give it up, Melanie. It's never going to happen. You're living in a dream world,' my dad would shout at me when he caught me half asleep on the sofa in our lounge in the middle of the afternoon. I know my mum was worried about me, but the day *The Stage* arrived, she'd comb through it before I woke up and would circle jobs she thought I could go for.

And then, one morning, I looked at two adverts she'd put a black biro circle around. One was an audition for a cruise ship, the other was for a girl band. It read:

RU 18/23 with the ability to sing/dance?
RU streetwise, outgoing, ambitious, dedicated?
Heart Management are a widely successful
Music Industry Management Consortium currently
Forming a choreographed, singing/dancing
All female Pop Act for a Record Recording Deal.
Auditions on 27 March 1994 at Dance Works
Opposite Selfridges. 11 – 4.

There was no way I was going to miss that.

14
EDDIE
—

There are in times in life – especially in my life – when unexpected things happen, and you go with it and it turns out to be something beautiful. The word that sums up those situations is (I'll check my thesaurus because this is a very long one for me) *serendipitous*.

Finding that advert for a girl band changed the course of my life, but there is one man who had – and still has – the most momentous effect on me, and that is Eddie Murphy.

I am going to go all Mills & Boon here (and honestly this is so not like me), but the moment I laid eyes on him it was as if a 2,000-volt electric current had passed between us. I felt a hundred different emotions at once, from confused to elated, to happy to scared, to relaxed to incredulous, and everything in between. I felt I had known this man all my life and that I was staring at my destiny in his face. And I felt terrified to be feeling like that because I wasn't prepared for something so massive which I knew was going to turn my world upside-down.

Before Eddie, I'd never believed in the idea of love at first sight. It had not happened to me before; it has not happened since. You may think it sounds ridiculous, but it was exactly like a moment in a movie when everything else in the whole world disappears but the boy and the girl; where birds tweet and music plays in your head and you are so thunderstruck you don't even remember your own name because your whole body is consumed by this one person whose eyes are locked with yours. And for me that was magical but petrifying.

But I've jumped ahead of myself because it's hard for me to think about that first meeting with Eddie without my emotions going straight back to that moment in his vast kitchen in May 2006.

So, this is how it all started. A few weeks beforehand, I'd bumped into Lisa, a friend of mine and the wife of Jimmy Jam. (Jimmy produced a few tracks on the solo album 'Hot' that I'd released after the Spice Girls split.) 'I've got to tell you this, Melanie,' she said. 'Eddie Murphy keeps asking me and Jimmy if we could arrange for him to meet you.'

I had to think who he was. 'The comedy guy?' I asked, Roladexing through my brain, trying to remember a name of one of his movies or picture his face.

'Yes,' said Lisa. 'I promise you'll really like him.'

'If he has a dinner party, I'll come,' I said jokingly, and thought no more about it.

An hour later Lisa called me. 'Can you make Friday?' she asked. 'I'll text you the address.'

At the time I was single. I'd come out of a very beautiful, loving, five-year relationship with a woman (one I will never, ever discuss because she was extremely private and I will always respect that). I was completely happy being on my own with Phoenix, but I guess I was a little bit flattered and a little bit intrigued to meet this Eddie Murphy guy. I never thought for a second anything would come of it, other than an interesting evening.

By now I had been living in Los Angeles for five years. LA suited me. I had never intended to move there – I have never been someone who makes plans and weighs up the pros and cons. If it feels right, I jump on in. Sometimes with disastrous results (shit storm), sometimes with great ones (serendipitous). America was a good decision. I went out for a holiday in 2003 after I split from Phoenix's dad, Jimmy, and basically I never went home.

I sold the large house in Marlow that I'd bought for myself, Jimmy and Phoenix, and I bought a gorgeous, spacious house in Los Feliz for me and Phoenix. I loved the weather, the fact that I could go to the beach with my little girl every day to relax and have fun. I didn't get hassled so much because in Hollywood there were way more famous people than me walking around. I'd stood in line in a grocer's next to a shimmering, perfect Nicole Kidman within a few days of being out there and laughed to myself as I checked out what she was buying. After six years of solid madness, LA felt right.

I did school runs; went to hot yoga classes; drank veggie juices; had coffees with other mums; made some great friends; meditated and got to know the weird and wonderful ways of the city where crisps were chips, and chips were things no-one (except me) ate. If I'm honest, I think I was always waiting for something to start up again with the Spice Girls. I did a few acting roles. I had no financial worries. My life was as chilled as the Midget Gems I kept – and still keep – in my fridge to remind me of home.

The 'dinner party' was at Eddie's gated mansion, high up in the Hollywood Hills, amid the giant cypresses and sycamores of the canyons. I arrived and was ushered into a huge room that was rammed with people. Believe it or not, I'm actually pretty shy when I'm in a room and don't know many people. I smiled at the other guests, and was thinking, Eddie must have a bloody big table for all these people to sit at. Then I wandered round the house, taking in the sumptuous marble floors and the pretty furniture. After about fifteen minutes or so, I found myself in Eddie's kitchen.

Again, the room was full of guests. I stood in the doorway trying to spot my friend Lisa, and then suddenly I noticed a man in a black tank-top who was looking right at me. I looked back at him, and that is when it felt like fireworks had started going off inside me. It was Eddie.

We weren't just 'looking'. It was as if there was no-one else in the whole world – let alone that room – but us. I know that's a cliché, but honestly that's how it felt. I couldn't tell you how long that 'look' lasted because even as I'm thinking about it now it felt like it went on for hours. Then someone grabbed me and I heard the words 'Melanie, you're here. Come and meet Eddie.' It was Lisa.

'Give me a minute, I need to go to the loo,' I said, and bolted from the room.

A minute later I stood in Eddie Murphy's large fancy 'bathroom' (as they call them in America), which was crammed with expensive soaps and scented candles with expensive-looking brand names I'd never even heard of. I was actually shaking but laughing at the same time. 'What the fuck happened there?' I asked myself. It was too weird and I had no idea how to handle the situation. There was no way I was going to walk back into that kitchen because I felt completely freaked out. 'Calm down, get a grip, Melanie,' I told myself. Had I honestly experienced some cosmic lovestruck moment with Eddie Murphy in his kitchen? Or had I imagined it or totally got it wrong? It didn't seem right. He was more than ten years older than me, and I never fell for older guys. I barely knew anything about him. And if I'd got it wrong, I had to stop acting like an idiot. In fact, I had to get out of there and go home before I did something stupid (yes, this is how my mind works). I needed to go away and think.

A few minutes later, I opened the door and, in my head, was going over my excuse to Lisa as to why I had to leave. But there in front of me, and to my horror, was Eddie, his head bowed, his hands in his pockets like a little boy. 'Hi Eddie,' I blurted out giving him an awkward hug. 'Thanks for a great party, but I've got to go because I forgot I've arranged to meet some friends at the Mondrian.' I was still blathering as I rushed away trying not to meet his eyes. My heart was pounding. Now I looked like a complete fool.

I drove home, took off my makeup and got into bed. I remember pulling the covers over my head trying to force myself to think about anything else apart from Eddie Murphy, me acting like an idiot, and whether it was possible I'd met the love of my life and then just done a runner. Within ten minutes I heard my phone buzzing: 'It's Lisa. Where are you? Eddie's moved the party to the Mondrian. But we can't see you.' I couldn't believe it. Clearly Someone Up There was making sure I had to deal with this. I got dressed again, into the same clothes, and put my makeup back on as fast as I could. Then I dashed to the Mondrian. There they were … about twenty people sitting at a huge table, and with an empty seat next to Eddie. I tried to be really casual and walked over to him, but as he turned round towards me I lost the plot again. What the hell was wrong with me? 'I'm just going to nip to the bathroom,' I said, thinking, 'Oh God, now he's going to think I'm incontinent or something.'

He stood up and shook his head. 'I know what happens when you go to the bathroom. So I'm coming with you to make sure you don't disappear.' He put his hands on my shoulders and walked behind me. I started laughing and laughing – we looked like a pair of complete idiots. He walked me to the ladies, and then back to my seat, with his hands firmly on my shoulders. Once I sat down, he took my hand and then held it under the table like a shy teenager. He didn't let go of it all night. I didn't want him to. I felt like my hand belonged in his. I hadn't imagined anything. This was real.

There was something solid beneath the formal Hollywood exterior that Eddie wanted me to see. I felt it in the way he held my hand. It felt at the same time protective, vulnerable and forthright. He didn't flirt or make sexual innuendos like most guys I'd gone on dates with. He was the perfect gentleman – even if the fact that he had my hand in his meant I couldn't use my knife to eat my meal. I didn't care. I couldn't have eaten a bite of food. When he talked to me, he would look at me, right in the eyes, as if it was just the two of us at this table for twenty people, and say, 'Are you happy, Melanie? I am very happy that you are here.'

He didn't talk to me constantly. Every now and again he would turn to me and say something like that. But all the time he held my hand. It made me feel special and quite shy. I didn't talk as much as usual. I didn't want to get engaged in any other conversations because I didn't want to miss a word that he said.

—

By the age of thirty-one, I'd had relationships with both men and women. I'd been married, dated guys in the public eye like Max Beesley, Lenny Kravitz and Peter Andre, and mixed with people from all sorts of backgrounds, cultures and beliefs. But Eddie was different to anyone I'd ever met. He was Hollywood. Old school. And I'm Leeds. Comprehensive school. We lived in two different worlds. He had been famous most of his life and had built himself his own private kingdom behind walls where he could look after and live with his family and friends. I spent my life trying to break walls down. In the very beginning of the Spice Girls, all the five of us ever wanted to do was kick down barriers.

When we were five little nobodies – or wannabes – who couldn't get a meeting with people in the music industry, we'd track them down and make them listen to us. We weren't going to sit there and take no for an answer. I remember us hijacking Simon Cowell in the carpark of his London offices. We'd heard his name by talking to the handful of people we'd met in the music industry through the little showcases Heart Management arranged for us where we would network our backsides off. None of us felt Chris and Bob from Heart had that much faith in us, partly because they kept telling us we 'weren't quite ready'. It drove us demented because we felt we were, and we didn't want to keep on doing vocal training, dance training and studio sessions – we wanted to get out there.

We would pester Chris and Bob to put on showcases. Various A&R men (Artists and Repertoire, the people employed by the record companies to find new acts) would turn up to the showcase gigs.

If they weren't interested in us, we were still interested in them, and we would pump them for information, shamelessly asking who they would recommend as the best managers in the business. Simon had his own little label called S-Records, and was known for being a sharp operator and having a perfect grasp of pop (nothing has changed).

Geri spent hours with a phone directory to track down an address for S-Records and work out how to get there from Maidenhead in her battered green Fiat Uno which we went everywhere in. We got there very early (if I'd known then what I know now about Simon, we wouldn't have left the house till after midday) and hung around for hours in this little carpark in west London all dressed up. When this long-haired, smooth-looking guy with a flash car ('It's him, it's him,' Geri screamed) finally arrived, I was yelling at Mel C, 'Quick, quick. Press play.' We had our knackered old silver beatbox on full blast, and we danced around him, singing and telling him we wanted him to be our manager.

'Sorry girls, I don't think it's going to work,' he told us, as he pushed past us into his office. Anyone who gets a rejection in this industry should bear that remark in mind ... We kept on going – bashing down doors – and eventually a man called Simon Fuller said yes.

If I got a letter from a fan and they included their phone number, I'd call them up. No-one in our record company could believe I wanted to do that. Why not? I love talking to people. 'But they are a fan,' I'd say. 'I want to say hello.' I'll talk to anyone whether they are royalty or a runner – there's no difference to me. I didn't want to be a celebrity who lived behind glass, I wanted to be touchable and knowable. I wanted to look my fans in the eye and say, 'Thank you ... Hello ... How's it going?' or 'Yes, that is an eye infection I've got. Do you ever get them? Bloody pain they are, aren't they?'

Eddie wasn't like that. He lived in a beautiful paradise in the hills, far away from the real world. Everything in his house was exactly as he wanted it and revolved around his kids (he had seven children back then but now has nine, including our daughter Angel), his mum, Lillian, and his older brother, Charlie. He talked about his family all the time and I loved that about him. I loved his shyness and his sweet, gentlemanly ways, and he made me laugh. The day after the dinner party he rang me and said, 'Melanie, do you mind if I see you every day for a few days? But I don't like going out, so will you come to my house?' It was such an unusual but honest thing to say.

I laughed and said yes.

—

As I child I was called 'The Wind', but to Eddie I was 'The Whirlwind'. The first day that I went to his house, I shouted, 'I'm here, where are you?' and then ran through his beautiful, pristine mansion, and ran around the garden, jumping onto the steps of the swimming pool, listening to my loud voice echo through the giant building.

'I'm here, where are you?' he yelled back.

'Come and find me,' I hollered back from the top of a giant *Gone with The Wind* sweeping staircase.

'Er, excuse me, madam.' A guy with a seriously anxious expression came running out of a room. 'Mr Murphy doesn't like anyone making loud noises,' he said.

'Melanie, I can't see you,' came Eddie's voice, bellowing from a room downstairs.

'I think he does now,' I said to the man who turned out to be a member of his household staff. And I ran down the stairs, yelling, 'I'm here,' before sprinting through another doorway and being chased by Eddie, who was laughing. Right from the get-go we were like two little excitable kids.

His place was gob-smackingly incredible. In the foyer there was a glass roof and a button you pushed to make the whole ceiling open up. There was a tiny, perfect Wendy house in the playroom, and a vast jacuzzi which I later discovered he'd never even been in. After a couple of days, I made him get in it. Naked. I sat in the kids' teeny Wendy house with Phoenix. Then I asked Eddie if the following day I could have a proper English afternoon tea with his kids in the Wendy house. I arrived in the afternoon to mountains of scones, jam (or 'jelly' as it's called in America) and sandwiches. His cook must have had one hell of a job on her hands finding out exactly how to make everything as she'd never even heard of a scone. And there were huge pots of tea (Yorkshire tea) in china teapots that looked like they had been specially bought for the occasion.

'Is this everything you wanted?' he asked.

'No,' I said. 'I need you to bring it to the Wendy house.' I got him to crouch down and join us, scoffing cucumber sandwiches and munching on the jam-covered scones. Phoenix – who came everywhere with me – loved being with his kids and having this children's paradise to explore. We'd spend days playing and having fun.

Eddie actually listened to everything I said – something that took me by surprise because so many guys I have dated never took much notice of what I said. I remember when I went into his gym for the first time. It was like some state-of-the-art gym that an Olympic athlete would use. There was a problem though. 'You've got terrible music on your workout playlist,' I said. The next time I went in there, every playlist had been changed, and all this '90s music I loved was booming from the speakers. I was switching things up!

'Melanie,' Eddie told me after the first day we spent together, 'I gotta let you know; you really make me laugh.' I was chuffed to bits. I made the world-famous comedian Eddie Murphy laugh.

Eddie had a plan for our relationship right from the start. He doesn't like surprises; he doesn't like disorder; he likes to know what's coming and when. That's why he's such a brilliant comedian. All those seemingly impromptu, mad performances are painstakingly constructed, second by second. No mistakes. All great comedians are like this. Nothing is left to chance. In that six weeks all we did was kiss, cuddle and have fun. We had a proper 'traditional' courtship because Eddie is old-fashioned. He was constantly telling me to slow down. 'I want to know all about you, and I want you to know all about me,' he said.

'Well, what bit don't you know?' I laughed. 'I'm Mel B., Scary Spice, and you're Eddie Murphy.'

He shook his head. 'But that's not who we ARE, Melanie. You know that.'

It takes me a while to drop my loud front, which I have always used as my protective armour. Geri used to call our Spice personas (Posh, Scary, Ginger, Sport and Baby) our 'Batman suits', because we could hide behind them. I will always make jokes, laugh and be loud, partly because I actually like to have a laugh, partly because I'm a Northern girl who tries not to take life too seriously, and partly because it gives me time to work out whether I can trust someone enough to open up to them.

'Tell me about your family,' Eddie would say as we sat around his pool, having iced tea and bagels with cheese and mayo (strangely I started craving these again as soon as I left Stephen) brought to us by a member of staff.

I'd tell him about working in a jeans shop in Leeds – funnily enough it was called Trading Places, which is the name of one of his most famous films – about my dad working in a factory, about my days dancing at the Horseshoe in Blackpool when I was sixteen, where we'd have money docked for coming onstage late or having a rip in our tights.

Sometimes he'd laugh, sometimes he'd ask me to repeat things. He would run through the names of all my mum's four sisters: 'Sheila, June, Di, Pamela.' He barely asked any questions about the Spice Girls. He was more interested in the prizes I'd won for Sports Day at school than the Brit Awards I'd won with the girls.

He'd play old Elvis movies and films like *Blazing Saddles*, which starred his hero Richard Pryor ('You haven't seen this, Melanie. You *have* to watch this.') He liked to talk about why a film was 'a classic', and what made a great director and writer. I would sit and listen, entranced. He'd talk about the movie business and his childhood in the projects in New York, living in foster care with his older brother, Charlie, when his mum was ill. He was fascinating to me. He'd had a life I could and couldn't imagine. His real dad had walked out on him when he was three, and had later been stabbed and killed by a girlfriend. His mum had married a guy called Vernon Lynch, the stepfather he adored.

Eddie was all about family. His beautiful brother, Charlie, who sadly passed away in 2017, was his closest friend because they'd done everything together. He bounced all his ideas off Charlie, who was also a gifted comedian and writer. But Eddie also needed space to think. We'd have discussions about God and spirituality. I don't think there was anything we didn't talk about. I felt completely safe with him.

His kingdom was magical. You'd walk into one room and Stevie Wonder would be there playing on a piano. I spent hours talking to Stevie about music, and he knew lots about the Spice Girls, which surprised me. Stevie and I would sit and hold hands because that is the way he connects with people, and we'd drink tequila shots together. But then everything and everyone at Eddie's was a surprise. Denzel Washington was another regular at Eddie's. He was someone I was totally in awe of until one night he knocked on our bedroom door (this was months later, when we actually made it to bed) drunk as a lord and talked and joked for hours like one of my uncles after a night out – he even tried to crash out in the bed with us because he could barely move. Eddie had an amazing chef, and every evening at 6 p.m. there would be a huge buffet, and tons of people would appear and sit around the house eating.

The more time we spent together, the more it became apparent to both of us that we had something incredibly special. Despite the age difference, there was something so young and innocent about our relationship. And like a couple of kids, we spent hours working out when to take our relationship to the next level.

We finally decided it would happen about six weeks after we met, and I was unbelievably excited. I remember going out and buying some green see-through underwear embroidered with cherries, putting it on and making jokes about popping my cherry. When it came to it, I felt more shy and nervous than anything else. It was like poetry, every touch, every kiss, every sense was out of this world. We were completely besotted with each other.

—

After a few weeks together, Eddie wanted me and Phoenix to move in with him but, as much as I loved being with him, I didn't want to give up my own little paradise in Los Feliz. I liked going home and hanging out with my great girlfriends, like the ballsy twin film-makers Nicola and Teena Collins who lived round the corner from me. Sometimes I liked sleeping in my own bed, cuddled up with Phoenix with her Labrador, Lordy, lying at our feet.

As incredible as it was, there was something about Eddie's house that was like a gilded cage, and I'm too independent to live like that. He rarely wanted to leave his house, and he didn't want me to leave it either. I'd tell him I wanted to go out for coffee and he'd say, 'What do you want, Melanie? I'll send someone to get it for you.'

After about two months of only ever seeing Eddie in his home, I couldn't stand it any longer. I told him he had to get into the real world. I told him I was taking him to Coffee Bean. No chauffeur. No assistant. Just us. We got into his Rolls Royce, which I could barely drive, and drove into the San Fernando Valley. Eddie was completely silent. 'OK, let's get coffee,' I said as we practically kangarooed to a halt outside Coffee Bean. As we were going in, I noticed him trying to open the door with his elbows – like the anxious germaphobe that he was – so I playfully slapped him and pulled him inside.

Once we got to the counter, the guy asked Eddie for his order. The place was heaving. There was a queue behind us and people bunched to the side of us, waiting for their coffees. All of a sudden, I saw something strange happening to Eddie. He looked at the guy, then he looked at the coffee menu with the dozens of different varieties of coffee, and he went into this completely off-the-cuff comedy routine about not knowing what the hell coffee to order. 'Latte, cold press, cappuccino, iced, vanilla, soy, Americano, Milano … Man oh man oh man … Flat white, espresso, almond milk, cold-pressed. What's happened to coffee!' He got louder and louder, and everyone was laughing, and I could see he was transformed by the interaction – absolutely in the moment. When we left, he looked at me and said, 'I love Coffee Bean!' After that he wanted to go to Coffee Bean again and again.

He was at his best around real people, his public. Every year he had a 4th of July party for all his friends. I asked my assistant Janet if she'd come. 'It'll be a load of celebrities and really fancy. I'm actually going to hang out with my mates,' she said. I felt exactly the same way, which is why I wanted her to come to hang out with me. And when I want something, I won't let up.

'I'd really like you to come. Please can you bring Lordy [Phoenix's dog] with you because if you're not at home, he can't be on his own.' I didn't let up and she agreed to come, 'just for an hour or so'.

When Janet arrived, she parked her little old Ford Explorer, came into the house and stood in the marble hallway. The party guests were in the entertainment area (Eddie's house was so vast you couldn't even hear the noise of the first fifty people who had arrived). I'd watched her arrive from the balcony of Eddie's bedroom. 'Come up here,'

I yelled. Five minutes later she appeared in the room, put a bag with a couple of bottles in it on a table and stood by his four-poster bed with Lordy. Eddie was in the shower (we were making a late entrance to the party) and walked into the room with a towel round his waist. They'd met a few times but had not really got to know each other.

'Hey,' he said. We all had a bit of a chat and I was trying not to laugh at Janet's 'MELANIE! THIS IS SOOOO AWKWARD' looks she was giving me. I actually made her sit down and eat some food with me and have a drink while Eddie was getting dressed.

'I'm going to go and see Phoenix and tell her I've brought Lordy,' she said. 'And then, I'm really sorry, but I'll have to love you and leave you because I promised I'd go to my friend's.' Eddie looked at me and I smiled.

'Have a great time, see you tomorrow.'

A few minutes after Janet left, Eddie looked in the bag she'd put on the table and said, 'I just want to do something.'

More and more guests had arrived and the huge front drive of Eddie's house was like a carpark. By the time Janet got downstairs, her little car was boxed in by cars that cost as much as – if not more – than a house in Leeds. Eddie ignored all the guests trying to grab him and went straight for Janet. 'You brought me a really nice bottle of wine,' he said. 'And you brought Melanie's favourite pink champagne. I want you to know that really means a lot to me. A lot of people here just turn up for the party.'

He looked out at her beat-up car on his driveway. 'Is that yours?' he grinned. Janet nodded. He grabbed one of his assistants. 'He's going to get my car for you to drive home. Keep it for the rest of the weekend and I'll see you when you get back.'

Janet – like me – will never forget that man.

15
LOVE
—

Eddie made me happier than any man I'd ever met. When I got pregnant with Angel, we jumped around his en-suite bathroom laughing and crying, bursting with the best news ever. My family thought he was great because they had never seen me so completely blissed out. Every day I would wake up and he'd tell me I was the most beautiful, incredible woman. I never felt so loved.

So why did it all go so spectacularly wrong?

I've thought about this a lot over the years. Much has been written about it and very little has even got close to the truth. Since May 2017 he's been back in my life thanks to his mum, Mrs Lillian Lynch, bringing about a reunion with our daughter Angel. I've watched Angel blossom as she's got to know her dad and – after years of silence – I know one day we will all sit together and talk. There's too much unfinished business to leave it.

Eddie told me when we had been together for a matter of weeks that he wanted to get married and he wanted to have a baby. It was written years later that it was a casual relationship, and it was also said that we were together for three months, but in total we were together for almost nine months and it was Eddie who pushed every step of the way.

He didn't actually have to push very hard because I was so in love with him. What started as a thunderbolt in his kitchen turned into the most beautiful, nurturing and loving relationship of my life. He definitely looked his age, but he had the toned, fit, lean body of a twenty-year-old, and no man has made me laugh like Eddie did. Obviously he's a comedian so everyone knows he's funny, but he could give me a look or make a little noise and I would be creased up in hysterics. He had a serious side too. He was serious about marriage and kids – in any order. I wasn't in such a rush. He would talk about finding the best gynaecologist in Beverly Hills to make sure we had a perfect pregnancy. I would want to do other things to show I was serious.

One afternoon, Eddie and I went to the Shamrock Tattoo parlour on Sunset. We wrote our autographs on a piece of paper, which the guy then tattooed onto the tops of our thighs. Eddie's scribbled name on me and my barely legible loopy scrawl on him. 'You're branded,' I grinned (although I had his autograph removed a few years later).

He liked me to stay as close to him as possible – within touching distance. He'd hold my hand, stroke my back, play with my hair. 'Melanie, I can't see you,' he'd shout if I disappeared from sight.

'But you can hear me,' I'd laugh back – because we both used to joke about how loud I was. I'd never met a man who wanted to possess me so completely. It was intoxicating because I had fallen in love with him, but also stifling because I've always been very independent, very much my own person.

Eddie was intrigued by my independence. He gave me a credit card to use, saying, 'Please, Melanie. It will make me happy if you use this card.' I gave it back to him after two weeks. 'Eddie, I have my own money. I buy my things. I buy Phoenix's things. I've never relied on a man to give me money,' I said. 'It makes me feel weird.' He took the card back, reluctantly.

He liked to do things his way. At night he had this routine of going round his house making sure everything was locked and double-locked, then he'd circle back and check everything again. I'd sit waiting in bed, shouting, 'You are such a loser' and laughing.

Eddie would shout up, 'Nearly done. Nearly done. Just one bunch more to check.'

Our first holiday was to the Four Seasons in Maui, Hawaii, with all his children along with a few friends. The boxer Sugar Ray Leonard is a great mate of Eddie's, and he came, too. Eddie made the plumber change the toilet in the room. I remember asking him, 'Is it because of your OCD?'

He looked at me and winked and said, 'No, it's because I can', and we both roared our heads off.

—

After the first couple of weeks, we had talked about getting married, but Eddie wanted to meet my dad to officially ask him for his blessing. Eddie was surprisingly nervous about them meeting and spent a lot of time worrying how he could impress my dad – a welder from Leeds who had seen every one of Eddie's movies at the cinema!

I didn't want my dad to have to come to Eddie's house and do the whole Eddie thing of buffets and crowds of friends. Eddie booked out the dining room at L'Ermitage – one of the best and most old-style, elegant hotels in Los Angeles – and organized flights (we had to work around dad's shifts as always). Eddie wanted to make the evening as relaxed as possible, so we invited a few people – including my friends Nicola and Teena Collins – and the whole night went off perfectly. Dad was on good form, chatting to everyone (he particularly liked one of Eddie's friends who knew all about British football). And when I was off talking to my friends, Eddie asked my dad if he could marry me.

Dad said yes. Which was a relief because I had already designed a beautiful wedding ring from Cartier. I remember sitting there that night, looking at my dad and Eddie across the table, trying to work out which one of them looked happiest. And then it struck me (another thunderbolt): 'Melanie! Eddie looks just like Dad!' They did. Look at photographs yourself; the resemblance is uncanny.

It's strange how it's only later that you see patterns in your relationships. Even with Eddie and my dad sitting next to each other looking for all the world like long-lost brothers. But the real similarity wasn't just the looks; it was that they both came from incredibly tough backgrounds and were both – under their family-orientated, charming exteriors – very controlling men. Dad – the welder from Leeds – and Eddie – the Hollywood superstar – both created homes in which they made all the rules. And if you couldn't follow the rules, you were going to find yourself in trouble.

I got pregnant in Mexico in July 2006. We'd gone on holiday together, on our own – no staff, no bodyguards, no friends. It was a first for Eddie and a first for all those people who expected they would be coming too. 'I want to have a holiday, but it has to be just us,' I'd told him, and within weeks we were sitting on his private plane. Alone. It felt amazing. It was just the two of us. I felt completely happy, completely free.

A few weeks later I sat on the toilet of my en-suite in Eddie's bedroom (his bathroom was on the right, mine was on the left), weeing onto one of the stack of pregnancy testers Eddie had bought. The line went blue in seconds. I rushed into his bathroom where he was brushing his teeth. I was waving the tester in the air. 'It's positive! I am pregnant,' I said excitedly, and he lifted me into the air, not caring that I was still waving the stick around (and this man is a total germ freak). I didn't know what else to do except run round the bedroom shrieking as he stood watching me and laughing.

Half an hour later, I walked downstairs and found his mother. 'Guess what Mrs Lynch? I'm pregnant.' As any mother would be, she was a little suspicious of this loud English girl who had bewitched her son. We'd met in May, and now – in August– I was pregnant.

She looked back at me and said, 'Well, that is clever of you, isn't it?' In retrospect I know I should have been more diplomatic. I could have waited, or let Eddie tell her in his own time. But everyone knows diplomacy has never been my style. 'Speak first, think later' pretty much sums me up most of the time. And I was so full of how happy we were.

Luckily, I did a lot better at getting on with Eddie's children and ex-wife. Eddie now has nine children by five different mothers, but then he had just come out of a divorce from his first wife, Nicole Mitchell, who became a very dear friend of mine. He had five children by Nicole, and two boys, Eric and Christian, from two previous relationships. Nicole would often tell me how well matched she thought me and Eddie were; she also loved the fact we were both just all about family. Phoenix and her kids got on brilliantly – that was so important to me.

I'd told Eddie from the start that, in order for him to be in my life, Phoenix had to like him, and that I thought the same went for his children with me. He liked that. He was all about what was good for the children. At the time, Phoenix was falling behind a bit in her grades at school. That worried Eddie because he thought the world of Phoenix and he also (like my dad) thought the world of education. Eddie is a very intelligent man, but he didn't have the best time at school. Education, for him, is an absolute privilege, and he gives all his children access to the very best – he wanted Phoenix to be part of his family. From day 1 she was included in everything – big and small. I remember him presenting her with a dressing gown, not something she usually wore. 'It's the same one all my kids wear,' he said. Phoenix put it straight on with a grin on her face. Being an only child, she loved being part of this family.

Eddie really cared about her, so much so that he read through all the past reports she had in her school. He studied them thoroughly and asked me questions about her teachers – her not getting good grades was a problem for him. 'Melanie. You need to sort this,' he said. 'Her grades are slipping and something needs to be done. The best thing is for her to be home-schooled so she can get the most out of her teacher. And it will give her confidence.' She started lessons at his house with two of his other children, Zola and Shayne. He had a whole classroom set up in part of his house like a mini-school. I remember that conversation in his bedroom, because I sat there thinking, 'This is a man who really cares about his kids. This is a man who wants to do the right thing.' I thought about how much my dad would approve. More than anything he did – more than the holidays and the laughs – it made me give my heart to Eddie.

But once I was pregnant, things started to change: everything got more serious. I'd still wind him up by getting up in the morning, sending all the staff away, and then telling Eddie to come and make breakfast with me in the kitchen, where he barely knew how to turn on his own cooker. We would lie together for hours with him stroking my bump, and me showing him all the designs I'd had Cartier make for the yellow diamond ring I was going to wear, to mark either the engagement or wedding.

We decided to call the baby Murphy Brown if it was a boy. I was convinced it was a boy. We'd sit and talk about what our baby would look like, who he'd be like. Eddie wanted me to watch his stand-up documentary, 'Raw', which is brilliant. He waited to see what I said about it and it was my opportunity to tease him. 'I don't like that jacket you're wearing,' I said. 'It makes you look like you want to be Michael Jackson.'

'Michael had that custom-made for me,' he answered, his voice going up an octave in mock outrage.

'Still don't like it.' And I'd laugh. I bloody loved winding him up.

We had managed to keep the whole relationship quiet, but a few things had started leaking out to the media. I didn't really care because I was used to my life being public property, though I was careful to stay as low-key as possible. We'd originally planned to get married that Christmas. When I became pregnant we decided to wait till after the baby was born. 'I don't want to walk down the aisle with a big bump,' I said.

'And I don't want you to,' he laughed. 'I want you to be the most beautiful bride you want to be.' On that issue we were totally in sync.

—

But there were other issues between us. I didn't always want to be in a house full of his friends. I'd ask him if we could have a few evenings on our own and he'd say, 'Sure, go and tell Charisse.' (Charisse Hewitt-Webster is Eddie's assistant and producer, and he's known her forever.) Or I'd call him from my house and say, 'Eddie, are all your friends at your place?'

'Just a few, honey.'

'Well, I'm not coming over till it's me, you and the kids.' I know it didn't make me popular with a lot of his friends who loved camping out at Eddie's. But I didn't like having a permanent crowd in the house. And there were people on my side. Jeffrey Katzenberg, the head of DreamWorks, who had known Eddie for thirty years, took me and Eddie out for a steak dinner one night. When Eddie was in the bathroom, Jeffrey said to me, 'Mel, don't know what you're doing to him. Eddie's nice. He's a bit of a funny geezer, but I've never seen him so happy. He is re-energized. He wants to work. He's excited about work and I know that's down to you.' I was acutely aware that a lot of Eddie's friends didn't like me (I was too loud and – they thought – had too much influence over Eddie, especially over how often everyone piled over to his house). To have a well-respected man such as Jeffrey show kindness to me was very much appreciated.

Eddie was a funny geezer because he expected you to know the way he wanted things to work. It had been similar back in Leeds when Danielle and I would automatically know how many inches of water we could have in the bath … or what nights we could watch the TV shows we wanted to because Dad was on a late shift. You had to learn Eddie's rules.

If I wanted to go to the outlet shops in Palm Springs to do a quick shop for the kids, I'd pre-warn his driver and have a conversation about taking my car, being driven or taking one of Eddie's cars. If I went out on a rare night with friends or if I wanted to get away, it was Eddie's people who sorted it out. It felt like nothing was really in my control. On Fridays he would do movie nights and decided that I had to pick the film we were all going to watch.

That was pressure. I felt it was a test. Eddie is very knowledgeable on black American culture; he was always telling me about various jazz musicians, actors, writers who had begun the difficult task of paving the way for others. 'Eddie says I have to choose a film. What the hell shall I pick?' I'd ask my girlfriends. 'They need to be the right ones.'

'Go for *Guess Who's Coming to Dinner*. Or anything with Sydney Poitier,' advised one of my friends. Every week I'd go to her to brainstorm the next movie choice.

I knew I could never live like this and be part of Eddie's kingdom. But I knew he would never leave his house with its swimming pools, his gardens, his park for his kids, his family, chefs and house managers, and his friends turning up all hours of the day. On a fundamental level, this was how he liked to live; it made him feel secure and comfortable. He wanted to be in the driving seat. He wanted to look after me, but I'd spent years on my own and I liked doing things my way. Once I was pregnant, I started worrying about all these things, driving myself mad about how it would all work out.

'Eddie,' I told him one morning, 'there's a great house for sale in Trancas Canyon. It's gorgeous. It looks right across the National Forest in Malibu. What if we each put half the money to buy it, and it can be the house where we raise our child? I can keep my house in Los Feliz. And you keep your house, so we have a bit of our own independence. But we can spend three or four days in Trancas as a family. What do you think?'

He looked at me like I had told him I was going to fly to a different planet to live with aliens. He wouldn't have it. 'Melanie. This makes no sense at all. Are you completely crazy? I'll buy the house and we both live there.' I point-blank refused. If Eddie bought the house, then it would turn into another Eddieland, and I didn't want that to happen. We started to row about it.

To me it made perfect sense. 'It's a compromise,' I'd say. 'Can't we at least think about it? Can't we try it?'

He'd turn it into a joke. 'Hey,' he'd say, 'why don't we buy Phoenix a house? And Lordy a house? And let's buy a house for a pet rabbit.' But I stuck to my guns. This was the only solution I could think of. Neither of us would back down and Eddie point-blank refused to even talk about it anymore. That drove me mad. I started to question my relationship with him and pick, pick, pick away at everything. I knew he was a father figure to me. I knew that in his own lovely, sweet, generous way he was as controlling as my dad was.

It was December, only a few months before our baby was due, and things didn't feel right. It could have been my instincts, it could have been hormones, it could have been cold feet. All I knew was that I felt myself being slowly but surely sucked into his world. 'I'm going to spend the day with MY friends,' I told him, and drove round to see Nicola and Teena.

'Hello stranger,' Teena had laughed when I'd called her from the car to check they were at home. I hadn't been in touch with them for weeks because as soon as I found out I was pregnant, I'd barely left Eddie's house.

They knew something was up as soon as I walked in. These girls make documentaries, they are very instinctive, and they knew me really well. 'How's the pregnancy going?' asked Teena as Nicola put the kettle on.

'Really good,' I said. Then in a matter of seconds I burst into tears. 'We are really happy,' I blubbed. 'But we keep having rows because I don't want to move in with him.' They both nodded and let me talk. Neither of them thought my idea about buying a house together was crazy. They knew how much my independence meant to me. As Teena told me more recently, 'We were very aware that quite a few of Eddie's friends were not huge fans of yours, so we totally understood why you needed your own space with him.'

'If he's not listening to you, give him the silent treatment,' advised Nicola, before I left. I thought about it. I could move back into my house with Phoenix. But I knew that he would keep sending someone over every day to pick us up, and Phoenix would want to go, and I'd end up giving in. Suddenly, I knew exactly what to do. I'd go home to Leeds. I'd have a bit of distance; I'd be able to think and be with my family. It was exactly what I needed.

16
THE BREAK
—

The following morning I told Eddie, 'I need a break for a few days. I need time to think about what we are going to do.'

He looked shocked. 'Are you insane?' he said. 'What do you need to think about?' I went into shutdown. I couldn't talk anymore. I had to get away. I packed a suitcase for me and another for Phoenix, walked out of the house and put the cases in my car.

I went back to the house to get Phoenix, who was inside having her breakfast. The door was locked. I went to a side door. It was also locked. I was furious. I started screaming and banging on the windows, yelling, 'Eddie, open the doors. You have my child in your house. I want my daughter now.' My voice is pretty loud. As secluded as his mansion was, you could probably hear me on Mulholland Drive about half a mile away. After ten minutes the door was opened by one of his staff – no sign of Eddie anywhere. I grabbed Phoenix and left in a fury.

I drove to the airport, still angry, telling myself I was doing the right thing. It had all got too much. I needed to go back to Leeds, the place where I was born, thousands of miles away from chauffeur-driven Rolls Royces, giant-sized jacuzzis and a private chef who would bring you perfectly prepared sushi at any time of the day or night. It was the first week of December 2006, and after the heat of LA, Leeds would be all chilly and cosy. I wanted streets you could walk on (no-one walks on the streets of LA; they drive everywhere). I craved Yorkshire accents, tea made with a tea bag in a chipped mug, and my mum to tell me she understood where I was coming from and that she'd help me sort it out.

Eddie was calling me on my mobile. I switched it off. I later discovered he asked his assistant to get straight on the phone to my friend Nicola Collins. 'Mr Murphy wants to know if you know where Melanie is. He's very worried about her,' she said.

'I'm very sorry, but I don't pass messages through assistants. If Mr Murphy wants to speak to me, ask him to call me,' said Nicola. A minute later Eddie called her and Nicola was ready. 'Do you love Melanie?' she asked.

'Completely,' he answered.

'Well, you have to listen to her,' she told him.

'But I don't know where she is.' It took him several more hours and several more phone calls to realize I had left the country.

When I finally walked through the door of my mum's house, she looked like the world had fallen on her head. 'What's going on, Melanie?' she cried, as I set my bag on the kitchen table. 'I've had Eddie Murphy on the phone for hours. He's been ringing all your friends and then he got through to me. He's in a terrible state. He wants you to go home, and I've told him I'd send you back to him.'

I couldn't quite believe it. My mum then told me that after I'd left, Eddie had called every single UK number I'd ever dialled from his house and had got through to my mum at about 2 a.m. UK time, as I was flying through the air on my way to Leeds.

'I love her so much, Andrea,' Eddie told my mum. 'I want her to come back. She's inspired me. We are so happy we're going to have a baby. I want to look after her and keep her safe.' And on and on for two and a half hours – saying he would even buy me a house in London if I wanted it, how he wanted my whole family to come over and stay with him, and how he wanted Phoenix to come back because she was missing lessons. My mum who was now ready to do battle for him, this Hollywood star who was calling her in the middle of the night. As she saw it, I was pregnant by a man I'd told her a million times I was absolutely in love with, and I should go back to him and be happy. But the way I saw it, she wasn't on my side; she was on his.

'Mum, I need time to think. I'm not sure I want to live with him. It's complicated,' I said.

She shook her head. 'Why are you being like this? He loves you. He wants to look after you. He's an amazing man. Your dad thought he was the bee's knees. He'll never let you want for anything. Go home and make it up. This is your hormones going crazy.'

In the emotional state I was in, this was the last thing I wanted to hear. I didn't need to be looked after, and I didn't want to lose my independence. I didn't really know what I wanted other than a few days to think. I didn't want my mum to be making a decision based on the fact that Eddie was a Hollywood superstar who had called her in distress telling her how much he loved her daughter. I wanted someone to listen to me and help me work out what to do.

The following day I called Charlotte and we went to Harvey Nichols. We didn't talk about Eddie. We had a laugh, and it was a welcome distraction. Charlotte remembers that Eddie kept calling me throughout the day, and I kept refusing to answer. 'He sounds desperate,' she said. 'Are you not going to pick up?'

'I'm giving him the silent treatment,' I said. She didn't push it. In the evening my family came over and we had a great time as we always do when we get together. Laughter always works for me; it breaks the tension in my head. It helps me get my life back into perspective.

——

A day later, I felt so much better and my head had cleared. My mum was right – not that I was going to tell her that. I was going to go back. I loved this man. He loved me and we would make it work. I would talk it through with Eddie, calmly and rationally. We would come up with the perfect solution and we would be a happy family. I missed him. I'd got myself completely wound up. Somehow we would get it right because love conquers all, doesn't it? I put on a leopard-print dress and knee-high boots (to channel my inner girl power) and boarded a flight to LA, telling Phoenix we were going 'back home'.

What I didn't know was that as I was on the plane, Eddie was going on the red carpet to promote his film *Dreamgirls*. As he walked down the carpet, a Dutch TV reporter asked him about his relationship with me. 'So are you happy with her?' asked the reporter. 'Because she is pregnant from your child.'

Eddie's response was this: 'You're being presumptuous, because we're not together anymore, and I don't know whose child that is until it comes out and has a blood test. You shouldn't jump to conclusions, sir.'

Those words – repeated on every cable channel and every Internet entertainment site – were rocketing through the stratosphere causing havoc in the media, who had discovered that I was about to land in LA any minute.

I do not – to this day – have any idea why Eddie would have said those words. It was completely out of character for him to talk about his private life, and it was even more out of character for him to say something so damning and nasty about someone he loved. The question 'Why?' has haunted me for more than a decade.

All I can think – and my friends who knew us both would agree – is that I had made one enemy too many among Eddie's entourage. I was absolutely, completely devoted to Eddie. I had never even looked at another man or even thought about any other man but him when I was with him. All I wanted was to be with him – just him. And that was the problem. If Eddie and I had moved into our own home, that would have caused a major upset for so many of his friends. 'The main thing, though,' Nicola said, 'is that he thought you weren't coming back, and no woman had ever treated him like that.'

As soon as he had spoken, Eddie panicked. I know this because he sent his security to the airport to get me – well aware that I would walk obliviously into a baying mob of reporters asking me all about his bombshell comments. Which is exactly what happened.

So the first I knew of Eddie's hideous comments were when they were shouted at me as I clutched my seven-year-old daughter to my side. It was like a hammer blow to my heart. I felt sick, humiliated and confused as I tried to get out of the airport as fast as possible. I saw Eddie's security man waving towards me and for half a second I thought, fuck you, but I had no option because I was being mobbed by the press and I needed to get out.

Once I was in the car, my phone rang. It was Eddie. 'I was caught off guard,' he said. 'I didn't know what was going on with us. I didn't know what to say.' I won't repeat what I said, but Eddie cut me off. Distraught, I told the driver to take me to the Four Seasons hotel (Janet had called to say my own house was surrounded by press and TV crews).

I called Eddie one last time. I was hurt, I was devastated, and I was raging. 'Thanks a lot,' I said. 'That was really fucking stupid of you to say that. I can't forgive you for this, and I'm going to make you do a DNA test.'

He said, 'Well, you left me.' He sounded cold. Distant.

'I left you, Eddie. But I didn't LEAVE YOU, leave you.'

'Well, that's what I thought you did.'

There was silence. I said, 'I'm going to have to leave you now because that is what you've done to me.' I ended the call, walked over to reception and booked a room. The staff could not have been more kind to me, and it was hard to hold back tears. I then walked into my hotel suite with Phoenix, sat on my bed and burst out sobbing.

—

How the hell had this happened? I was pregnant. On my own. Dumped in public and made to look like a complete and utter slut and gold-digger who'd got pregnant to trap this multi-millionaire star. The man who told me he would love me till the end of time had turned on me and turned me into a punchline for jokes that would run and run on Saturday night TV shows for months to come.

I held Phoenix against me and put my other hand on my bump as my five-month-old baby – Eddie's baby – kicked against me. There was no call back from him. I tried to call him and was told by his assistant, 'Mr Murphy has the message you called.'

Silence.

It was us three against the world.

17
DUMPED
—

Vulnerable. Not a word I would ever think of to describe myself. If anyone had said it to me back then, as I sat in that hotel room, or used it to describe me a few weeks later when a crazy group of Eddie Murphy fans started to pitch up outside my house in Los Feliz, screaming vile insults, I would have shouted back at them, 'You're wrong. I'm not vulnerable. I'm fine.'

But I wasn't 'fine' (except in its other meaning, as in Fucked up. Insecure. Neurotic. And Emotional) and I was vulnerable. I was a joke. I was a gold-digger. A tramp. A woman who had conned a man into having a baby. A thirty-two-year-old woman soon to give birth to a child whose father refused to acknowledge or claim it.

The press had a field day, and comedians on 'Saturday Night Live' (all of them idolize Eddie) lost no time in coming up with humiliating sketches, gag after gag, about me. In the olden days I'm sure I would have been dragged out into the streets to be put in the stocks and had rotten fruit thrown at me by the whole of Hollywood. And if you have a burning desire to be famous (a study by Dr Patricia Greenfield at UCLA found that 'fame was the number one value communicated to pre-teens on popular TV'), please be aware that this is what can happen to you.

Fame has a way of dehumanizing you. The Greeks and Romans had their gods, and today we have celebrities. We are adored; offerings of designer handbags and free clothes are laid at our feet; we don't queue; we fly through the air in first-class cabins with scented towels and lie-down beds. Men scream at you on the street that they want to marry you. It's all an illusion because you are still the same you that got shouted at by the maths teacher or got turned down again and again in auditions. And then, when something terrible happens in your famous life, it's as if there is a collective realization that you are not actually a god. You can go from Fame to Shame in a heartbeat. You've seen it all in the *Mail Online* or TMZ.

To be fair, being famous means you have a lifestyle where you can block out a lot of the noise. You move to a gated community so no-one can get to you. And thank God Los Angeles has so many delivery services (thank you, Postmates) that you can stay behind your own four walls. One week after I left Stephen, I bought my own laptop from a shop in Pasadena and quickly discovered the joys of Amazon. I could order hair bows for Madi, lunch boxes, rucksacks, dog collars, pet beds – I didn't even know Amazon existed before April 2017, and within a matter of weeks I was their best customer. Fewer reasons to leave the house.

I wasn't prepared for that tidal wave of vitriol crashing over me after Eddie dropped me. I'd been a Spice Girl. I'd been loved, adored, and even when I did silly things like jumping on tables at Virgin Music HQ in London, in a room full of music lawyers, shouting, 'I'm bored! Let's all dance!' everyone had laughed and indulged me. I had to learn to start blocking negativity out of my life. But I still can't forget being heavily pregnant with Angel and dropping Phoenix to school and a man driving past in a car yelling 'Whore!' at me in front of all those LA mums. I can walk out onto a stage in front of thousands, but I am completely overwhelmed with anxiety walking into my daughters' schools. What do those other mums think of me? Circle Time for me is way more terrifying than Wembley Arena.

My most recent embarrassing moment happened – in the spring of 2018 – at Angel's school. She had not mentioned she was performing in a morning assembly until we were about to get into the car to drive

Wedding bells: Mum and Dad, the rebel couple, in all their 1970s glory
with matching platform shoes. Mum couldn't quite hide her baby belly:
they got married just a few weeks after I came along.
I was a scandal before I was born. Some things
never change.

White Grandma and Black Grandma who, despite a sticky start,
did become best of friends.

Mum and me and the only other mixed race girl we knew for miles around, my lovely friend Sherrell.

Little brown girl from a backstreet council estate in Leeds with big dreams.

Showing off my splits and suede kickers in the back garden in Leeds.

Bikini Spices ... On our first holiday together in Maui. We all looked so young we had to keep showing our ID cards to prove we were old enough to be in the hotel without our parents!

Turning the Oxford Street Christmas lights on, followed by champagne overload and a hangover Charlotte and Danielle took days to recover from. I woke up the next day at the crack of dawn for work and managed a full English at the airport.

Messing about in Brighton. We never took ourselves too seriously, although Vic was always practising her fashion pout.

Happy days with Eddie, the man who will always be the love
of my life.

A fool in love and a man with a diamond wedding ring, bought by his bride. My Vegas wedding.

Eyes down, face forward. Desperate on the inside.

When the whip comes down! In my element, on stage and in control. Loving it.

With my beautiful daughters and my sweet step-daughter Giselle.

A fabulous moment on my infamous yellow sofa in Beverly Hills, surrounded by my Spice shrine. If only that sofa could talk.

to school. Ten minutes into the journey, right in the midst of the LA morning rush, I get a call on my phone: 'Ms Brown, this is Angel's teacher. Where are you? Everyone else is here rehearsing.' I looked out of my windscreen at the bumper-to-bumper traffic and clocked that my estimated time of arrival on my sat nav read twenty-five minutes. 'Er, I'm so sorry, we are on our way. We should be there in fifteen minutes.' There was a sigh. Thirty minutes later, I had fended off three more calls and a final warning of 'Everybody is here now. Angel's dad is here. We are waiting to start assembly.'

All I'd actually heard was, 'Angel's dad is here.' Aaaargh! I was in track bottoms and a T-shirt with no makeup on. This was going to be the first time in a decade that I'd seen him – the man is still the love of my life – and I was late, a mess and mortified. When I got into the hall, I crawled – literally – on my hands and knees like an army recruit until I got to the very front and sat among the little kids, trying my best to ignore the stares of the other mums. I then got a tap on the shoulder from Eddie's polite youngest son, telling me they'd saved me a seat so I could sit with them. My face was so red hot with embarrassment you could have fried an egg on it. 'That's so kind,' I whispered. 'But I'm fine here.' In my next life I'm coming back as one of those women who does everything perfectly. I know Eddie is happy with his girlfriend, I would never expect him at any point to run over and declare undying love for me (honestly, I'm not that deluded), but I did at least want to look like an organized and together mum instead of a complete buffoon.

I can – and believe me I do – laugh about Angel's assembly. But the root of it is that I so often feel judged because I have so often been made to feel ashamed about myself and the choices I have made.

Shame is the age-old stick used to beat women since Biblical times. It works on many levels. When I went to court against Stephen, I seesawed between feeling like the warrior queen Boadicea, fighting for freedom, justice and my family, and feeling desperate, shamed and humiliated by the newspaper headlines: *Mel B Battles Cocaine Addiction and Agrees to Take Medication So She Is Safe Around Her Kids.* That is how my overdose in 2014 was played out in court by Stephen, who released his text exchanges with our family therapist, Dr Sophy, in his legal papers, making me look like a mad, out-of-control woman to the whole world in open court. The truth is far more complex. I did take cocaine because I was living in hell and I used it as a crutch. I wasn't proud of what I'd done, but no-one knew the real truth behind those headlines, and I just had to stay silent and suck it up.

I'd swing from Boadicea to angry, ashamed, frustrated and powerless, spending my days in my bedroom, hidden behind security gates. Going to court doesn't always mean getting justice, but I refuse to be shamed.

You do – to be truthful – have several options. You can take up one of the scores of offers like those that flew through my agent's hands to do a 'tell-all' interview on television or in the press. (But if you are going through a court case as I was with Stephen, you can't do this.) You can play games with the media – leak stories and stage 'impromptu' little interviews with television reporters. You can even hire a whole team of very clever brand and image consultants to do it for you. They call them 'fire-fighters' because their job is to put out all the fires in the media. And they make sure you will only ever walk away with a little bit of smoke damage. The cleverest of all throw fires in other directions, distract from the big story with lots of little firebombs. In the media fire-fighting world, it's called the 'look over there' technique.

That is not my style. Never has been. And with Eddie I made a decision not to do any of those things. I didn't call in a super-smart university-educated public-relations person to advise me. I called my mum, who'd left school in Leeds at the age of fifteen. I was too raw, too humiliated to even start thinking about how this could impact my career or my brand. I felt smashed to pieces. And, being honest, I felt ashamed. Not just for myself but for my family, for my daughter and for my unborn child. All my insecurities flooded to the surface. Who was I kidding, thinking I was someone who'd done something with their life? Underneath it all, I was still that mixed-race kid who was too loud, too difficult to be really loved.

Eddie still did not call. I set a timer on my phone and I'd call him at the same time every three weeks. I would leave messages with Charisse, but I'd get the same response: 'He is aware you have called.' Eventually I stopped calling. What was the point? I behaved probably like any other woman who has been dumped and disgraced: I replayed every moment of our relationship, every conversation, to work out what I'd missed. How I'd not realized he was someone capable of being so unkind. It was just like with my husband Jimmy Gulzar. Falling for them fast and not seeing what they were really like.

Although I felt mortified about everything that was being written about me, it was nothing compared with how hurt I felt. I meditated. I played with Phoenix. I prayed. I tried to believe that people would see the truth. In public I would smile, but if you ever look closely at any pictures you can see how forced those smiles were. There were – as my mum and Janet can tell you – many times when I would fall apart and like a jigsaw puzzle have to piece myself back together again.

—

It's amazing what pulls you through things. I found a house to rent in Pacific Palisades, away from the paparazzi and reporters who gathered round my house. I called my mum. I needed her to make me roast chicken, roast potatoes, Yorkshire puddings (half her suitcase was taken up with Yorkshire pudding mix) and gravy. But I also needed her to not talk about what was going on. As much as I love my mum, if there's a drama going on she ramps it up times a hundred, and

I will always end up being the one having to calm her down, stop her crying, tell her everything will be okay. 'What are you going to do, Melanie?' she'd say ten times a day. 'Can you not call him?' 'What's going to happen when you have the baby?' 'Have you seen this story in the paper now?'

'No, Mother.' 'It'll be OK, Mother.' 'Yes, Mother. Ignore it.'

Geri, Emma, Vic and Mel C helped. They would call and we would all talk. When something goes wrong, if you let your friends into your life, it brings you closer. We started making plans to get back together. Vic was moving to LA because David had signed to LA Galaxy. All of them know me well enough never to do the 'Poor you' speeches. All of them knew me well enough to know the best thing was for me to focus on moving forward, on work, on the future. And so we finally started planning the thing I'd wanted for years – a Spice Girls reunion.

Eddie moved on. He started dating Tracey Edmonds, the ex-wife of Madonna's record producer. It was a punch in the stomach when I saw them together on the red carpet. I heard he took her on a date to that same Coffee Bean in Studio City, and that he has taken all his subsequent girlfriends – and current partner, Paige Butcher – there. I wondered whether he thought about me when he walked through the doors.

The Christmas before Angel was born, I knew I had to get away. It was a few weeks after Eddie had made his shocking claim that he did not know who the father of my child was, but it was also the time we had originally planned to get married. And it would have been our first Christmas together. I couldn't be in Los Angeles. I couldn't be in the same city as Eddie; it was too painful. After the craziness, the tears, the headlines and the shock, I needed space and I needed to be on my own.

My mum took Phoenix to Leeds, and I flew to the remote resort of Tulum on the Caribbean side of Mexico. People think that I have this overpowering need to be loud, shouty and crazy all the time, but I also have a need for silence and solitude. I like my own space. I like my own company. I had a tiny beach hut that opened directly onto the sea. I saw no-one apart from the people from the resort who would come every day with my breakfast, lunch and dinner. I spent most of that time completely naked in the sea, stroking my growing belly, bonding with my unborn baby and trying to get Eddie out of my head, out of my heart. In all the hysteria, I felt the thing I needed most was to really connect with this child inside me and give her some calm and attention. I would lie on my back in the ocean with tears leaking from my eyes into the warm waters all around me. 'Eddie, Eddie, Eddie,' I would repeat, and then I'd hold my belly, feeling our child growing within me.

I still think of those days surrounded by all that water. It was the best thing I could have done. Remove myself. Be with myself. Feel my pain, feel my heartbreak but hang onto the hope that was growing inside me – my child, our child. I tried not to think how much I loved him, I stopped myself trying to analyze, question and pull apart those last few weeks we spent together. Because I would never be able to understand what made him behave like that. 'If he did that,' I told myself, 'what else could he do?' I was going to be okay on my own.

My mum cried when I spoke to her on Christmas Day. 'Melanie, you are all on your own and it's Christmas,' she said. I could hear Christmas music in the background and the sound of all my relatives having a good time. It made me smile. 'I'm good. I'm happy. This is what I want,' I said. I could feel myself getting stronger and more sure of what I wanted to do.

This for me was now about Girl Power. No woman should be treated like Eddie had treated me. I had loved him. I had done nothing wrong. I wasn't going to give a story to the papers, but I was going to get the best lawyer I could and I was going to make Eddie take a DNA test after my baby was born to show the world he was the father. I would get myself a lawyer to force him to take that test. I would do that reunion tour with the Spice Girls and show my children and the rest of the world who I was and what I did. But first I would have my child.

The gods were laughing when she came. She was due in the second or third week of April. I started having pains on the morning of 2 April. I ignored them. My baby had two weeks left to go. My mum took Phoenix out for the day, and at home I felt the labour pains starting. 'I'm in labour,' I called her from the car. 'You have to come to the hospital with Phoenix.' I drove, having contractions all the way. Lord knows what people who looked into my car window thought as I pulled faces to brace myself against the pains. When I arrived at the maternity wing of Cedars Sinai, I was yelling at anyone and everyone, 'If the baby's coming, it has to be today. Tomorrow it's Eddie's birthday. I need the baby out now!'

The pains went on. I asked to be induced, but still she didn't come. I had my mum and Janet with me, and Phoenix, who was tucked up asleep on a little bed, but all I wanted was Eddie. He didn't call, he didn't come. But Angel did. One hand raised in the air came out followed by this perfect baby with huge, almond-shaped eyes. My mother cut the cord. It was eleven minutes past midnight on the same day of the year that Angel's father was born.

Happy birthday, Eddie. The joke was on us both.

18
STEPHEN

—

STEPHEN … Even just saying the name makes my body shake with a mixture of anger, dread and a blurry series of half-buried flashbacks. I had been married previously to a difficult man. Jimmy Gulzar had a temper, and we had some dramatic, blazing battles. But he never had the hold on me that Stephen did.

Before Stephen, I never had moments when I disgusted myself. And that was what made me weak. That was what made me powerless.

So how did I ever let a man like Stephen into my life? I'd met him a few times. First, years ago when I was with Max Beesley, and then he was one of those people you'd see on the fringes of Hollywood parties blagging his way in.

Stephen once came up to me in LA airport when I was six months pregnant with Angel and asked me if I would talk to him because he was trying to impress a group of Spice Girls fans. 'Act like you really know me and then one of them might have sex with me,' he said. I told him not to be so disrespectful, but I laughed. To be honest, I admired his cheek. At the time, a lot of people in LA would either give me dirty looks or not speak to me. I gave him my cell-phone number. Hollywood is full of players and I knew that was exactly what he was.

The next time I heard from him, I was in the Bel Air Hotel with my mum, Phoenix and my newborn Angel. My hormones were all over the place. I was ping-ponging between being unbelievably happy because I had this beautiful, perfect baby and desperately sad because her father wouldn't call.

My heart was broken. As angry as I was and as much as I told myself and my mother I hated him, I couldn't stop myself being in love with Eddie. But I had messed with the wrong man. Eddie, proud, proud Eddie, couldn't pick up the phone and say, 'Let's work this out.' We'd gone from him following me round his house, sitting in the bathroom with me because he couldn't bear me to be out of his sight or stroking my hair while I was reading a book, to communicating only through his management team. 'How was the birth?' was the first call. 'Can you let us know that everything is OK with the baby?' I couldn't deal with the cold realization that he no longer wanted to be part of my life.

The press was full of stories that I'd got pregnant on purpose, that I'd tricked Eddie. It was the most devastating thing that had ever happened to me, harder than my marriage breakdown with Jimmy, harder than the Spice Girls ending. Little did I know then there were going to be far worse things I'd have to deal with in my life.

So in the Oprah Winfrey Suite of the Bel Air Hotel – the plushest hotel suite in the whole of the city – I flipped between being happy, crying and deciding to contact the infamous LA lawyer Gloria Allred to make mincemeat of Eddie. I was crushed and she was going to help me rise. Gloria's whole reputation is built on her burning desire to get justice for minorities and underdogs – and that's largely women! She is fearless. She is the woman who finally nailed Bill Cosby for sexual assault, and she's gone up against everyone from Donald Trump to Harvey Weinstein.

I had stayed an extra day in hospital just to give Eddie the chance to call me – even let me know his full official details so I could put it on our baby's birth certificate ('Eddie is aware of your request,' the message came back, but nothing more). I was crushed, but Gloria told me to be strong for my baby and all other women who are cast aside by a man refusing to acknowledge their child.

It was Gloria's idea to call a press conference and announce the results of the DNA test. I wanted justice, I wanted my baby to be acknowledged, and I wanted Eddie's attention. He could not treat me like that. I wasn't going to stand for it. I named our child Angel because she was my angel, Iris after Black Grandma to channel some of her strength, Murphy because Eddie was her dad, and her surname on the birth certificate is Brown because I was her mother and I was going to look after her – whatever happened.

So when Angel was about three weeks old and I was seesawing all over the place emotionally, I got a call from Stephen Belafonte. He was really cheerful. 'Hi Melanie, I'd like to come and see you if I can? I wondered if I could bring my little girl, Giselle?' He had to remind me where we'd met, but he wasn't put off; he just joked a little bit and said he was going to be in my area. The next day he turned up. He was immaculately dressed in designer gear with a Gucci belt and expensive-looking shoes. It made me laugh because I was in bed breastfeeding Angel with no makeup on and my pyjamas. He was super-charming. 'You look amazing,' he said, which was hilarious because I knew I didn't. 'This is my little girl, Giselle. She is so excited.' She was a cute four-year-old who looked more terrified by being in this room full of strangers than excited. She spent the whole time her dad was there wrapped around my mother's knees.

'I don't like that guy, Melanie,' my mum said within seconds of him leaving. 'There's something not right about him. He's a Suavo,' which is my mum's word for any guy who's smooth, slippery and not to be trusted. My mum and I had been cooped up together for months by this stage, and, as much as I loved her and wolfed down all the roast chicken dinners she kept making for me, we were also really getting on each other's nerves. My mum is a catastrophist. That's a word I've learned recently from my English thesaurus.

What a catastrophist basically means is that if something happens you always think the absolute worst. 'Oh, Melanie, You can't do that,' she says. 'Oh my God, you can't wear that,' she says.

'Melanie, what are you doing?' I've heard it all my life, and it's probably the reason why I always push things one step too far, or why I went out as a teenager wearing just gaffer tape stuck to my boobs and a fishnet catsuit, and, if I'm honest, if I could get away with doing that now then I very probably would. Just dare me. Or better yet, tell me I can't, then I'll do it.

—

Stephen popped in the next day. And the next. Always with Giselle, and always with a confident smile on his face. I'd just seen on the news that Eddie had proposed to Tracey Edmonds and she was wearing a Cartier yellow-diamond ring – almost a replica of the one I'd designed. Talk about a punch in the stomach! Part of me was still trying to believe he was still in love with me, and that him giving her my ring was sending that message to me. But I was deluding myself. He'd moved on with humiliating speed, making me look even more of a loser. At least I had someone trying to get my attention.

Stephen made me feel like I was the centre of his whole world. He didn't focus on anyone except me (and Angel) but – I realized later – he was sucking up everything he heard and saw in the room. He clocked the tension between me and my mother (it still niggled at me that she'd been on Eddie's side). He clocked that both me and my mum were absolute traditionalists, so to have two babies by two different men and not to be acknowledged by one was such a difficult thing for me. He saw every single one of my weaknesses, and he wrapped them up with full-on charm.

'Why don't we go on a date?' he said the second time he came round.

'I'm not going anywhere,' I replied.

'What about the bar downstairs?' he said.

I thought about it. Even the absolute luxury of a fabulous hotel suite can feel too stifling. 'No,' I said.

'Let's go for a walk in the gardens with the kids,' said Stephen. My mum looked at me, horrified because Stephen had already picked up Angel and was holding her in his arms.

Janet remembers how he always called Angel his 'golden goose'. 'Where's my golden goose?' he would say, as he walked in the room. My mum was shaking her head at me. 'Don't let anyone get pictures of you,' she whispered. I told her to stop being dramatic.

As we were walking, Stephen stopped suddenly and looked at me. 'I'm going to make you fall in love with me because you need a really good man,' he said.

I laughed, and then I said, 'Good luck with that.' I didn't notice the photographer, but the next day there it was: a picture of me with Stephen protectively holding Eddie Murphy's baby.

We did go to the bar. A couple of days later. Stephen worked really fast. On the way back to my room, he randomly kissed me. I wasn't expecting it, but I knew he was after me, and some part of my brain was telling me not to go there. 'That was weird,' I said. 'And it was a crap kiss by the way.' I could see he was annoyed, but he was amazing at covering up. He laughed and made a joke. He wasn't going to be put off easily.

Honestly, I was flattered. But more than that, I was intrigued by Stephen. Apart from his blue eyes, I didn't initially find him very attractive at all. But I've never really been about looks, I've always been hooked in by the way a man's brain worked, the way he is in himself. If you lined up all the men I've been with in my life, none of them look in any way alike. I initially thought Stephen was smart, way smarter than me. I was fascinated by his confidence, his fearlessness, this bulletproof way he had about him, completely resistant to insults or knockbacks. I watched the way he was with other people. If he wanted to charm them, he would instinctively hone in on some thing that they wanted or were fascinated by. He'd tell me how much research he'd do on people when he had meetings with them. He'd get to know what they liked, which restaurants they went to, what music they liked, where they worked before so he could find connections.

My friend and assistant Janet, who was with me all throughout that time, recognized Stephen's surname because she knew that in America Harry Belafonte was a really famous singer from the 1950s and '60s who was known as the 'King of Calypso'. My mum also knew of Harry Belafonte because he'd had a few top 10 hits in Britain. I didn't know about him. But Janet, who like most Scousers I know is as sharp as one of my stiletto heels, thought she was onto something. 'I want to find out if Stephen's a member of the Belafonte family or not,' she said.

It turned out Janet had a friend in New York who knew Harry's wife, Julie. 'Call her and ask about him,' I suggested. A few hours later Janet told me there had been issues between this guy from Los Angeles who was calling himself Stephen Belafonte and the Belafonte family. He was no relation of theirs. They didn't like the fact that he was using his name and that people might think he was related to them. 'Big deal,' I said, catching the looks between Janet and my mum. 'That's not exactly a crime, is it? I've never heard of Harry Belafonte anyway so it makes no difference to me.'

Stephen said he was a movie producer with a credit on the Katie Holmes/Aaron Eckhart film *Thank You for Smoking* – but isn't everyone in the movies in LA? He talked like a player and I knew so much of it was bullshit, but he was also playing me like a pro, talking about the music industry in America, telling me I could turn everything to my advantage, on and on saying all the things I wanted to hear. He knew this person, that person. If the sales pitch was getting too much, he'd switch in a second to flattery: 'You've got the greatest laugh I've ever heard – and the best butt' or 'I can see your mother is getting on your nerves. Do you really need her around? I can help with the kids and I know a great nanny.'

The insane thing is that I thought I was in control. My mother knew I wasn't and that little by little I was relying on his opinion, saying, 'I can get Stephen to do that' or 'He makes me laugh, Mother, leave it.' She didn't. She kept on and on about him. 'Please don't get with him, Melanie,' she'd say. 'I don't trust him with his Gucci belts and his smarmy talk. All he's interested in is fame and money.' I'd roll my eyes.

I knew I was still in love with Eddie and desperately hurt that not only had he publicly denied our child but he had moved on so fast with another woman. (The marriage, by the way, lasted only two weeks, but I'm not gloating about that. I found it sad.) Stephen was – I genuinely believed – a distraction. Again, I was a fool. My mum left to go back to my sister, Danielle, in Leeds on 4 June. On 5 June, two months after Stephen had first come to the hotel, he was down on his knees proposing and the words 'Okay then' were coming out of my mouth. The next day – 6 June 2007 – we got married in Vegas.

19
I DO

—

I actually laughed as we exchanged vows in a tiny Vegas chapel, standing there in my jeans, baseball cap and white tank top in this tiny church with only my assistant, Janet, as our witness, Stephen's younger brother, Daniel and a guy introduced as 'Stephen's best friend', who we never laid eyes on again after the wedding. 'I want another night in the hotel booked for me' was all this man said as we tucked into a slap-up post-ceremony feast at the Wynn in Vegas. Stephen didn't so much as blink. Janet – who was convinced he was an actor hired for the day – sorted it. I paid. That was it. The first hint that all my marriage was ever going to do was cost me money.

I wish I had been warned.

We'd been drinking champagne and vodka. I felt like I was doing something really reckless and crazy and I didn't care. All I'd been thinking as I stumbled giggling into that church – whose name I can't even remember – was, 'Ha! Look at me, Eddie. I beat you to it.' I was also foolishly thinking, 'I'm so rock 'n' roll.' But let's face it – like I've had to over this past year of endless, humiliating, traumatizing and expensive court cases – I wasn't really thinking at all. I was walking into a fire that was going to burn me and my family for ten years till I got the strength to get the hell out of it.

Your wedding day is meant to be the happiest day of your life. And looking back, every wedding day I have had (the first with my backing dancer Jimmy Gulzar on 13 September – the 13th!! – 1998, and the second and third [in Vegas and then our renewal service in Egypt a year and a half later]) has been a total disaster. And they followed the exact same pattern.

There could not be two people in the world who could seem more different than a weed-smoking Dutch dancer called Jimmy Gulzar and a New Jersey-born hustler called Stephen Stansbury Belafonte. They were both born in the same year – 1975 – and both birthdays were on the 18th of the month (18 February for Jim and 18 May for Stephen), but the real similarity is how the relationships began and ended and how every single person I trust told me – both times – not to get married. Sometimes it was little hints I would ignore. Sometimes it was 'What are you doing, Melanie?' (my mum of course). They all saw the red flashing warning lights and each time I raced on through.

Jimmy was my backing dancer for the Spice Girls Spiceworld Tour, which went into rehearsals in January 1998. I chose him from a group of dancers who lined up in open calls by our choreographer, Priscilla Samuels; it was Priscilla's idea to introduce the Spice Boys dancers into the show. Each boy was meant to reflect one of us. Jimmy with his tattoos, his piercings and his background as a go-go dancer couldn't have been more perfect for me.

Everything in my life back then seemed perfect. I was riding the wave of the Spice Girls. Every day was a different adventure, and – even though we had our occasional bust-ups – we were all as tight as the Spanx that made our butts look so perfect on stage. 'What's his name, Priscilla?' I asked after I'd told her he was the one. 'He's called Jimmy and he's from Amsterdam,' she said. 'Why don't you ring him and have a chat?'

Intrigued, I did. 'Hey, it's Mel B here. You're my dancer, aren't you?' Long pause. 'I'm not YOURS. But yes, I'm your partner.' At the time, I was used to people falling over themselves to be friendly and men desperately trying to flirt at any opportunity. Jimmy did nothing of the sort.

When I laid eyes on him again about a week later in the gym we were using for rehearsals in the K Club in County Kildare, Ireland, I was completely taken aback. He was the absolute double of my first-ever boyfriend, Stephen Mulrain, who was my head-over-heels love when I was a teenager (although Jimmy was way shorter). 'You're my dancer,' I said again by way of introduction (No, I don't ever learn). 'I'm not YOURS,' he said again. But then he looked at me with his light hazel eyes and grinned. That was it. 'Girls, I fancy my dancer,' I announced to Geri, Emma, Mel C and Vic, who all laughed and rolled their eyes. I was actually with my Icelandic boyfriend, Fjol, at the time. 'Melanie, you're terrible,' giggled Mel C.

Jim wasn't interested in me. I thought he was terribly European and cool in all senses of the word. He had a beautiful blonde girlfriend (another connection; the men I marry always prefer blue-eyed blondes). I flirted with him outrageously, but he never responded. He had his Dutch girl and I had my Viking. The only flash of a connection was when I gave him a Jean Paul Gaultier top on his birthday and he tore his top off to put it on. His body was insane. 'Mum, I fancy my dancer,' I told her after the first show in Dublin. She looked at him across the bar where we were all celebrating – David and Vic, Emma and her mum, Mel C and her family, me and my mate Charlotte, my sister Danielle. 'Noooo, Melanie, noooo,' was all I needed. That rebellious desire to show my mother I knew what I was doing and I was in control of my own life.

Jim and I started dating on 13 March and by 13 May he'd proposed in Paris (after exactly two months, just like Stephen). He set the scene for his proposal perfectly; unbeknown to me he had help from Emma. We went back to the Buddha Bar, where we'd gone on our first date. He'd asked the chefs to prepare exactly the same meal we'd eaten then, and he wrote out the words to the Luther Vandross song 'You're the One', which he placed on the table. He got down on one knee and gave me a thumb ring engraved with the words *To be or not to be*. Grace Jones was in the restaurant and we had a drink and a laugh with her (she is louder than me, honestly). I was thrilled that I'd made this distant man fall in love with me. He reminded me of my dad, he would go from hot to cold emotionally, he was serious, he had his own rules he lived by. 'Be quiet, Melanie, calm down', he'd tell me. 'Can you listen to people and stop talking over them?' It was like being with my dad. 'Can you give me space? You don't understand people need their space. You have to have more respect, Melanie.' I persuaded myself he was trying to make me a better person because he cared about me so much. His criticisms were all well meant. But just like my dad he was able to confuse me emotionally by switching off, giving me a long, cold stare for no reason like he didn't even like me at all.

I had so much going on in my life at that time. I bought my first beautiful house in Little Marlow. I was told Sarah Ferguson had her eye on it so I bought it outright in cash. There were issues between Jim and the other dancers who felt he'd got above himself because he was with me. And I was also trying to get pregnant.

I wanted a baby. Some of the girls I'd been at school with in Leeds were having their second babies and I wanted that too. I wanted solidity in my crazy life. So much was going on that I didn't realize my fearless, gorgeous Geri was having problems. I was too wrapped up in Jim. Her weight was yo-yoing, she came out with us less and less, and then two days before my birthday – after we'd flown back from Helsinki – she left the group. In a lot of ways, it pushed me closer to Jim. Vic had David, Emma had Jade (Jones from the band Damage). I felt if it was getting less and less about us five against the world, I wanted it to be me and Jim against the world. A team.

'Stop buying Jim presents, Melanie. Just stop it.' That was Mel C's way of trying to warn me to be careful of him. My friend Charlotte raised her eyes every time she saw him with a whole heap of designer bags and my American Express Gold Card. 'He likes to shop doesn't he, Melanie?' she'd say pointedly. I wanted him to be happy. 'So what, it's only money, don't get so uptight,' I'd reply.

I was more worried about other things. Everyone on the tour knew we had a problem with our sex life because I was often confiding in the other dancers and the girls, saying how worried I was and wondering what it meant. Me. Mel B. My sex drive is like a bloody Formula One car but - with a few exceptions - Jim kept me at arm's length. It drove me crazy. My mum thought I was crazy. I flew her out to New York for her forty-second birthday with her best mate, Bernie. By then, I'd paid for my own engagement ring (she was NOT impressed) and she couldn't let it lie. 'I think you are marrying my daughter for her money. And I think you are gay,' she told Jim with classic Yorkshire bluntness. Jim was horrified. I was mortified. I felt everyone needed to mind their own business, but I started to have my doubts. Someone leaked to the press that we were having problems, and the front page of *The Sun* newspaper announced we had split.

Timing is everything in life. Just as I was getting used to the idea of splitting from Jim, Vic came running into my room holding a pregnancy tester and screaming, 'I'm pregnant!' I got up yelling and danced around the room with her. 'I want to try a test too,' I said. I ran back to her room with her, did a test and watched in disbelief as a blue line appeared. I called Jim and said, 'We're gonna have a baby.' That was it. Destiny – and I was going to make it work. I was going to make us a happy family.

I don't know if you ever saw the photos from that day. I was dressed up like a queen and everyone who came wore white. Jim looked beautiful in a white Stetson and my dad looked so cool in his immaculately tailored white suit, with the diamonds pierced through his ears that had been my birthday present to him (something precious, something painful). We got married in the old church next to my house in Marlow, and on the outside – as it so often does in my life – everything looked totally perfect. I knew it wasn't quite perfect.

Geri wasn't there to hug me or grab my boobs and make me laugh, and when I saw my dad walk towards me outside the church, I wanted him to look at me and tell me I didn't need to marry Jim. That's what dads do, isn't it? 'Ask me if I'm doing the right thing, Dad?' I said. He shook his head. 'It's too bloody late now, Melanie. Everyone is waiting,' he said, and we went inside.

The photographs of that day are gorgeous (although I do laugh now at what I was wearing; it was so over the top). Everyone is smiling. The food looks incredible, the reception in my lovely manor house was to die for. Vic and I both kept squeezing each other because we were pregnant and about to be married or just married. We'd had a huge hormonal fight backstage in the loos on tour in America, and literally we were about to lamp each other when Mel C calmly came out of one of the toilets and said, 'Evening ladies' and walked out, which made us start clutching each other laughing our heads off. Now here we were, two pregnant Spice Ladies with our men. 'You beat me up the aisle,' she laughed. I laughed too.

But something felt wrong. Throughout the whole day, Jimmy barely came near me. Apart from our kiss at the altar, he hadn't come close for a romantic sneaky snog. That's what I desperately wanted – a sign that he was really in love with me.

We drove off in a vintage Rolls Royce to The Hempel, but somehow a message hadn't got through about flowers, champagne and music, and our bridal suite was bare and minimal. Pretty symbolic really. Jim got into bed, turned his back on me and fell asleep. 'He doesn't love me.' I pushed away the thought. 'He's exhausted. It's been a mad day. Maybe this is what really happens on wedding nights.'

My Uncle Barry told me later that Jimmy had come out of one of the bathrooms in Marlow after the wedding and said to him, 'That's it now. I'm a rich man.' I remember hearing those words. My uncle was trying to look out for me, but it completely broke my heart. Everyone else could clearly see that Jim was marrying me for money. I wished my dad had dragged me away from that church by my feathered butterfly headdress. I also knew I'd ignored all the warnings.

—

And this is what happened in Vegas on the day I married Stephen. I paid for the flights, the hotel; I bought the wedding rings – gold versions of the Chrome Hearts rings I was obsessed with, complete with the words FUCK YOU LAS VEGAS written on the outside. And I bought a beautiful diamond engagement ring from Caesar's Palace. Yes. Yet again. I bought myself my engagement ring and put it on my finger.

After fifteen crazy minutes in the chapel, we celebrated in the casinos, and then at midnight we went up to our suite overlooking the lights of Vegas, which are a sight (remember my professional days started in the lights of Blackpool) that never fails to fill me with absolute awe. Unlike the honeymoon suite I shared with Jimmy, this time we had everything – flowers, music, candles, champagne. Stephen threw bubbles in the bath, then crashed out in the bedroom and refused to get up. Janet looked at me as I pretended to think it was funny. 'Let's go back down the casino and have a laugh and a dance,' I said.

'I've made a mistake,' I told her as we sat at the bar. 'I think I should get the marriage annulled.' She jumped off her seat. 'Let's go do that now. It will be really easy to do it in Vegas.' I was about to go running back to the chapel with her or whatever we needed to do, but something stopped me. I'd look an even bigger loser than I already did. 'Let me think about it,' I told her. I could see her face fall. She was genuinely worried for me. 'Melanie,' I told myself. 'You have got to make this work.' What was I playing at? I couldn't be the woman who was dumped by their baby's father who then got married and divorced in a day. 'And he definitely loves me,' I told myself. 'We can be a family. Just make it work.'

20
HONEYMOON'S OVER

—

It happened a few months after we got married. I woke up with a shock. The night before, Stephen and I had had a threesome with another woman. Remembering that it had been videoed, I jolted awake. A video. A sex video. In my mind, I could see my husband smiling at me, and something in his smile didn't feel right. I felt as if I was falling in slow motion down a black hole, like a little girl in a nursery rhyme. 'What if the video gets leaked,' I thought. 'What have I done?' A thousand images flashed through my brain, some from the night before, repeats of scenes of naked bodies, alongside screaming headlines in the tabloids and my dad crying. This was my dad who was mortified by pictures of me appearing in The Sun newspaper (the paper he and all his mates read at work) when I'd been snapped sunbathing topless a decade earlier. But would this man that I just married, this man I was convinced was completely obsessed with me seriously want to ruin me, take me down and control me like this? How could I get this so very wrong?

My head was spinning for hours and I couldn't get rid of the horrible lurching feeling. If you ever experience this, you need to realize that this is what is called a gut feeling and you need to listen to it. Just stop and get the hell out of whatever relationship you are in that makes you feel like that. I didn't. I felt I must have missed something, that something might have gone wrong and I hadn't noticed.

—

At school, I never found lessons easy. I didn't get a lot of what the teachers were talking about, and the textbooks seemed to make everything more complicated. I've subsequently been diagnosed with dyspraxia, dyslexia and ADHD (obviously I have to have the whole spectrum), but years of struggling with schoolwork and scraping through tests have left me with that vulnerable feeling of being the kid who didn't 'get' things. It's an insecurity of mine. I know I'm not stupid, but I think people think I am. Now, lying naked under my white duvet, I anxiously ran the night before through my head.

Stephen and I had been messing around, enjoying ourselves, asking each other what turned us on in bed. It was fun, really intimate like one of those first giggly dates with your partner when you tease and compliment each other, and open up – not just about sex but about other stuff. He talked about his dad. How growing up as a kid in the projects in New Jersey he'd been terrified of the man he called his 'drug-dealing' father who'd been in and out of prison all his life.

Stephen claimed he had been the favourite child because he had light skin and blue eyes, but that meant he had to spend more time with his dad, who would sometimes beat him for no reason. The fact that he skimmed over a lot of stories actually made me feel protective of him. I knew there was damage behind the loud, confident exterior, and I thought I could help him by showing him how much I loved him, by making us a family. I wanted to be everything to him, to show I could listen, I could help him, I could make his dreams come true, and I could make his fantasies come true too. 'I'll tell you my sexual fantasies and then you tell me yours,' I said.

The threesome was my idea, but of course my then husband was well up for it – as long as there were no other men involved. It had to be women, which suited me fine because I love women. I've always found women's bodies so much more beautiful than men's bodies. I have no issues with my sexuality. I've been in relationships with men and women. I don't think it's shameful to like sex, I don't think it's shameful to experiment – as long as it is all consensual – and I believe women can enjoy and initiate sex just as much (if not a whole lot more) than men. I made a call and a friend of mine came over. We had a lot of champagne and a lot of fun. I fell asleep happy because we'd fulfilled a fantasy.

Sexually, Stephen was my match. To me, after Jimmy, after what I'd been through with Eddie, this made me feel completely desired. I had no problems reciprocating. A three-minute quickie can be as much fun as a twelve-hour marathon if you are both on the same wavelength and you know what you are doing.

I thought about this as I tried to block out what had happened with the video. Did he actually film our sex session? He must have done. It had added to the kick. But sex tapes are private. I would never, ever in a million years show anyone else a sex tape. That's between the people involved. End of.

By now we were home in Los Angeles. I'd called my parents, my sister and everyone from Las Vegas, saying, 'Surprise! I've just got married.' The news was about as unwelcome as dog poo in a swimming pool.

'Oh Melanie' (my mum). 'I don't even know him' (my dad). I tried to make Phoenix excited about how me, her, Angel and Stephen were going to be a family. That she had another half-sister, Giselle. I tried so hard to make it all fabulous and exciting, but I could see from her face, as I tried to explain the situation, that she wasn't happy.

'What do you mean, Mum?' she kept saying. She missed Uncle Eddie, the little talks she would have with him about her day at school or some funny thing her dog, Lordy, had done. The stability of the life we had with him and all his kids, who had become her friends. Now it was just me, her, Stephen and Angel. In the past few months, she'd had so much to take on, and at the age of eight she had another sibling to share me with. Phoenix has always been an incredible kid. She loved her baby sister from the get-go, but a hand grenade had gone off in her little world.

'That's completely normal, Melanie. Stop fussing round her. It's a big change and all kids get used to change.' It wasn't just Stephen saying that, it was lots of people.

Janet, who had been around me for the previous five years, wasn't so convinced. As much as she tried for my sake, she couldn't hide her suspicion and dislike of my new husband. And he felt it from the moment he walked into my house. I was living on Mulholland Drive then, I moved around many times in LA. He walked in with two sports bags (mainly full of black T-shirts, jeans and a couple of designer shirts) and dropped them on the floor. Janet, bless her, tried her best to be pleasant, but she's an honest, plain-speaking Liverpool lass who couldn't take this very loud, strong man who was now calling all the shots.

I knew Janet. She was loyal, smart, and went above and beyond her job description in terms of what she did for Phoenix and me. I can't speak for her, but three months after Stephen and I got married, she quit. She could not stop herself berating him. I had one of them on each side of me, kicking at each other non-stop. 'He goes in your bag and takes your credit card to go shopping,' she'd say. 'He's left porn magazines open in Phoenix's bathroom.' 'Melanie, he picked up your phone and went through all your messages.' I can't explain why I didn't rise to what she was saying. I was torn. Within days of us coming back from Vegas he wasn't just my husband, he was my manager. It had never actually been officially discussed; it simply happened.

He was good at two things. Telling me I could do something and telling me how completely shit I was. 'You are so rubbish with money,' he said, removing credit cards from my purse. 'You need someone to sort you out. You're a washed-up old has-been Spice Girl with two kids by two different men. You are lucky you have me, now.' If I looked upset he'd say, 'I knew you'd act like that. Don't be an idiot. I'm telling you this because it's what people think, and I care about you. They think you fucked Eddie and got pregnant for his money, they think you are low rent scum. You have to know the truth.'

———

Stephen treated me like no-one else ever had done – except probably my dad. If I'd had a fall-out with one of my friends, if I'd been in trouble at school or work and I was trying to explain my side of it, my dad would glare at me and say, 'This will be down to you, Melanie. Only you.' Or my endless issues with money back in the day in Leeds, when a five-pound note had to last me a week and I'd somehow manage to spend it all in one go after a sneaky night out with mates (yes, back in the '80s you could have a good night out on a fiver). 'Do you think money grows on trees, Melanie? You have to learn how to look after your money, and don't go asking your mother for anymore. You can't be trusted.'

And then I got famous. Money did literally seem to grow on trees, and that money – millions of it (in 1998 alone we earned £29.6 million) – was my retort whenever anyone tried to criticize me. The first cheque I ever got given was for £200,000 in December 1996 at the Christmas party at Simon Fuller's management company, 19. I'd gone from scrounging money from my mum to holding that cheque and counting all those noughts. All five of us Spice Girls kept going into a corner of the room to pull out our cheques and look at them.

'See, I clearly DID know what I was doing,' I'd tell my dad. 'I can pay off your mortgage now.'

But money and fame do change things. Slowly, slowly you enter a bubble where the people around you don't tell you that you're being stupid, or that you can't wear a Dior dress with a pair of trainers or stay out all night before a magazine cover shoot (thank God for makeup artists). Everyone is on the payroll so it's their job to keep you happy. If you want a chip butty at 4.00 in the morning, washed down with a bottle or two (or three) of Lambrusco (a Spice Girl tradition … and yes, even Vic used to eat those chip butties), no-one tells you to go to bed because you have an early call in the morning. Someone goes and gets it and then makes excuses for you when you are running late.

Stephen wasn't like that. He pulled no punches, he sugar-coated nothing, he said exactly what he thought when he thought it, and he never stopped talking about setting up meetings, telling me I should be doing this deal, that deal; who I should be hanging out with; which restaurants we ought to be eating at; what dishes we should be ordering and which celebrities I should be hanging out with. He was all about being seen to be in the right place and with the right accessories.

I thought he was pure Hollywood, someone who was smart enough to know exactly what you should be doing. I found it entertaining that he actually knew which Birkin handbag Kate Beckinsale was carrying or which stylist J-Lo was using and which watches everyone was wearing, but his constant jibing and jabbing at me was starting to get to me.

Initially I found it refreshing because I hate people blowing hot air up my arse all the time, and I always know when I'm being bullshitted. 'You are not wearing that, you look a mess,' Stephen would yell, as I pulled on a pair of crazy leggings and a T-shirt. I didn't care if I didn't look up-to-the-minute perfect. I like to dress how I like, whether it's a hotchpotch of different-coloured clothes or a designer dress. I have clothes in my wardrobe from Primark and Target, as well as vintage Christian Dior and Jean Paul Gaultier. In the Spice Girl days, I remember being given a Gucci dress that was too long to dance in, so I tacked it up with safety pins and went out in it. On the shoot for 'Wannabe' I refused to wear the very expensive top that the stylist had picked out. I walked into Mr Buyrights and found a fantastic green top for £2 and wore it with the Jean Paul Gaultier trousers. It's still in my bedroom today, in my Spice Girl shrine. It's a bit tatty, but I still love it. It's my style.

'Your style is disgusting,' my beloved husband told me. There was a particular tone he used which, at first, I couldn't quite put my finger on. I now think it was probably contempt. He would go through my wardrobe and throw out anything he didn't like when I wasn't there. He pulled up images of Jennifer Lopez and Kate Beckinsale looking groomed and glam. 'Dress to impress' was his 24/7 mantra.

—

It was Stephen's idea that I do 'Dancing with the Stars'. I was approached a few months after Angel was born but always said, 'I'm not doing that show! Not happening.' It was out of my comfort zone. I'd already been talking to my girls Geri, Vic, Emma and Mel C about a reunion. That was my comfort zone. If I was going to do a tour, it would mean a massive amount of work and lots of travelling, but it would also mean the Spice Girls being back together again, and I was really excited about it. I'd be performing in front of my fans with my friends next to me onstage. The idea of doing a top-rated television show was crazy – too hard, too much to commit to. I had other things to deal with, such as being married and being a mum.

Stephen stood in front of me and shook his head. 'It's one of the biggest shows on American television,' he said. 'You have to stop hiding. When people think you are a scumbag, you get out there and you show them what you can do.'

'No,' I said. I was adamant. I was not doing that show. More than ten million people watch that show. It's like 'Strictly Come Dancing' but pumped up to the max, and all I could think is that every single one of them would hate me. I'd been humiliated, called a gold-digger, dumped by the man I loved when I was pregnant with his child. I still had my baby belly and my excess stone and a half, which was fine by me because my plan was to hunker down at home with my kids and, in private, get in training for the Spice Girls tour.

Even though I hate to admit it, going on the show would turn out to be the one brilliant decision Stephen made for me because that show put me back on the map. People saw who I was behind those awful headlines. They got to know me, to see me struggle, fight and rise. And they saw me dance – the great passion of my life since I was a little kid. To this day my Pasa Doble is one of the most-watched dances ever on YouTube.

It took a few days getting to know everyone on set for me to realize that – whatever my fears had been – I was in the right place and that I could really do this and show America who I really was. Not only would everyone get that it took guts to take on that show a few months after having had a baby, but they'd all have to acknowledge it took balls to face a big, fat, prime-time television audience when my reputation was in the toilet. And – to my mind and his mind – Stephen had made that happen.

So he really does know what he's doing. He really does know what is best for me, I thought to myself. This threw me again because it made me think he was some kind of business genius. It was me who put myself out there, me who chatted away on screen. It was me who danced like my reputation depended on it. But doing that show turned my life back around in America. And doing that show made me see exactly who I was married to.

21
SMASH

—

What I remember most is the sound of the vase as it hit the wall of our hotel suite in Minneapolis. Broken glass spinning across the polished wooden floor. It was 4 a.m. on 29 May 1999, the morning of my 24th birthday and my present from my husband – who was there to support me as I made my debut solo album – was a soundtrack of absolute fury as his shouts and curses cut through the still night air.

'Please go home, Jim,' I sobbed. 'Just leave.'

'Why should I?' he roared back. 'I'm your husband and I'm not going anywhere.' He stood, staring at me, his hand still raised, his eyes motionless and filled with absolute loathing.

It was less than a year after our dramatic wedding. We were parents, celebrity millionaires with a beautiful baby girl, a fabulous house in Marlow and a golden future. I had everything I'd ever wished for as a kid but the reality was nothing like my dreams and I had to face the fact that my marriage had gone past the point of no return. Fame puts pressure on anyone. If you marry someone famous, there will be pressure on you and pressure on the marriage. You believe you can deal with it because you believe love conquers all, but it's amazing how fast the rot sets in.

The row was just the latest in a long line of fights marking our 16-month marriage. Our marriage was not easy. He was 'Jimmy Goldcard', a figure of fun in the tabloid press who snapped him here there and everywhere on his shopping trips, laden down with designer bags. He 'spent money like water' as my dad – who'd trailed round the shops of Oslo for hours with him on one infamous occasion – said. My dad couldn't actually believe a man could walk into one shop after another, spending thousands on clothes. And when Jim kept presenting the shop assistants with my gold Amex card my dad was boiling over with fury.

There were so many reasons why we rowed. I never challenged him about the money – all the attention on that irritated me – but I challenged him about smoking too much weed, about doing nothing all day long, about refusing to have sex with me. He said he didn't want to have sex with a pregnant woman. Pregnant women are beautiful. And being pregnant made me feel extra frisky, but Jim would push me away. 'I can't.'

I tried to get him work, but it was just more 'Mr Mel B' handouts. He was proud. I was working non-stop, flying all over the place with the girls and even doing other crazy, wonderful things like interviewing Prince (I was requested specifically). I sympathized with that , but I have limited tolerance for people who sit around all day long, looking as miserable as a Blackpool donkey, when they've actually got the world at their feet. Get out there. Shout. Knock on doors and don't take rejection like a kick in the teeth; take it as a kick up the arse and move on. There will always be people to put you down, always be people to tell you, 'No, you can't – you're not good enough, you're not thin enough, you're not smart enough.' Just prove them wrong.

—

When the Spice Girls first got put together in 1994, we were called Touch. Emma Bunton wasn't part of the group, and there was another girl called Michelle Stephenson who was nice enough, but she didn't have the same attitude as the rest of us. We weren't all the best singers and we weren't all the best dancers, but we all had that same 'I'm gonna show you' attitude. Michelle was sweet and very well turned out but she didn't seem as hard working as the rest of us. So she left and a cute little blonde with pigtails turned up at the train station in Maidenhead (where we lived) with her mother, Pauline. Through the girly hair ribbons and pink lipstick, what we all recognized was a kindred spirit. Underneath that pretty, giggly surface, Emma is a warrior woman and far naughtier than anyone would believe. Emma was – like the rest of us – forged with ambition of steel.

There were times when we'd put on shows in front of half a dozen totally disinterested 'music industry types', but every time we'd walk out onto the floor as if we were at Wembley Stadium. We did lots of showcases where no-one gave a damn, but their bored, jaded expressions and their shrugging shoulders didn't faze us. They made us more determined. We knew we were going to be massive, we were going to show them – and we did.

If you want to be a winner, you have to believe you can win. Just put it out there in the universe. I do it all the time. At the age of thirteen, when I was supposed to be doing my homework, I'd be up in my room practising signing my autograph. I was determined I was going to be famous. There was no Plan B. I was sure I was going to make it. Again, this is a split in my Gemini personality. When it comes to anything to do with my work, I'm on solid ground. I know what I'm doing; dance steps, costume changes, cameras, live performances – none of that fazes me. I can run into a live show late, panting, completely unprepared, and I will be fine. I won't even break a sweat. I'll just laugh a lot. I actually love the excitement of cutting everything fine and going to the wire. It gives me a buzz to this day.

But that's only part of my life. It's not enough being happy on a stage. I want happiness offstage. I'm much closer to that now, thank God. I can see myself more clearly, see how desperate I was for someone to show me unconditional love. See how I ignored the ones who did actually care for me and went for emotionally unavailable and controlling men like my father because the little girl inside me was always mourning for the man who loved me so much as a child then shut me out as a woman. So much of my need for attention comes from that single, deadening loss. It makes me demanding, it makes me want to push and push and test all the time how much you love me.

It's very hard when you throw fame into the mix, throw in the fact that so many people are prepared to do anything for you. It made me want even more proof of love from the people I loved. My way of showing absolute, unconditional love was by trying to give them the world. I am a drama queen. I love grand gestures: 'You want a Ferrari? I'll buy it for you.' I didn't think I was buying their love, I thought I was sharing what I had. If they jumped up and down with delight, I was pleased because I had made them happy. But in fact it was my money that had made them happy.

When I bought my mum and dad a beautiful stone house in Horsforth in 2000, my dad didn't want to move in. For another six months he stayed in the house they bought in Kirkstall for £18,000 when I was seven, and after him and mum divorced a few years later, that was the house he lived in till he died. 'I like it here, that house is too posh for me. I don't want to live anywhere else,' he said.

On my wedding day to Jim, before I got into my dress, I took my sister, Danielle, into the garage, where I had a brand new yellow Punto complete with leather interior and a number plate which read DAN 800 (she was born in 1980) and shouted, 'Happy Birthday!' She just stared, dumbfounded. 'Do you like it? Do you like it?' I asked, grabbing her arm and dragging her towards the car. I wanted her to stroke it, leap into the front seat or burst into tears, but she barely reacted, which actually upset me a bit because I'd thought so hard about what would be her perfect car.

A couple of years later, Danielle was dating Jay-Z, who had chased her for years to get her to go out with him. He took her to Paris and – because I was away at the time – she borrowed some of my clothes for the weekend. And then, much to both our surprise, Max Beesley and I walked into Hôtel Costes where she was with Jay-Z and all his mates and where we were also booked in. She didn't say, 'Oh yes, I took these clothes because you've got loads of designer clothes.' She was mortified because she'd nicked her big sister's outfit without her permission.

'Nice belt, Danielle,' I said jokingly when I walked over to her. I didn't mind; she could keep those clothes. But she wouldn't ever do that. The next week, they were all dry-cleaned and hanging back up in my closet.

In September 2017, when my mum was staying with me at my house in Coldwater Canyon, I was so happy she was back in my life after nine years of distance because of Stephen. I hatched a plan with my friend Gary Madatyan. 'Tell my mum I want her to go and make us all a cup of tea in the kitchen,' I said. 'And then I'll call her out and we'll give her the biggest surprise of her life.'

I was standing in a pair of white pyjamas, hiding with Gary in the corner of the landing against the wrought-iron balustrade, overlooking the beautiful marble hallway where I could see Angel's French bulldog puppy, Axl, sniffing around the kids' schoolbags. 'Mother,' I yelled. 'Come here, now.' As she came out into the hall, we threw $5,000 on top of her. She stood there underneath twirling ten- and twenty-dollar bills, which flew on her head and around her like something out of a movie. Then – ten minutes later – she gathered up the money and gave it back to me. 'Here you are, Melanie. You keep your money.'

I find it harder to accept when people don't want me for my money. 'Take it. Spend it. Buy yourself something.'

'Melanie, I just want you,' she said.

—

Jim had a temper (a few years later, in 2002, he was fined for smacking a three-year-old autistic boy who had pushed Phoenix in a zoo). He would kick off with the photographers who followed us around, but he'd never hit me. He'd always been very protective. In fact, most of his fights with photographers were because they were trying to get a picture of me.

I sat on my bed in my hotel room in Minneapolis, sobbing. It was my 24th birthday and for remaining few days of his visit I felt utterly miserable. All my famous confidence and ballsiness seemed to have leaked out of me like air from a balloon. The following week I had to fly to Los Angeles to do the video for my single 'Word Up' which was going to be in the Austin Powers movie, *The Spy Who Shagged Me*.

I felt unattractive and uncomfortable with my post pregnancy body. Now that's just not like me, but Jim would make little comments about how I spoke or what I wore and it chipped away at my self-esteem. I remember telling the stylist at the video shoot that I needed to wear a corset so I could look right in the silver catsuit they'd chosen for me to wear and her telling me I looked amazing.

I didn't believe her. In my eyes I was a woman whose husband never wanted to have sex with her. How could I even try to be sexy … Who was I kidding?

Los Angeles saved me but it ended my marriage. I enjoyed myself on my video shoot, I went out with Mel C a few nights later for the premiere of *The Spy Who Shagged Me* and we had a laugh. I felt more like myself. One night in my hotel room in the Four Seasons in Beverly Hills I made myself think back to moments in our marriage that I had never resolved.

I am a Gemini. There are moments I deal with life head on (honestly, I love nothing more than sorting out a crisis for a friend. 'Right, book this flight,' 'I'm calling this doctor,' I'll yell with my phone in my hand making calls and sending emails like a woman possessed) and then there are times when I refuse to deal with a problem at all.

A few months later, in the midst of yet another row about yet another stupid, insignificant thing, I twisted away from Jim on the landing as he stormed off to our room. I lost my footing and fell down the stairs. I was seven months pregnant with our daughter.

Jim didn't even look back and I heard the bedroom door slam.

I lay completely motionless, covering my belly, whispering, 'Are you okay?' to our unborn child. I could hear Jim's footsteps upstairs. And I felt Phoenix kick inside me. I put my hand up to my face and felt it was wet. I looked at my palm, expecting to see blood, but there was none, just the dampness of tears. I had no idea I'd even cried.

When I finally stood up, I knew there was no way I was going to stay in the house with Jim a second longer. I didn't want to be on my own. I didn't want to call my mum because I knew my dad would want to tear Jim to pieces, and I didn't want any more drama.

I knew exactly who I could turn to. I picked up the phone and dialled Mel C's number. 'Melanie, it's me. I need to stay with you,' I said. I was trying to keep my voice from shaking. She knew instantly that I was in trouble.

'I'm coming to get you,' she said straight away.

'No. I'll come to you.' I picked up my car keys and left. I didn't even pack a bag. I knew that Mel would take care of everything.

A few nights before I'd been laughing and joking with Mel. It felt more than a coincidence. It felt significant. I had to work out exactly what it meant.

—

In my marriage to Jim, the vicious rows were a wake-up call. We lived in the most beautiful home. I had spent nearly all of my money turning the Tudor-fronted Grade II listed house – originally built for the Sheriff of Marlow – into the most stunning place.

The ten-bedroom house was set in 10 acres of land with garages which I converted so there were two cottages within the gardens. The Thames ran past the bottom of my land. I had a bathroom with gold baths, a downstairs toilet with two loos in it (because girls always go into loos together, right, so why not pee at the same time and carry on talking?), a hand-painted nursery, and a piano room with a gorgeous white piano and a huge golden harp. There was also a cottage in the grounds; that later became my sister Danielle's home for a few years.

On the walls were my treasured Andy Warhol Marilyn Monroe original Pop art prints, and every single thing in that house was chosen by me to make it the perfect place for us to bring up our child. I knew Jim wasn't happy. He was angry with the world. But there was no way I was going to be treated like this. Look at the life this man led. No way was he going to ruin mine.

I decided right there and then – sitting on my cream-carpeted stairs in Marlow, and before I phoned Mel C – that I was going to get out of the marriage. Every shred of respect I had for Jim was gone.

I wasn't going to do it right then – we'd only been married a few months, for God's sake, and I couldn't face the backlash. 'I knew it, Melanie' – I could actually hear my mum saying it. I was going to wait. I would wait till our child was born. I would wait to see if that changed things. I would wait to see if we had some sort of breakthrough in our relationship, but in my head I knew it was pretty much over. I needed time to think and I needed time to work out a plan. There was no way I was going to let a man treat me like that.

—

People think I am so tough, and to some degree I am. I can stand my ground against the likes of Sean 'P. Diddy' 'Puffy' Combes, who – back in 1998, when I'd been asked to host the MOBO awards in London – wouldn't get off the stage to let me start my rehearsals for the show. I had to perform as well as host the show. He'd turned up with a massive entourage and then run into my rehearsal time with the clock ticking less than an hour before the doors were due to open. I was watching, fuming as he said he wanted another run-through. I marched out towards him. 'No, I need to rehearse my song NOW,' I said.

He didn't even look at me, just raised his mic and said, 'Get this bitch off the stage.'

I was livid. This was a British show, and we don't behave like that over here. No-one has the right to say that about anyone. I went up and poked him in the shoulder. 'What did you say? Get WHAT off the stage?' He tried to ignore me, so I said, 'Listen, I'm introducing you tonight, so I'd be nice if I were you. The doors are opening in ten minutes. I need to rehearse. Can you get off the fucking stage!' I got my rehearsal, and about half an hour later one of his bouncers turned up in my dressing room with a peace offering: a jacket with P. Diddy's name splashed all over it. It looked like a bloody cagoule. And there's no way I'd be walking around with his name on my back. 'Thanks,' I said with a fake smile, then I threw it back at the bouncer. I wanted to send a message back. Nobody has the right to treat anyone like that. And some crummy jacket was not an acceptable apology.

And then there was my row with Robbie Williams – who has, along with his hilarious, brilliant wife, Ayda, become a good friend and neighbour of mine in LA. In 2000, me and the rest of the girls were performing at the Brits because we were winning a Lifetime Achievement Award (even though we were all under thirty) and Robbie was also going to be there. Now Rob had said something not very complimentary about a friend of mine (turns out he's just as bad as I am for shooting his mouth off, but I didn't know that then). I walked past his dressing-room door, which was open. The Brits was always a pretty mad occasion. Back in the old days it was like some reunion, with everyone pumped up on booze, adrenalin and whatever, with kids from various different schools (or bands) all wanting to settle scores on the day.

In 1997, Liam Gallagher announced he was going to 'smack' us all if he ever bumped into us, so when we stepped up to collect our Best British Video award, Mel C leaned into the microphone and shouted, 'Liam Gallagher, come on and have a go if you think you are hard enough.' Another year, all of us ran into Mark Morrison (who had a hit with 'Return Of The Mack') and we sprayed rude graffiti over the walls because he'd slated us in an interview. Now it was Robbie's turn.

'Robbie Williams, get out here, you twat. I'm going to batter you,' I yelled. I expected Robbie to race out and confront me in a fury. I psyched myself up for the fray, quickly glancing to see where the rest of the girls were. But he didn't. The door slammed, and then one of his security guys came out and stood in front of it. I walked away, laughing my head off. Now I go round to his house and tell him off in front of Ayda, like when he announced he'd slept with four of the Spice Girls. 'Well, he never slept with me,' I said. He has since amended the number to 'three out of five'. That's Rob.

—

When it comes to men I fall in love with, I am not tough, I am a pushover. I will let them get away with things that everyone else can see because I love them and I desperately want to be loved back. I should never have married Jim. We brought out the worst in each other. We divorced in 2000, almost a year after Phoenix was born. I was sad my marriage hadn't worked out because my dream has always been to love and to be loved and to have a perfect family unit. I knew in that moment on the staircase that I had made the wrong choice. And I knew I had – as ever – ignored the warning signs and refused to listen to those who knew me best. By the time I filed for divorce, in my head and in my heart I had already moved on. That's the way I deal with things. I propel myself forwards. By then I'd met the actor and musician Max Beesley, who was smart, talented and, best of all, made me laugh. He was from the North, like me. He was full of ideas, full of ambition and full of life.

And in 2007, a year short of a decade later, I was married again, to Stephen. And once again after those first few weeks, after my bad feelings about our sex tape, I no idea whether he actually loved me. Once we got back from our few days of honeymoon, I gave him the keys to my £200,000 black Bentley and within weeks he had a whole new wardrobe, boxes of shirts and designer bags (Gucci, Gucci, Gucci of course) piling up in our walk-in wardrobe in a way that was all too familiar. 'If I'm representing you, I have to look the part,' he said, shucking a brand new Rolex out of its case onto the bed. He bought Rolexes like other people buy packets of crisps. I think I just nodded. I was never going to argue about money.

That was not my world. And I never wanted it to be my world. I am not one of these people who like to show off about their material possessions or flash lifestyles. A few weeks after my divorce from Stephen was finally granted, I flew to Leeds and turned up at the reception for my cousin john's wedding to a gorgeous girl called Danielle. It was held in a small club in Leeds, there was no ice at the bar, no fancy food or designer goodie bags but I had the best time I'd had for years. In fact my mum and I were two of the last people to leave the party. I do not take my lifestyle for granted. I am so, so lucky to have what I have.

When Stephen and I were first married, we lived in a beautiful house off Mulholland Drive where the first thing you saw when you looked out of your window was a gleaming, crystal-blue pool like something out of a David Hockney painting. Stephen had previously been living in a small rented one-bedroom apartment in Larrabee Street and driving an old Audi. Now he was living like a lord and acting like a king. He moved in his brother, Jeremiah, to work as a chauffeur so we could go out to clubs and mingle with all the celebrities Stephen wanted to meet. That drove me insane. I'm not a networker. I've always been a very private person, and I don't barge up to people in clubs and ask them to hang out just because they are famous and I am famous. Stephen wouldn't have it. His eyes were like trackers hunting down anyone of celebrity status. Then he'd push me in the back. 'Go on, say hello. Get over there now.' I hated it because you could see very clearly that people didn't like him. I'd pretend not to notice and just laugh a lot. So awkward.

Jeremiah didn't appear to be like Stephen. Often he'd say to me, 'Don't worry, Melanie.' He's since spoken out in many interviews, claiming he witnessed how abusive his brother was to me; how he witnessed Stephen punch Phoenix's golden retriever, Lordy (who was eight at the time and a bit fragile) so hard he collapsed while Stephen laughed; how he got one of our nannies in the hot tub; and how he used to feel sorry for me when his brother would grab the keys to the Bentley and announce, 'I'm going out to get my dick sucked.' When the neighbour's cat went missing, the little boy who owned the cat was beside himself. Stephen thought the funniest thing was to hide on our balcony and make miaowing noises and laugh when he heard the boy shouting to his mum: 'I think I can hear the cat.'

—

If Jim was controlling, I would have to invent another word for Stephen. He ruled by clever, manipulative domestic terrorism. This was the way he had been brought up and the only way he knew.

Born on Pulaski Drive, one of the roughest streets of Point Pleasant, New Jersey, Stephen Brian Stansbury (known as 'Steve' or 'Stevie' to his family) grew up with his white mother, Sheryl – a teacher in the Shelby County, Tennessee school system – and five siblings, with a father he told me was 'the toughest man on the streets'. He walked like he was bullet-proof, and – when he was in a mood – he talked like he was pelting you with gunfire.

Stephen – which was the name he introduced himself with to me, pronounced with a final 'a' as in 'Stephan' – had told lots of stories about who he was, I soon discovered. And his new surname – changed from Stansbury to Belafonte – created intrigue and a connection to stardom.

He'd had a terrible childhood, he'd made mistakes. So what? So had I, so had most of the kids at school I'd grown up with. I live in the business of transformation. I've seen it first-hand. Girls brought up on fish fingers, baked beans and fizzy pop changing their accents, sending back vintage wine in Michelin-starred restaurants because 'it's not the right temperature' or 'it doesn't taste like it should'.

It makes me laugh because it's never something I've been tempted to do (I brought my Yorkshire accent all the way to America), but I get it. Reinvention. Everybody in show business does it in one way or another, whether it's lying about your age, having surgery or making people believe you are someone you are not. 'This is Hollywood, this is what you have to do,' Stephen said. Of course, he was right.

I have no idea whether Stephen's stories about his father being a drug dealer are true. I do know (from his brothers and sisters) that there were an awful lot of drugs consumed in the house by him (largely LSD and marijuana), and that his dad, Kenneth Stansbury, a black African American, was a Golden Gloves-winning boxer in New Jersey (he won the title in 1964) with a record of violence and abuse. At the age of 18, Kenneth was charged with trying to kill his own father, Theodore (the charge was later dropped) but he went on to build up a rap sheet which included domestic violence, assault and threatening police. In 1968 when Kenneth was 21, he was charged with malicious mischief, fornication, using profanity and threatening a police officer telling him, 'I'll put a bullet in you.' Steve was his father's son. He comes from a line of criminals. His grandfather, Theodore, has criminal history for adultery, not paying child support and abandoning his wife. But even his only family would say – and they did – that Steve was the nastiest of them all.

'Look at your arms. They look flabby and saggy. You're old and you're ugly.' 'Get your face out of my sight.' 'Your fucking arse, Melanie. It's fucking disgusting.' He would get louder and louder, pushing his face right in front of mine to tell me how stupid and ugly I was. 'You should thank God you have me because no one else would want you.' When we were out he was constantly checking out other girls. I would see Janet in the back of her car, shaking her head as he leered at girls crossing the street. It made me feel as if I wasn't good enough, as if I repulsed him. 'Now she's a real fuckable bitch,' he'd say, looking at me as if I repulsed him.

Ten minutes later he would be shouting for me to have sex with him, telling me I was his princess, his queen, how much he loved me and couldn't live without me. He'd tell me I looked stressed and needed to wind down. He'd bring out a bottle of vodka, pour me drinks then an hour later scream, 'You're drunk, you disgusting bitch. You look like a derelict.' My brain was scrambled. I told myself he was insecure, he had a damaged background, that I hadn't given him enough attention, that he didn't mean what he was saying, but I was still hormonal after giving birth and felt completely crap about myself.

One of my problems is that I can't admit to having made a mistake. I toughed it out. I pretended it didn't bother me, shouted back and tried to work out what was going on in the head of this man. I was sure I could actually help him; I was also certain that I was strong enough to deal with him. And I wasn't going to let anyone else know I'd got myself in too deep. I was ready to go to the extreme. On a trip to Hawaii, I cringed as I heard him asking Janet to go and find girls to bring over to our table. She refused. I laughed, saying he was a massive pervert like me. That is what I was telling myself.

—

The fact Stephen pushed me into doing 'Dancing with the Stars' had, however, paid off. Suddenly, everything was coming together in my life; a few small pieces of positive press already had started. On 27 June 2007, Geri, Vic, Mel C, Emma and me got together for a press conference at the O2 in London and announced *The Return of The Spice Girls* tour. I was so happy to see the girls, but I wanted them to think everything was going well in my world. I've always hated people feeling sorry for me. It was time to introduce them to Stephen.

22
SPICE REVISITED
—

I am standing in a black fabric box that is held together by Velcro. It is 2 January 2008. I am covered in sweat, struggling into a leopard-print catsuit and leather buckled boots. I can hear Vic on stage – a few feet from where I am – singing along to 'Like a Virgin', the crowd at the O2 in London is going crazy and I am laughing.

I wait to hear the last strains of Vic's solo spot – a remix of RuPaul's 'Supermodel (You Better Work)' – and then it's my turn. I run underneath the stage and get on a platform riser that will lift me up through a hole back onto the stage. On this tour, we decided to give ourselves a solo spot each in the third act of the show, partly to sort of reflect what we'd done since we split and also because – let's face it – we've all got massive egos and each of us wanted her own moment in the spotlight.

Vic went out and did a kind of catwalk strut because now she's the queen of the fashion world. She didn't need to sing. All she needed to do was walk up and down and the crowd went completely berserk. Every night it brought the house down. People loved seeing the newly-turned-fashionista Victoria Beckham onstage, camping it up as a Spice Girl – and she loved it too. 'What did you think of Mummy?' was the first question she asked her boys Brooklyn, Romeo and baby Cruz, twirling around in her stage gear in her silver-and-black dressing room (mine was leopard-print, of course, and Emma's was bubblegum-pink).

Geri did her hit, a cover of the Weather Girls' 'It's Raining Men' with a bunch of scantily glad guys, Mel C sang the huge summer rave smash 'I Turn to You', and Emma sang her solo hit 'Maybe'. I was the one who followed Vic (the toughest slot) and – because this is me you are talking about – I made sure I gave a knockout performance.

Every night I would do a version of the Lenny Kravitz song 'Are You Gonna Go My Way'. I have to say it was a choice influenced by the fact Lenny K is one of the sexiest men on the planet. After I split from Jim, I was invited by Nancy Berry, the uber rock chick and super-successful record-company executive, to her place in Italy, along with Meg Matthews . I took Phoenix and my best friend Charlotte, and I would watch Lenny in the pool, thinking how bloody gorgeous he was. On the tour, I would emerge on the stage on a riser, with my microphone slotted into a whip, and I would stomp into the audience with a couple of male dancers, grab a likely-looking guy (most of the poor sods were there with their girlfriends, which made me laugh) and then handcuff him to a ladder contraption that was bolted to the middle of the T-shaped stage. I would then proceed to bump and grind all over him, up and down the ladder, lashing my whip and getting the crowd into a frenzy.

'Melanie, are you ready?' It was the stage technician, checking I was in the right spot on the riser. I am not nervous. I am never nervous. I left my stagefright behind years ago when I was a kid doing dance shows around the north-west of England. My heart is pumping and I am thinking (as I always do), 'This is almost better than sex.' 'Go, go, go!' shouts the stage technician, and I feel the riser kick into life beneath my leather boots.

After months of non-stop training and performances for 'Dancing with the Stars', I was super-fit and toned. My boobs (I'd had a boob job after I'd had Phoenix because I'd wanted my boobs back after breast-feeding) were looking great, and whatever I felt in front of Stephen, onstage I felt amazing. I loved singing live. And as I rose up in front of the packed audience at the O2 – our homecoming – with the thudding baseline of 'Are You Gonna Go My Way' belting out at top volume, I felt completely free.

In every form of meditation or spiritual enlightenment, the aim is to try to get the mind to the present and in the moment. Onstage, that is exactly where I am. In the moment. Nothing else matters. Geri and I could have a row backstage (usually about me having a go at her about her dancing – *'You bloody went wrong again, Geri!' 'No, I didn't!' 'I think I actually know the steps and you bloody did!'*). I can be way too direct because when you go to dance schools you get used to taking criticism (but you forget it can come across so harsh if you haven't had that training). But onstage it's all forgotten. We will be giggling at each other, hiding behind the life-size hardboard cutouts we had made of each of us where we had to keep perfectly still – except me and Emma would be pushing and shoving each other for a laugh, just before the lights went up to make it even harder.

'What's your name?' I yelled to my 'male catch' for the night and helped my dancers drag him to get strapped to the ladders. 'Have you been a good boy?' I'd yell at him … I was playing up to the audience – I love connecting with the people who come and see us. Sometimes I will seek out someone in the crowd and keep eye-contact with them throughout an entire song (hilariously, people nearly always look away after a minute or so because they don't quite know what's happening).

Tonight, for the three precious minutes of my solo, I was focused entirely on my whipping boy, focused entirely on the music. But even in that moment, that inexplicably, insanely wonderful moment of being on a stage in front of a twenty-thousand-plus crowd, there was a message in my brain telling me not to look down to my right, at the point where the catwalk met the stage. That was where Stephen was watching my every move with his beady eyes.

I'd invited some journalist friends of mine to the show, including Louise Gannon, who I'd known since the very early days of the Spice Girls, and Rosie Nixon, the editor of *Hello!* They were seated in that exact same spot, right next to Stephen, and they were due to come and see me after the show. But they never came backstage. Years later they explained why. They told they had been freaked out by Stephen stalking back and forth in front of them, slamming his right fist into his left palm as I performed my ladder dance. He was steaming with rage that his wife was shaking her booty all over some guy onstage. Throughout the rest of the show, he didn't even watch, kept making calls on his mobile – despite the fact you couldn't hear a word even when you were right next to someone because the music was so loud. Louise and Rosie didn't want to go and have to stand in a room with Stephen, making small talk. As journalists say, they made their excuses and left. I got a text saying, 'Sorry, had to rush back home.' I also got a far less polite message from Stephen. From then on, only my gay fans were allowed to get up for my routine.

I think I probably knew – deep down, that is – why my friends hadn't come to see me. Anyone who is in any form of abusive relationship gradually starts to accept that friends slowly peel away.

Initially, this 'peel away' makes things easier. You don't have the embarrassment of seeing really good mates such as my great friend Kim Deck – she lived across the road from us on Mulholland Drive – look horrified when, in the middle of some social gathering at our house, Stephen started screaming at me, calling me a whore. Kim was one of the first people I met in LA. Lovely woman, lovely family – she's a lawyer; she's funny, smart, well-educated but not in any way patronizing or smug. Her son, Julian, was the same age as Phoenix, and for years they were inseparable. Then Stephen came along ...

You fall into the cliché of telling yourself they are like this because they love you. Jealous because they love you so much. You pick your battles and you think, 'If I can get to the root of what makes them behave like this ...' And if you show them they are front and centre of your life ... If, if, if ... Then it will all work out. And you avert your eyes or pretend not to notice the looks and the no-shows, and, to be honest, the sympathetic gazes were both mortifying and infuriating. 'I'm fine, absolutely fine,' I'd say. I would laugh incidents off. Or I'd pretend that they never happened. I got so bloody good at pretending.

And I got defensive. 'Leave me alone, I can handle this. I can sort this out.' Those were my go-to responses. People who know you well become difficult to be around. Everyone feels awkward. So you let them go. You think, This is just happening, this is my life now. You don't realize that you are in a programme. You are being isolated. The strings are being pulled, but someone else – not you – is pulling them.

—

The Spice Girls performed seventeen nights at the O2 in London. It was the biggest and most successful concert of 2008 – those seventeen dates alone grossed $33.8 million in sales. You couldn't open a newspaper without pictures of all of us, or one of us splashed over the news pages. After years of doing our own thing, we were back together, and after two intense weeks of dates in Canada, America, Germany and Spain we were – when we were all together backstage or on our Spice Jet – slotting back into our old ways, all of us wearing our Juicy Couture tracksuits in black or white with our names embroidered on.

Me, Vic and Emma would share one hair and makeup room, Geri and Mel C another (they like to do lots of vocal warm-ups, while the rest of us like to chat, eat and mess about). I'd find myself turning back into who I was in my teens. Emma would be there recording a little backstage piece for our website (she and Geri always get asked to do that because they take things like that VERY seriously, and I'll do something like go round filming the toilets – which never gets used). And I would find myself photo-bombing every little set, throwing myself in front of the camera, trying to take over.

I could – in these moments – forget Stephen. Almost. He would call endlessly, of course, but I would pick up the phone: 'Hiya, I'm in the middle of hair and makeup' or 'We're about to go on telly.' If he wasn't there, there was nothing he could do, which meant I could go back to being Mel B.

I could go back to being the girl I was when my life was carefree and breathlessly exciting. With these girls whose ticks and habits were as familiar as my own. I could tell what mood Geri was in simply by the way she walked into the room first thing, the tone in her voice. I could watch Vic making a really serious, sensible business call and knew I could make her wet herself laughing in a second by flashing in front of her. There is no part of any of their bodies I don't know. We have never been shy.

One of our favourite tricks, when we were stuck in a hotel suite and bored, was to ask for room service. Mel C would answer the door in just a T-shirt and then a waiter would walk in and see Emma, Geri and Vic standing there in bras and pants. I'd then walk in naked (again, always me doing the maddest bit) with a towel around myself. I'd pretend to be shocked and – oops! – I'd accidentally drop my towel to the floor.

I also remember a night when we were in the same hotel as Elton John, and Geri and I were drunkenly giggling outside his door. We didn't know him then, so we didn't actually knock. But we did wee in a pot plant right outside his doorway. We thought it was the most hilarious thing in the world – you have to remember we were still all just kids. Now that I'm older, I reckon … it's still quite amusing.

—

It is always strange at first when you meet up for a life-changing period of time with a group of girls you have lived and breathed every moment with. Like when you walk into a school reunion (not that I have ever been back to Intake High in Leeds or the Northern School of Contemporary Dance in Chapeltown, where I got kicked out after a year for being too loud). It feels weird. We all knew each other 'before Spice'. We all bonded together 'before Spice'. I will never forget how much my Spice Girls influenced me. Little things like Mel C showing me how to sort washing. I was pretty undomesticated and had no idea that if you put something red in with something white it would mess it up. Duurh. Vic would never let me near her washing. I was totally fascinated by her because she was unlike any other girl I knew.

Even back then, Vic had a definite sense of style. Her clothes were immaculate and she looked after them, always hanging them up, always making sure buttons were sewn back on if they fell off. At weekends in Maidenhead, Emma and Vic would go back home to London, and Mel C would meet up with some dancer friends she knew who lived a train ride away. Geri and I would try to spice up the local clubs. We were always nicking Vic's clothes, and we'd try to put them back perfectly, brushing them down. 'There's a mark on that skirt,' Geri would hiss. 'I don't think she'll notice,' I'd say. She always did. In the end she started taking most of her clothes with her.

Emma was always my easy-going, smiley little sister. She and I were usually rifling through cupboards for food or making shopping lists – largely doughnuts from Cullens, and lots of crisps. Geri was my terrible twin. We'd bomb around the place in her bashed-up green Fiat Uno, flashing our boobs at strangers on the motorway, howling our heads off and making crazy plans about 'when we are famous'.

And now that we were famous, years and years later, I wanted everyone to see that I was okay and that I had my life back under control.

On 2 February 2018, we met up again to discuss a Spice Girl Reunion, and it was that same feeling, times a hundred. I felt nervous. I felt raw. Sordid details of my marriage to Stephen had played out in headlines since my eight-month court battle with him, which finally ended in November 2017. '*Mel B – 56 sex tapes!*' … '*Mel B cocaine, Spice Girls and her threesomes*' … '*Mel B claims she was drugged throughout her ten-year marriage*' … '*Mel B blew £38 million – where did the money go?*'

—

This reunion in February 2018 was a massive deal. It was the first time we'd been back with our old manager, Simon Fuller, since 2007, and it was he and I who orchestrated the whole thing. I'd call Geri, he'd call Vic (because he still managed Vic and David), she would call Mel C, and we would all speak to Emma.

I should add that Geri, Emma and I had tried getting everyone together in 2016, but it hadn't worked out. At that time, Vic was busy with her fashion career and Mel C was recording her own album. Then, when we thought we could at least mark the twentieth anniversary for the fans with Emma, Geri and I doing our own mini tour … Geri got pregnant with her little boy, Monty. She'd been desperate to have a baby with her husband, Christian Horner, and we were all just really happy for her – even if we didn't get to do our tour.

But this was all of us. Back with Simon Fuller – 'the sixth Spice Girl', as he liked to be called. We arranged to meet at The Connaught, that five-star hotel in Mayfair. I flew in from LA in the morning, a mate picked me up, and we went to another friend, Dean Keyworth, the interior designer. He has a gorgeous flat in Kensington where I freshened up after my eleven-hour flight. The plan was to get a black cab to The Connaught, so I called Simon to say I'd landed. 'We're all at Geri's house,' he said. I was totally thrown. The story of the reunion had leaked out and there were press all over The Connaught. I got that, but I was completely thrown that no-one had texted me to tell me about the change of plan, about going to Geri's house.

Like I say, I was raw and emotional. I felt like I'd been left out of the loop, even though it was me and Simon who'd spent months organizing the meeting. I was so upset that for a moment, I actually thought about not going. Then my friend said, 'You've *got* to go.' I made her drive me there, which was pretty funny because she had a battered silver VW Golf, with gaffer tape holding the wing mirror on. One reporter wrote that the car we pulled up in 'looked like it was worth less than Mel's coat'. But that's me. I don't give a toss about material things. I wanted to have my friend there – I didn't care about the car.

Outside Geri's it was mayhem, but by now I was laughing because my friend was getting all panicky and I had two massive suitcases with me. I felt like Pippa in the movie *Rough Night* (played hilariously by Kate McKinnon) who is constantly dragging her luggage around with her. I got out of the car and was ushered by Vic's security (who were also looking a bit taken aback by the car) into Geri's fabulous house in north London. All the girls were inside drinking champagne. Geri had called in caterers to do the food. It looked more than a 'last-minute change' to me, but I wasn't going to make a fuss. I love being a Spice Girl. I'm proud of being a Spice Girl. Nothing will ever stop me putting on a leopard-print catsuit again – I don't take myself too seriously, I don't think I've 'moved on'. I think the fans would love it. And what a message. Never has Girl Power been more important.

The funny thing was that we spent less time talking about a reunion and more time taking photos. Vic started it, getting everyone in groups to do snaps, and then everyone was doing it. It was a pretty chaotic day and when we did get round to talking, we were all throwing ideas at each other. Poor Simon was having to be the referee. Then there was sushi for us and edamame beans, balsamic and sea salt for Vic, and by late afternoon what was clear was that – however many disagreements there may have been in the past – put us in a room and there's an energy that still burns. It made me happy and it made me sad because we don't get together enough.

And, true to form, four months after that meeting at Geri's, we all fell out again. We are not easy. We are five women with strong personalities and strong wills. Vic said she didn't want to go on tour, and the rest of us were unhappy that Simon hadn't pushed hard enough to make it happen. It will happen – in one form or another –

at some point in the future because I am going to make sure it does. The Spice story – like mine – is not over yet.

The last time we'd all been together was at the closing ceremony of the Olympics, the maddest, most brilliant performance – dancing on top of London cabs. I had a costume malfunction because I'd had a catsuit made up for me, with a pair of shoes to match, and when I got hold of them – an hour before the show – I hated the shoes that had been designed for me. I was wearing a pair of 8-inch Louboutins so I shouted to my hairdresser, Randy, 'Let's improvise!' We picked off some of the sequins from the catsuit and started gluing them onto the shoes. I was still fixing them on as we were spinning around in the cars just before we jumped out onstage.

'Bloody hell, Mel,' Emma said when she saw them. 'They are so high. You know we've got to dance on top of the taxis. Make sure you don't fall off.' As if! I can sprint in heels. But the whole event wasn't much fun for me. Stephen was there; the mix of Stephen, the other Spice Girls and me was always a problem. It was part of the reason why I hadn't been the one to keep in touch. It was part of the problem of isolation. It was easier to stay away – even from my girls, who were the biggest and greatest part of my life.

23
WALL
—

The introduction between my husband and the rest of the girls had not gone well. We were in London, and there are two occasions I clearly remember. The first was at a photo shoot. Everyone was polite, smiling, giving him a hug. And then, within a matter of minutes, Stephen started to go into his 'wheeler dealer' mode.

I could see what Geri was thinking: Who is this idiot? Emma did a lot of smiling and picking up her phone whenever he came near. Mel C – bless her – did spend time talking to him. Not that he particularly appreciated it because whenever Vic walked past, he would jump up, even if Mel was mid-sentence. He seemed obsessed with getting Vic to talk to him, and she avoided eye contact.

I was cringing. I was angry with him for being such a jerk. The patter I'd thought was so impressive in Los Angeles fell flat on British ears. He sounded crass, making inappropriate jokes and talking about sex. I would laugh every now and again to break the embarrassing silence, but inside I was raging. I was also – if I'm honest – raging that the girls were judging him. And I was raging with myself: 'Another mistake Melanie. Another fuck-up.'

The British press had turned up story after story on Scary Spice's Scary Husband. First off, his ex-partner, Nicole Contreras (the mother of his daughter, Giselle, who he had brought with him when he first met me to show what a good dad he was) gave an interview. Nicole didn't hold back. She talked about how abusive Stephen had been during their six-year relationship. She talked about how he had tried to choke her and that he had – in 2003 – pleaded 'No Contest' to a charge of battery against her, admitting beating her in a 'malicious, drunken frenzy'. And there was more. Lots more. The tabloids went to town.

—

Looking at it in black and white, it is impossible for me now to understand why I didn't walk away there and then, especially after Nicole's chilling account of the battering she'd had at Stephen's hands. He told me at the time that they had had a row which had got out of control. I believed him. I didn't even question his story. I've since become a good friend of Nicole's, as Giselle remains a fixture in my life and the life of my girls, and I know the truth.

I had no idea of the extent of these incidents when we got married – Stephen had simply told me he'd been a bit of a 'bad boy' in his youth. I didn't judge him because I'm no angel either (although I have never had a criminal conviction or so much as a caution from the police), and a few guys I'd grown up with in Leeds had got themselves in real trouble. My very first boyfriend, Stephen Mulrain, had ended up with a nine-month prison sentence in 2002 for grievous bodily harm.

Every time a screaming headline about me taking drugs, or drinking, or being involved in threesomes came out about me in court, I was set up for judgement by the public. *Piece of filth.* Only my family and my true and oldest friends, as well as my beautiful, loyal fans, held off all judgement, and showed compassion and understanding. I don't say it enough, but there will never be adequate words to thank them.

And so it was thanks to the British press that I found out about Stephen's past. Drip by drip. But it was still too late for me to really take heed of all the horror stories. As much as I respect the British press, I know all too well how stories can be twisted and misrepresented.

You always have to know your own truth. I was in love and I believed the version of Stephen he sold to me.

'They've got it all wrong. They are out to pull us apart,' he'd say. I believed him. I loved him and I was in too deep. I wanted my marriage to work, and I was doing anything and everything to make that happen. Stephen had control of the finances, chose where we lived and who looked after the kids; he had strong views on what we ate, what I wore (he always liked me to wear black), what handbag and shoes I had on, where we went. I lost my perception of what reality was.

It has taken me a long time to see how I lost control of my mind, my reason and my future from the moment I said 'I do' in Vegas. I was a strong, independent woman. I had been the one who called the shots. Of the Spice Girls, I was notoriously the one incapable of holding her tongue, incapable of being made to do anything I didn't want to do. My whole Scary Spice persona was built on the fact that I was intimidated by no-one.

'You're all going to wear tracksuits in different colours – that's your look.' That was what the five of us were told by our very first managers, Chris and Bob Herbert, in 1994. Imagine that. Five Sporty Spices! Vic looked down, Geri looked at me. 'No bloody way,' I shouted back at these professional managers giving us bunch of skint wannabes our 'big chance' in the business. 'Not happening. We're all different. That's the point.' No-one was going to tell me what to do.

Now I was constantly questioning myself. The voice I heard in my head was not my own but Stephen's.

As I have mentioned, I told myself that – in his own way – he was trying to protect me. If I got upset, he'd sometimes laugh, or he'd sometimes grab me and take me into the bedroom, where he'd tell me he was addicted to my body, obsessed with me. We'd have unbelievable sex for hours and then I'd think, 'Yes, he loves me. He does really love me. He just talks like that because – as he always told me – he was a ghetto kid from the rough streets of New York. He doesn't mean it.'

The way I felt inside most of the time was the same way I felt at fourteen, when my dad would say to me as I ran down the stairs on a Tuesday morning, 'I will see you on Friday, Melanie.' Which meant I was in trouble for something I'd done. I felt confused, unsure of myself, upset, angry and insecure.

My default is to cover those feelings. As a kid, I might then walk into the kitchen and start berating my mum for some imaginary crime. 'You didn't wash my PE kit! It's PE today!' I'd scream, once I heard the door slam behind my dad.

'Melanie, you have PE on a Wednesday,' she'd say with a sigh (she always knew my timetable better than I did). She knew I was rattled because I was in trouble with Dad. I've always covered up my true emotions when I feel bad. Put on a smile, laughed my head off, pretended not to notice or not to care …

—

… And now, in that room with these girls who are still sisters to me, I was mortified by their evident dislike of my new husband. So, I chatted to my assistant, Janet, or showed off to the girls some fancy new designer bag. 'He got me this,' I lied (not mentioning that it was with my money). One by one, I'd take them aside. 'He's got the most massive cock you've ever seen,' I'd say, and laugh. 'I've never had such incredible sex with anyone.'

David turned up at one point in the late afternoon with Brooklyn, Romeo and Cruz. Janet had been to get Phoenix and Angel. Jade (Emma's husband) came in with baby Beau (who was born two months after we announced our tour) and Geri's little girl, Bluebell.

But as everyone rushed to coo over each other's kids, Stephen had his eyes fixed on David. He had been badgering me to introduce him for months. 'Get Beckham to meet up with us,' he'd say every time I was going to call Vic. 'We should go out on our own with them. Can't you even sort that out, Melanie? I thought she was meant to be your friend.'

'They're busy,' I'd tell him week after week. 'They're not around.' I didn't want to put them through a night with Stephen. Would you?

I have known David since he and Vic got together when he was this shy twenty-one-year-old footballer completely besotted with Posh Spice. Back then we'd vet each other's boyfriends – often giving them the Spanish Inquisition (or even the Spice Inquisition, hence the lyric we wrote in 'Wannabe': 'If you wanna be my lover, you've got to get with my friends') when we were all together. Poor guys. David got an easier time than most because Vic fell for him straightaway. 'Don't be mean to him,' she'd say, so I'd just tease him gently about his hair or his clothes – something VERY mild for me. In the following two decades, he would go on to be one of the most famous men in the world, and one of the most successful footballers of all time. But David is still David. He's pretty unassuming. There's still that shyness in him, and he is most relaxed around his kids.

So there he was. He said hello to everyone, we all had a little chat, and then David went off to the kitchen area to make some ramen noodles for his sons. We left him to it. You could sense he wanted some space and time with his kids. Stephen didn't get that at all. I cringed as I saw him immediately barge into the tiny kitchen. And out of the corner of my eye, I could see that Stephen was just following David around, being loud, telling jokes, trying to get him to go out on the town with him: 'What do you say we hit a few bars? You must know the best places?'

I could also see he was pissing David off. 'I knew he was bad news the moment I met him,' David later told my mum. Stephen couldn't get the hint. Humiliatingly, I saw one of the assistants walk up to my husband and suggest David be given 'a moment with his boys'. I didn't want to look at the other girls. I didn't want to look at Stephen, who would be seething with me for not making it okay.

Even worse for him was that Vic – who had avoided him most of the day – was making the biggest fuss of Phoenix.

—

Remember, Phoenix is the first Spice Baby – born in February 1999, a month before Brooklyn – and I don't think many babies had as much of a fuss made of them at their birth as Phoenix did. She was born at The Portland Hospital. I started the trend, as it became the hospital where Vic, Geri, Emma and Mel C all had their first babies. We also all had the same consultant, Dr Edward Douek, deliver our babies. I used to go round to his house for dinner, and I'd make jokes about his being the only guy ever to have seen every single one of the Spice Girls private parts. He'd just laugh and tell me he was a professional. What a lovely man.

Emma and Mel C were there to hold my hand at Phoenix's birth and Vic came to see her within hours of her being born. There were so many flowers and gifts that, before I left, I went round giving them to other patients in the whole hospital. My great mentor and friend, Alan Edwards, who was my PR for many years and represented everyone from David Bowie to the Rolling Stones and Blondie, remembers the day of Phoenix's birth very well. He arrived at the hospital as soon as he heard I was in labour, only to be mistakenly ushered into the birthing room at the precise moment that her head appeared between my legs. 'You looked at me and said, "Alan, I believe in working closely with the media, but this is ridiculous,"' he told me a few years later. Which always makes me laugh, and makes me very chuffed that I was able to come out with a funny one-liner at that crucial point. It was such a happy, happy day. She was a gorgeous, easy, laid-back baby (she still is), and she was the first baby in all of our young lives.

'Mel, can I have a day with Phoenix? I want to do a whole girlie day with her,' Vic asked as Stephen glared at me. 'Course you can. Sounds lovely,' I said.

There were plenty of other incidents in which it was made very apparent that Stephen was at best tolerated and at worse absolutely loathed by the girls. Whenever he was with me, Geri remembers that he had me doing loads of club appearances (to make more money) so I couldn't spend my downtime with the girls.

I tried to make out I was having the best time. I didn't fool anyone. Alan – who was with us as always – remembers feeling very sad for me, as he told me years later. Alan, who is a father to two wonderful daughters, has always treated me like one of the family. Apart from being there when Phoenix was born, he was one of the first people I called when Angel was born.

'I could see you weren't happy,' he said to me recently. 'You were trying to spin so many plates: being a mum to a new baby, being a wife, doing the show. And then all these other commitments you were having to make. And because I know you so well, I knew you were going to try to put on your loud, laughing Mel B front and make it seem all okay. But I could see it was too much pressure for anyone. I was genuinely worried about you. We all were.'

As much as I could, I would try and make sure Stephen wasn't with us as we flew round Europe. But he desperately wanted to be part of the Spice tribe, and it was hard to come up with reasons why he shouldn't be with us.

I remember – again in London (where bad things always happened with me and Stephen) – being in a restaurant with all the girls and their partners and Simon Fuller, and Stephen kicking off at the waiter, causing a scene over nothing. Simon had to ask me to get him out of there. A lot of other occasions I've blocked out. It still makes me cringe. I still think of the look on my dad's face when he came to visit me in LA a few weeks after the Vegas wedding. My dad had witnessed a few bust-ups between us, but I told myself everything was okay. And Stephen kept telling me, 'I like your dad. He's a cool guy.'

Then, I was in the car with my dad, Stephen and my dance partner Maksim Chmerkovskiy from 'Dancing with the Stars'. For some reason they had blocked off the stage entrance and we were told by the show's security that we would have to walk across the carpark. Fine. Not fine. Stephen yelled and swore at the poor security guy. My dad was so shocked. He kept staring at me in disbelief.

That night, he phoned my mum on his mobile to say, 'He seems crazy. How could she be with him?' My dad was the most careful man on the planet. He NEVER would have dreamt of calling abroad on his mobile. He was so traumatized that, for once in his life, he didn't think how much every minute would cost. My mum told me later that she was more shocked he'd called her long distance than that he thought his new son-in-law was horrible (which was no surprise to her).

'I know,' she told him. 'And now you've seen it for yourself. Just try and talk some sense into our Melanie because she won't listen to me,' she told him. Later that night, I saw him pull out of his ancient suitcase the plane ticket I'd bought for him to come and visit us.

'Is this transferable?' he asked me. He only had two more days with us, for God's sake. I bit my tongue. My dad didn't even want to get into a conversation with me about my husband. He simply wanted to go home. Get away from me and Stephen.

'No, Dad, it's not,' I snapped. He spent most of the rest of the time in his room.

—

I'm sitting in my rented house in Beverly Hills, which is in a private estate where the likes of Gwen Stefani and Hilary Duff also live. I'm packing up to move to a smaller, cheaper apartment for me and my girls. That's life and I embrace it. Downsizing, upsizing – we're all strapped to a wheel of fortune, and I accept that. I don't have the money I used to. Every aspect of my life has been ripped to shreds, thrown into either a tabloid or a legal meat grinder. But I have my kids, I have my freedom, and every choice I make for the rest of my life – good or bad – will be my own.

We will be close to The Grove, where all the shops, cinemas and food markets are – you can imagine how thrilled my girls are about this. And as I look around at my clothes and photos, my Spice memorabilia (some of which I got back from my husband in one of those court battles), all this with Stephen seems so long ago.

I'm thinking back to those times, trying to pull apart all the emotions that pushed around in my head. For many years I blocked many emotions, and now it's hard to remember not only everything that happened to me but what my thought processes were at the time. In common with lots of women in abusive relationships I've spoken to, different emotions were smashed together in my head. And I remember even then – even when I caught one of the girls looking at Stephen in this 'please get him out of here' way – that I did feel anger towards him. But I also felt sorry for him and protective of him all at the same time. But ultimately I chose him. They were my sisters, but he was my husband. I wanted to show him I was his ride-or-die bitch.

Geri remembers a moment when I almost broke my cover. It was on the penultimate date of the tour in Toronto, Canada. We were supposed to do a 'meet and greet' before the show where a hundred sponsors, VIPs and superfans get to chat and say hello, and we all make a effort to make everyone feel special. Except I didn't. After fifteen minutes or so of anxiously waiting for me, with everyone calling my mobile and trying to track me down, Geri came to find me. 'I didn't want people to think you were standing them up,' she told me later, 'because I knew that's something you wouldn't do. So after no-one could get you on the phone, I came to look for you.'

Geri said: 'I walked into your dressing room and shouted for you. But there was no answer. And then I went into the bathroom, and I saw you crumpled up in the foetal position, naked on the floor of the shower. You were just sobbing and sobbing. I got into the shower with you and put my arms around you, saying, 'Melanie, it will be okay.' But you just carried on crying.

'I know you. I knew if I told you that you had to come with me to do the meet and greet, then you'd get up because going into work mode makes you feel focused. I put a towel around you and helped you get dressed, thinking we could talk later. And then we went and chatted to everyone. I kept looking over at you, but you were smiling and acting as if nothing was wrong. Then afterwards, after the show, I tried to gently talk about it, but you put a wall up and I could see there was no way you were ever going to discuss it.

'It made me sad because I know when you are at your most vulnerable that's when you put your Batman suit on or your Scary suit and make like there's nothing wrong. And I know underneath everything you are the most sensitive woman with the softest heart. But on that tour we could all feel the distance.'

If you want to know the reason why that reunion tour was cut short by three months, that was the reason why. It was me. I couldn't take it anymore. After three months and forty-seven dates and hundreds of hours on our Spice Jet (we had one and there was a second Spice Jet that took catering, technicians and crew; a tour is like the army, you travel in planes and juggernauts around the world), the tension was getting too much.

There was so much talk and gossip about Stephen, about how he was trying to take over as manager (that would never happen) and how people (i.e. the girls and the Spice team) didn't like being around him. They could see how I had changed around him. One minute I would be the girl they knew, the next I'd cut them off, distance myself or be difficult. We told the fans, 'We are so sorry, but we wanted to leave it on a high.' The truth was – it was left on a low. And I'm the one who owes the apology to the girls, the fans, to everyone.

Then why was I so angry? Why did I feel sorry for Stephen and protective of him? I'm pulling apart those feelings now like trying to untangle hundreds of tiny knots in a ball of matted wool. It's so complicated. Even though I was, on the inside, one of the famous Spice Girls, I would catch those looks and hear those whispers and it cut me. It cut me because I knew those looks and whispers all my life, and up until I became a Spice Girl I had no protection from them. Only then would everyone laugh at my jokes or put up with my hyper behaviour. 'Please shut up, Melanie Brown' – I'd heard it from friends, teachers, dancing instructors. I was that loud, in-your-face girl who people talked about because she never shut up and she never knew when to stop. The girl who did cartwheels in front of the telly when all her cousins were watching 'Dr Who' … 'Go away, Melanie. Move.' The girl who was often dropped by friends or got bitched about by the other dancers at Blackpool. The girl who seemed so supremely confident on the outside but was so often hurting inside. And I was – like Stephen – brown. Not black, not white. The brown ones who didn't quite fit in anywhere and didn't get to belong to any group. So somewhere, underneath everything – as crazy as it sounds – I convinced myself, Stephen was just like me.

24

INSTA-SHAM

—

It is November 2008 and Stephen and I are on the sun-kissed beach of the Jaz Makadi Golf Resort in Madinat Makadi in Hurghada, Egypt.

The ocean – a perfect blue – is sparkling in the background, and there is not a single cloud in the sky. I am wearing a white bikini. My body is looking toned after months of endless working out and a season of 'Dancing with the Stars' and a Spice Girls reunion tour. I am holding a glass of champagne and puckering my immaculately made-up lips to kiss my husband, who is smiling down at me like a man madly in love.

A photographer catches the moment and then shouts, 'OK, can we do the kiss again? Melanie, can you put your hand on his chest? No, not like that … Someone move that sunbed back a bit … Both of you tilt your bodies towards me … That's it. Got it.'

And that is how – back in the days before social media – you created a picture to show the world you were in love. I am the expert at showing the world how happy I am, how in love I am, how fabulous my life is. I look back at the magazine shoot I did two weeks after Angel was born. I look wonderful. I'm smiling, my skin is glowing. You would never have guessed I was totally broken inside and had been killing myself to look good for the photo shoot by exercising pretty much from the day after she was born with Joey Kormier, one of the most ruthless personal trainers in LA. What pushed me on, as I wept on the running machine, was the thought that Eddie would see those photos. And the message I was sending was, 'Look at what you are missing' (mixed obviously with a bit of 'fuck you').

In show business we've been using the cameras to sugar-coat our lives (or should I say *lies*) for decades. We've had the tools to airbrush, elongate, whiten teeth and erase body hair, and we've had the platform (glossy magazines) to get our messages across. We are not above using the people we are meant to despise – the paparazzi – in order to show the world how good we look in a bikini, or how upset we are (with good hair and a great pair of sunglasses of course). And now – since it was first launched in 2010 – we have Instagram, and everyone can do it. You can airbrush and tint, and even write your own messages! Stephen loved Instagram. He was always posting.

I call it Insta-sham. Dress it up and fake it and you can make anything look beautiful, anyone look happy. Life's not like that though. At the time those photos on the beach in Egypt were taken, that is what I wanted my life to be like. That is what I wanted everyone else to think it was like. If I believed it was like that, if I pretended to myself that bad things weren't happening, then maybe it would be. It wasn't though. Only I couldn't admit that to myself.

The marriage renewal in Egypt was, in all fairness, a bit of a laugh. It was a laugh because my family came out, along with Charlotte and my other great mate from home, Maya, and all my aunts, uncles and cousins. My mum and dad had not long separated, which was a little weird, but they were still on good terms, still completely united as a family. They always were. I don't think a day went by in their lives when they didn't speak to each other on the phone (except if my dad was abroad on holiday). She even used to go round with his Sunday dinner. Stephen's mum, Sylvia, and his five brothers and sisters were also flown out to join us, as was Giselle, who spent all her time with either Charlotte or my mum.

I think even God was trying to send me a message in Egypt because as I stood on the beach with Stephen, in the late afternoon before the Big Day, my dress still hadn't arrived at the hotel. It had got lost somewhere in transit. I was in a massive flap. My mum laughed. 'Let's have a drink and stop worrying. It'll turn up,' she said. So we did.

I spent most of that romantic breakaway in my mum's room with my family. I barely saw Stephen. By 9 p.m. my dress still hadn't arrived, and I was torn between laughing about it and having a breakdown. My mum finally explained the situation to a waiter who spoke reasonable English and who miraculously had a cousin working at the airport. The cousin, even more miraculously, tracked down the dress in Cairo, where it had ended up. We then sat up till about 5 a.m. in Mum's room getting more and more drunk. There was a bit of an incident with a fire extinguisher between some of my cousins and Stephen's brothers, but everything seemed OK. The whole weekend was going to be a success.

There was, of course, an undercurrent swirling away. In the week before we all flew to Egypt, Phoenix had been staying with my mum and sister at my sister's house in north London. She had broken down in tears several times, telling my mum and sister how much she hated her life. Both Danielle and my mum were beside themselves.

My mum knew she had to be careful how she handled this. 'I knew he had an absolute hold over you,' she told me years later. 'And I knew you wouldn't want to hear it. I was scared for Phoenix and I was scared for you.' In Egypt she said nothing. Nor did my dad.

The following day, we all flew back to London. At Heathrow, Stephen got a flight to Los Angeles. I had another day with my family because I had to sort out my visa. (I refused to take American citizenship after I married Stephen and wanted me and Phoenix to keep British nationality. 'That's who I am,' I'd say.) My mum voiced her concerns about Stephen. 'He's bad news, Melanie.' I sat there in my hotel room, listening, emotionless. A new trick I'd learned in my marriage was to block out all emotions. I didn't want to hear it. But as she talked, I knew I wanted Stephen to hear it. There was part of me that knew my mum was right; there was part of me that was too scared to say it – or even acknowledge it – myself. I kissed my mother goodbye.

'I'll sort it,' I said. 'I promise.'

On the flight over to Los Angeles with Phoenix, all I could think of was what my mother had said. I watched Phoenix. We were in first-class seats and she was fast asleep, cuddled up with her blanket. How many nine-year-olds get to travel first class? My child was a privileged child, shielded by money, beautiful cars and pretty clothes from the harshness of the world. Her world was a million miles away from my world as a nine-year-old. But what was it like really? Should I be very worried for my child? I needed Stephen to hear what my mother had said. And how did I begin that conversation when we got home? I admit I was scared; I knew it wasn't going to go well. 'Stephen,' I said. 'My mum thinks …'

I would not see my mother again for eight years.

ANDREA'S STORY

I was asleep in bed and I heard my phone ring. I looked at the time; it was 3 a.m.. The first thought in my head was: Melanie. Is she okay? I picked up the phone and I heard Stephen's voice. The words coming out of his mouth were unbelievable. 'You fucking c*nt. You fucking bitch trash whore.'

I started shaking. I don't know why. I think it's because – up until that point in my life – I had never, ever been spoken to like that, and those words just kept spewing out of the phone. I can't even describe it. It was torrents and torrents of filth and the most hurtful, evil, wicked words you can possibly think of. And all of it was so loud because he wasn't speaking, he was yelling. 'Stephen,' I said. 'Stephen … ' He wasn't listening. He was screaming and screaming at the top of his voice. I was in a state of shock, so much so that I didn't put down the phone. I didn't even understand some of what he was saying. I'd never felt that actual words could be like weapons before. So many of them hitting me like bullets. They just did not stop.

'You have been fooled by a nine-year-old child, you fucking bitch.' My mind was spinning. It took me a few minutes to realize Melanie must have been in the room with him, standing next to him. I could hear him telling her, 'So your bitch mother said this, right?'

I couldn't interrupt or stop him. Then I heard Melanie say, 'Phoenix, go out of the room. Go to your bedroom.'

And I heard him say, 'No. She needs to hear this. She needs to hear what fucking lies she's told and she needs to know what a stupid c*nt her grandmother is. And she needs to know she will never see her again. And you need to know, you fucking bitch whore, you will never see your grandchildren again.'

I heard Phoenix sobbing, which made me completely break down. 'Don't let her hear this,' I was begging. The line went dead and my heart seemed to stop. I don't know how long it took me to call Melanie back. Maybe five minutes. I'm not sure because it was a blur. If you have never had an abusive call from that man, you would have no idea of the effect it has on you. I felt traumatized. Violated. Melanie's phone was switched off. I called Martin. I could hear him groping for his specs as he tried to take in what I was saying.

'I'm going to call him now,' said Martin, sounding more stunned and upset than angry. He called me back a few minutes later. He couldn't get through on their mobiles or the house phone. I got up. I was freezing cold. I couldn't stop crying. I spoke to Martin again and both of us kept trying their numbers hour after hour. I had a million thoughts running through my head. I knew they were about to move or had moved, and I didn't know the address. Would Melanie call me? I went downstairs to my computer and emailed her.

'Please, please call me Melanie.' I sent her about ten more emails. I was even writing, 'Sorry, sorry,' even though I'd done nothing wrong. I couldn't bear to think of poor little Phoenix hearing that filthy language, being told it was her fault. It wasn't right. Martin was in bits every time he said her name. By the morning, all my emails had bounced back with a 'failed delivery' message – the email address Mel had had for years had been erased.

We got a different message from Melanie's mobile.

'This mobile number is no longer in use,' a computerized American voice buzzed down the phone. Our daughter and (back then) our only grand-daughter had been cut out of our lives.

—

I am watching Phoenix rooting through clothes in my closet. 'You're not wearing anything black,' I'm shouting at her, as she looks for something to wear for a date. 'You have to pick something colourful or you're not having anything.' She is nineteen years old, and she is laughing and telling me to stop bossing her around. She is taller than me, she is kind, she is funny, she is beautiful and has a killer body. Sometimes it's hard for me to look at her because a part of what I feel when I look at her is bottomless guilt.

For ten years, I convinced myself that I protected her, that she and her two little sisters were all cushioned from the emotional horrors of my relationship with Stephen. It is very hard as a mother to admit that they weren't.

It's hard to see when you are in it (although it becomes horribly, blindingly obvious when you are out of it) that the emotional upset you feel with your partner doesn't just exist between the two of you or in your bedroom. It is an energy that fills a house. You carry it with you wherever you are, and it changes you and it changes them. I was so emotionally blocked and messed up, and self-medicating with drink and drugs, that I didn't realize that they did see, hear and feel things no child ever should. And of all my children, Phoenix had it the worst.

I know I am inviting absolute damnation by admitting this. But I also know this is the truth. And if we keep silent, if we don't tell the truth, we will never break the cycle of abusive relationships. I would rather risk vilification if it helps another woman in an emotionally abusive relationship to admit her children have been damaged and those children to get therapy and help.

I will also admit it wasn't until half way through my court case against Stephen that my brave daughter chose to talk about what she had witnessed that I realized what she herself went through. To this day I have still not read every word she has said. I can't see the words on the page because there are too many tears in my eyes. What breaks my heart is that never, in ten years, did she once cry out to me.

—

It is amazing what you don't see as a mother. My mum never saw me teasing my little sister mercilessly on the days when I was 'babysitting'. She never saw me crying when I got called 'Paki' in the playground. She didn't ever notice those looks or sneers from other kids when we were out together. I knew what they meant: 'Look at that brown kid with that white woman!' I used to think it too. I'd think if I sat in the bath long enough I might turn white like her because she was my mum and she was white and I was brown. It's also amazing that you can convince yourself everything is totally all right. 'They're just looking at you because you're so pretty, Melanie.' Yeah, right.

Janet, my former assistant, reminded me of one of our first holidays with Stephen. 'I'll spend a couple of hours bonding with Phoenix,' he said. Phoenix had an absolute phobia about crabs, so he (either for a joke or because he said it would cure the phobia) thought it would be a great idea to take her off, into the middle of a load of rocks crawling with crabs, and then leave her there screaming … Until Janet saw what was going on and went to get her.

And when I was in London in the summer of 2018, an old friend of Phoenix recounted a tale that made my blood run cold. She was a close family friend who remembered me taking her to plays on Broadway, and going to see the Harlem Globe Trotters on Phoenix's birthday. Then she came on a rare play-date to our house in Mount Olympus and spent most of her time in Phoenix's room listening to her talking about how terrifying Stephen was. She was already scared of him because he was rude and dismissive of her.

Phoenix told her about his gun, and then took her downstairs. The gun's lock box was sitting on the end of the dining room table. She could barely force anything down when they had to eat, especially as Stephen kept telling her, 'This is black peoples' food. Here you eat black peoples' food.'

It was the first and last time she visited. 'I never want to go there again,' she told her mum.

—

I missed a lot of the little things that happened because my new manager (Stephen) kept me busy working. If I wasn't in rehearsals for 'Dancing with the Stars' or the Spice reunion, I was going with him to a business meeting or we were out at a celebrity party. As I've said, I've never been one for those people, except maybe for a mad phase in my twenties when I hung out with the London 'It' crowd – Kate Moss, Meg Matthews, Noel Gallagher, the All Saints girls and the MTV presenter Donna Air. But since I'd had Phoenix and moved to LA, I tended to hang out with other mums or people I got to know through work. I loved my house in Los Feliz so much, I hardly ever left it. I had a massive purple sofa specially built to hold twelve people; there were always kids sprawling on it playing games, or my girlfriends sitting on it, having a glass of wine. I painted the walls all different colours because I love colour and because I read that it would stimulate a baby's brain like playing classical music to her and Baby Einstein CDs.

My greatest pleasure in life, though, was always being with Phoenix. Not so long ago, Janet reminded me of a Friday night when Phoenix had gone over to stay with her dad and I was so upset because I missed her. Janet got out a bottle of wine and I had the bright idea of decorating her bedroom ceiling with stars and moons in a fluorescent paint that I'd bought. We got two ladders and two paintbrushes, took in the wine and spent the whole night turning her ceiling into an incredible night sky. We finished as the sun rose, and we sat on the floor and looked at our workmanship. 'I think we went a bit mad,' laughed Janet (we did have another bottle of wine as we worked). 'But Phoenix will LOVE it,' I said. And she did.

I never saw the cruelty that was inflicted on my daughter's sweet, gentle dog, Lordy. He was old, he had bad hips. He would not hurt a fly. Stephen would beat him in front of Phoenix. Lordy was her best friend. They were inseparable. It broke my heart when I read in her court statement in 2017 of how Stephen had picked up Lordy and thrown him hard into the swimming pool, and at Phoenix who was in the water. Poor Phoenix, poor Lordy.

——

There were so many rules. Phoenix needed to ask before opening the fridge to get a drink or a snack. She wasn't allowed to switch on the television without permission. She had to make her own lunches for school if I wasn't there. Stephen decided when and if her friends came over, or whether she was grounded and for how long.

From being an independent single mum, organizing two lives, I became a woman who didn't have her own computer, didn't drive herself, didn't know her bank details, didn't make decisions small or large, and had no friendly relationships with any heterosexual men or any of her old friends or her family.

By the time we were living in the house that Stephen built and designed in Cordell Drive, off Sunset, the children were not allowed out of the house to play (Stephen said going to a park was dangerous). He wanted the house pristine and worried the children so much that they ate on the floor, so as not to damage the expensive dining room table and velvet chairs. They had to keep their rooms tidy.

There was an added layer of paranoia instilled into them. Food dropped on the floor would be full of germs which could kill you. Going to a park was dangerous. Bogeymen were everywhere. I remember at one point going to Ikea and buying a small fold-up table which I kept hidden in a storage room on the kids' floor so they could at least sometimes sit at the table. Ridiculously, we had to keep it a secret.

Angel was the exception. She and Stephen had a special bond – or so he told me. Where Phoenix would be punished, Angel, his 'golden goose' would be spoilt, cuddled and praised. Phoenix was told that she was stupid and ugly.

People did try to intervene. Kim – my neighbour – saw Stephen whizzing down the road near our house on a skateboard with Angel in his arms. Crazy. People called our house 'Nutts Landing'. Kim did try to speak to me when she was told Phoenix couldn't play with her son at her house, and that he couldn't come to our house because she was grounded for three months. 'What's Phoenix done that deserves that?' she gently asked me. I shrugged it off.

Kim could see that Phoenix was already a changed kid. She'd gone into her shell; she walked 'hunched up'. Kim recalls that her eyes looked sad. Meanwhile, Janet, my loyal, lovely assistant, left. She says now she couldn't bear Stephen, how he'd come into my house and taken control. She couldn't bear the way he treated Phoenix, she couldn't bear the way he treated the dog. Kim remembers trying to talk to me but also worrying that, by expressing her opinion, it might make things worse for me. She had known me forever. She cheered as I came runner-up in 'Dancing with the Stars' – laughing on the small screen in her living room. That wasn't the face she saw in private when she tried to talk to me. 'You looked so closed off and sad. I was so worried for you, but I was also worried that somehow I might even be making things worse,' she told me years later.

This happened in a street full of multi-million-dollar houses in Los Angeles to a famous woman with gorgeous kids and her new husband. It happens here, it happens in your road, wherever you live. But probably you will never see it.

Now, smile for that Insta-post. 'Happy families.'

25
BOOMERANG FROM HELL
—

You probably think I've forgotten where I started with my story. I haven't at all (and in case you have, I began with my overdose during the run of 'The X Factor' in 2014). But life is a series of footsteps, and what I've been doing this past year – amid my court cases, judging on 'America's Got Talent', sorting out my kids and finances, and re-bonding with friends and family – is taking myself back over those steps. Some good steps, some very bad, some very, very ugly.

This is the way my mind works. It jumps. I have ADHD. I don't think like a lot of other people. I think about one thing that happened and it takes me back to other places, and then I link them together like beads on a string, looking for the patterns and how one step led to another.

In March 2017, soon after I walked away from my husband, I began a court case. The initial charges involved domestic violence. But by November 2017, as part of a mediation settlement, I agreed to drop domestic violence charges in order for all the 64 sex tapes he had made during our marriage not to be shown in open court. I couldn't deal with it any more, I couldn't deal with him anymore. If they were shown then they would enter the public domain. Such are the deals we make. Looking back now that was a deal I regret.

That was the most difficult time for me. You see, I had to sit down and watch those tapes. It was a legal requirement, believe it or not. And you might think, 'So what? You're in them, aren't you? Having sex with whoever. It's no big deal you had to watch them.' I understand why you might think that, but what I am trying to do for myself, and for any other woman who has ever found themselves going through anything like my situation, is to explain that nothing is ever that simple or clear-cut.

Follow this line and see where it becomes blurred. All these statements are true. I like sex. I am adventurous with sex. I have enjoyed threesomes. I have initiated threesomes. I enjoy a woman's body and I enjoy a man's body. I have participated in threesomes while being videoed. I have taken drugs. I have drunk alcohol. I have had threesomes to please my partner. I have no memory of some of the sexual situations I have seen myself in on video. I am frightened when I see myself in some of these videos. I have seen myself used sexually in a way that I did not enjoy or want.

Traumatized. It is an understatement. I could not watch those videos in my house. I couldn't have the children anywhere near them, or near me, when I saw them. I went to a small hotel in Koreatown with Gary, my friend. Initially, the videos made me feel uncomfortable. There were hours of them. And they were not only sex tapes, they were videos Stephen had made on his phone when I was visibly out of it, with him shouting, 'Get up, Melanie,' again and again, as I struggled to get to my feet or even comprehend what he was saying. Phoenix was in a few of them, dragged in to see her mother in a state. I saw her face. I saw my face. I didn't recognize it. This wasn't me.

—

One of Geri's nicknames for me was 'The Ox' because I could operate perfectly on the most outrageous hangover, or even do a full performance faultlessly after several bottles of champagne. While she would be throwing up in the loo, I'd be laughing and telling her to hurry up and get ready. I could easily hold my own with the Gallagher brothers. Ask them. I was one of the regulars at Supernova Heights in the excessive days of Brit Pop. I was never an angel, but I was always able to handle my drink and my drugs.

Charlotte, the woman who has known me and my family nearly all my life and knows me best of all, always used to say, 'You might have been in a pop band, Melanie. But you were never pop. You were always hardcore rock 'n' roll.' She would say that. Since the age of fourteen we'd been out partying (when my dad was on lates), from underground illegal blues dives in Leeds like Sonny's to Mr Smith's in Warrington. I'd go to bed with conditioner in my hair, tie it in a double knot, wait till midnight for the sound of Charlotte's car (she's three years older than me and passed her test at seventeen) and then creep out, making sure not to wake Danielle, whose bedroom overlooked the drive and whose head would occasionally pop out of the window. A mop of frizzy curls, eyes blinking in the streetlights, yelling, 'What you doing, Melanie? (she could never say my name properly) I'm telling!' She got an eyeful once when we discovered the crazy, brilliant Hacienda Club in Manchester when I was fifteen. I turned up on many occasions with fishnets and hot pants.

By the time I was a Spice Girl, Danielle was part of the gang. Charlotte remembers coming to watch us turn on the lights in Oxford Street on 7 November 1996. It was at the start of Spice Mania, and Oxford Street was gridlocked. We were all hustled into the top floor of Debenhams, where we set about opening the crates of champagne to wait for the crowds to die down. After several bottles, the rest of the girls called it a night, but me, Danielle and Charlotte swiped a couple of bottles each and returned to my hotel, where I said, 'Right, let's get drunk on the minibar.' I woke up to catch a 6 a.m. flight. Charlotte could neither speak nor walk and finally got back on a train to leave after emptying the contents of her stomach several times. I polished off a complimentary full English breakfast at the airport, along with a couple of glasses of Buck's Fizz. Geri could barely look at me from behind her sunglasses. 'What?' I said.

'Aren't you going to have one? It's free!' I was definitely the Keith Richards of the Spice Girls.

I was recently reminded of an episode by a former assistant who knew me in the early days of my relationship with Stephen. Stephen liked to spend the evenings drinking wine, vodka or whisky. We would try to outdo each other in how much liquor we could hold. Now, I'm not exactly proud of this story, but it illustrates my point. My assistant came into the house in the morning to find half-drunk wine bottles on the kitchen counter. He then turned to see me walk down the stairs in my dressing gown, sit at the counter, pour myself a glass of wine and smoke a cigarette. 'Then, you got up to go to a two-hour Barry's Bootcamp session. You came back sweating and glowing. I remember thinking, "This woman is made of kryptonite,"' he said. Check out my great-grandmother, Celian. I am made of tough stuff. This person stumbling up the stairs in the videos was no-one I had ever seen.

And then I saw the sex videos. Some I remembered. Some I did not. 'Gary, that's not me,' I told him, pointing at myself on screen.

'Don't watch it, my love,' he said. He couldn't even bear to look. I was transfixed, horrified. Who the hell was this woman with my face and my body? I have watched porn videos many times, but these videos were not porn. They were dark, they were out of control. I started to shake.

'I have to watch them all,' I said to Gary. 'I need to watch everything. I need to see what happened to me.'

I know it's a thing, a horrible thing these days on social media for kids who are videoing each other; as much as I know drug date-rape is on the increase (even back in 2014 an ITV survey said one in ten girls had had their drinks spiked, and if you talk to any young girls the whole club scene is rife with date-rape drugs). Revenge porn has become a social media weapon. I cheered and cried when the brave YouTube vlogger Chrissie Chambers won her four-year court battle against her ex-lover (he managed to legally remain anonymous!) who put six sex tapes online without her knowledge. Throughout those four years, she suffered from depression, anxiety, sleep paralysis and PTSD. She became an alcoholic by the age of twenty-three because she couldn't emotionally deal with what she was going through. She was called a whore and slut (and far worse) online. It makes my head pound to think of it. She is a Boadicea. And I salute her.

I remember lying on the bed in that hotel room in Koreatown in the foetal position. Other images played across a screen in my mind, dredged from the vaults deep in my brain that I had previously blocked myself remembering. I saw in flashes. Me waking up in pools of piss, vomit, shit and blood, being mortified, dragging myself up and rolling up my white sheets. Stuffing them soiled and filthy into bin bags, showering over and over again. I wasn't crying because I was in a place beyond tears, but I was making strange, uncontrollable animal whimpers.

I knew Gary was there, I knew he was scared – I could feel that – but sometimes I couldn't even see him. Eventually he lay on the bed and held me till I stopped crying. And then I was silent. For hours I lay there with my eyes wide open. Nothing was in my head. I have learned the word from the thesaurus I carry around with me. *Catatonic*. I was catatonic. It felt like I was lying on the floor of one of those movie sets about a post-apocalyptic world, where everything is grey and dark and there is just a big misty, murky nothing all around you. Gary later said he spent ages talking to me, softly, asking, 'Are you okay? … Melanie, can you hear me? … You need to drink some water, you need to eat, my love.' And then – because he is a very intuitive man – he understood that I just needed to be. And he never left my side.

I fell down a hole. I had been doing so well. I had been happy. I'd been up, running round the house in the mornings: 'Madison, Angel! Breakfast!' I liked the routine of my new life with my girls. And, thinking back, I was proud of myself for being so together. I was conscious of being happy. Properly happy for the first time in ten years. Not just when I was working; it was all the time. It was like feeling an emotion I recognized but didn't quite remember – 'Oh, I know. That is happiness.'

I had friends over. I played music loud and I danced, and I discovered that I can make the best home-made ice cream, and the best cream cheese and turkey bagels (the secret is adding a small amount of finely chopped red onion). I took a photograph of myself writing my first cheque in a decade. Opening my own bank account. Going and hiring the car I'd always wanted, a white Range Rover – I'd show the man with the bullet-proof Bentley. I felt like I'd been living in that Jim Carrey movie *The Truman Show*, when he realized it had all been a fantasy and there was a big bubble surrounding him that he had to break through into the real world.

I was in a new world. As if I'd been a character in one of those computer games, running about in a beautiful fantasy world then falling through the floor into a hell. But it felt so real. It was a world which I'd later be told by Dr Sophy was textbook PTSD (post-traumatic stress disorder). It was emotional. Hard. Horrible. I wanted to scream, I wanted to fight with anyone and everyone. I wanted to cry. I wanted to hide in my room. I wanted to try to get out of the way of tidal waves of frightening emotions that kept hitting me. They were coming so fast for days on end that it felt at times as if they were stopping me breathing. I couldn't do the school runs, I couldn't make the breakfasts. It was enough just to feed the dogs. I wanted my mum and I didn't want her. I wanted her to know what I'd been through – see my pain, watch those horrible videos – and yet I didn't want her to know anything. I seemed to have gone from the land of hope and happiness to the land of grief and shame.

I tried doing the emotional blocking that had served me so well for almost ten years of my marriage. But now that facility had gone like a faulty lightbulb: sometimes it was on, sometimes it was off. It did my head in when it was flickering on and off. The crap kept coming, a sewer pipe exploding into my life. My lawyers' bills were out of control. And then came that black thought again, like a boomerang from hell: 'Just end it, Melanie. It's the easiest way. Life is too hard.'

—

I didn't do anything. I didn't start secretly stockpiling pills. I sat with those thoughts. I wasn't giving it a name – depression, anxiety, PTSD, insomnia – then. I was letting it run through my system because I couldn't fight it. It had a hold of me. I had to learn to live with it and ride the storm. I tried to cleanse my chakras, I gave myself Reiki healing, I meditated. I talked to my dad and I cried to him at night. 'Help me,' I said. Gary told me he would handle Christmas (God bless Gary – we had an Armenian feast), and even though Phoenix and I were rowing badly at this time, I thought of her in that hospital in Northwick Park in Harrow and I told myself, 'No, no, no, Melanie. You will NEVER do that again.'

I was going to let myself cry. I was going to let myself fall, but I was not going to let myself check out. Never again. I had to believe that this was all for a purpose. That my power would come back to me, my light would shine again. A layer had been ripped off me, but I had faith I would emerge stronger and better. I had my friends. I had my family. I was going to get through it.

26
BACK TO BLACK

—

Christmas 2014 was a turning point. After my brave, dramatic statement to the world on 'The X Factor' that my marriage was over, after all my plans for a new life, there I was pushing turkey round my plate as my husband took photos of his happy family reunited once again.

It was the most surreal day. I had returned to Los Angeles with Phoenix and Angel, but for two days we stayed in a hotel because I could not face Stephen or my own defeat. I sat in my room, thinking. Probably drinking. Definitely drinking. Phoenix looked after Angel and then sat for hours by my bedside. 'Mom,' she said tenderly. 'What are we going to do?' I had no answers.

Stephen had hired a house in Malibu for Christmas Day. There was a real fire in the fireplace even though it was boiling hot outside. He had made a massive Christmas feast with huge bowls of candies and snacks all over the place. An hour after we arrived, he disappeared for a couple of hours and then came back with boxes and boxes of presents (the shops never shut in LA). Barbie dolls, plastic toys, clothes for Phoenix, electronic games, a designer bag for me, insane amounts of bright, shiny things that the two little ones fell on with absolute delight. He knew I hated our children being spoiled like that. I am very strict about our children appreciating what they have and not expecting too much, but he knew he could do what he liked. I felt like I had no control.

I don't remember talking much. Stephen was on a high. I could sense he was nervous, but I could also sense he was savouring the moment. I'd been made to look a fool. I'd gone back to him. I couldn't look at the stories in the press, and I couldn't speak to anyone because I'd been given a new phone with a new number – it was a relief in a way, not to have to say anything. Phoenix remembers the two of us avoiding each other, but with the occasional insult passing between us. Even though Stephen had won the battle, it was Christmas Day and he knew not to push me too far.

Sometime in the afternoon we sat down and ate. I don't remember speaking. Phoenix doesn't remember speaking. What she does recall is Stephen picking up her phone at the end of the meal and taking a photograph. *'Can everyone just chill he didn't hit my mom don't know how that stupid rumour came up,'* he posted on her Instagram page, alongside a photo of the two of them together and all of us sitting around in our Christmas show-house.

He took my phone and posted, *'Have a merry Christmas #familytime #funday'*. And I felt I could do nothing about it.

I did do something. I continued to drink too much. I continued – on and off – to use cocaine. I continued to have threesomes with my husband. And I continued to work. Good Mel at work. Alive, firing on all four cylinders, happy. Bad Mel at home. Dead inside. Buried under the oblivion of sex and alcohol. Amazing what you do to stop yourself from thinking. Amazing what you do when you believe – beneath the laughs and the smiles – that you are a worthless piece of crap.

—

I'll tell you about the sex. It's what a lot of people want to know. 'Tell us about the threesomes, Mel.' I've made you wait long enough, haven't I? But I'm only going to tell you the times I remember with women I remember.

It was pretty much always pre-arranged with women we knew,

lap-dancers we'd come across, or one of the very many LA party girls. Stephen was desperate to make me entice other celebrities into our little sex web. Some girls said yes, some girls said no; I'm not going to mention names because I'm happy to reveal my darkest secrets, but I will never hold anything over anyone else and let them think they have anything to fear from me.

In the very early days it was fun. We'd go to a nightclub and pick out girls we found attractive. We had similar tastes – toned bodies, an air of confidence, a couple of tattoos and a sexy way of dressing. I preferred blondes. Stephen would watch the way someone danced and moved – you can tell everything about a woman's sensuality by the way she dances. I'd invite them over for a drink. It's pretty easy when you are Mel B; people are really happy to talk to you. We'd have a drink and a chat and I'd see if I liked them. I have to feel comfortable, feel I can trust someone and have a rapport beyond the physical. If it felt right, I'd ask them, 'Do you want to come back to our room?' It was usually me who asked because Stephen would say it's more threatening for a man to ask, and I have no problems when it comes to asking someone if they want to have sex. Unbeknown to me, Stephen already knew a lot of the women already.

Sometimes it would all play out with us in one room together. Sometimes we would invite people to our house. We were always on the top floor, several levels above the children who would be asleep. At home it was a different pattern. It was a game I had grown tired of. I wanted to stop. He didn't. Things would get nasty and I'd give in.

I would always make sure I got the girl home, that she was OK, that everything was OK. I grew quite close to some of these girls. I still see them every now and again and we talk. They are glad I've left him.

I know there are a lot of people out there (my mother included) who would never find this funny. Just seedy, sordid or another word beginning with 's', like *sleazy*. And I know there's another layer of people thinking, 'What about her kids?' And that's where you have me. That's what I'm dealing with now. I wish I had a degree in the psychology of emotionally abusive relationships to explain how it damages your whole perception of motherhood. But I don't have a degree. I have the waves of realization that have hit me over the months since I left Stephen. And I have snippets of information I have picked up from kind, compassionate and helpful people along the way. People who know who I really am, women who have known me as a mother before and after Stephen.

—

I thought, I genuinely believed, that my children were completely protected from the toxicity of our relationship. I thought I could soak it up for all of us, that I could work hard to give them a good lifestyle, that they had clothes, good schools, decent food, fabulous holidays – so that meant my children were absolutely OK. I kissed them, I hugged them, I told them I loved them, and every single day I would try to think how I could build a different life for them. 'Just wait,' I'd tell Phoenix. 'I know what I'm doing. I have a plan.' I don't think either of us realized ten years would pass before that plan came to fruition.

I did bad things as a mother. I drank in front of my children. According to my husband, I passed out in front of my children. My daughter Phoenix was regularly brought in to witness me incapacitated, and to witness my then husband filming me and making me sign 'I will not drink again' documents.

These are indeed totally shocking moments. Shocking that a daughter has to see that, shocking that a mother would behave like that. But what I want other people to understand is that you have to look deeper and see further. Why would anyone do that to a loved one or a child?

I don't want anyone to think I am making excuses for my behaviour. But I know I am not alone. In 2016, Australia's National Research Organisation for Women's Safety released a research review conducted by La Trobe University and the Australian Institute of Family Studies. The review suggested that 1.9 million children in Australia are affected by what becomes labelled as 'bad mother' syndrome.

The research showed that emotionally manipulative people will tell their partner she is a bad mother so many times that she becomes less able and less confident in her ability to parent effectively. Causing a rift between a mother and her child fundamentally rocks this relationship, empowering the position of the other parent. And because women in these situations are more likely to self-medicate with drink and drugs, the whole issue can spiral out of control with threats like 'I can get your children taken away from you' thrown at you.

I read every word in that report (which, given my dyslexia, took a long time). A lot of the words and expressions I didn't get, but the meaning I did. If a man tells a woman she is a bad mother, you start to believe him, you start to close down, you start to spin out in other ways. And if that man – slowly, cleverly – starts trying to turn you against your kids and your kids against you – then you are lost. But you are not lost forever because you are still their mother, and when you have the strength, the confidence and the belief, you can bring yourself back to being the mother you want to be.

I am not going to ever call myself a bad mother, and I will always stand up for myself if anyone tries to beat me with that stick. I will stand up for any mothers in a similar siutation. I vividly remember all the occasions at airports and on planes, zooming from one job to the next, where I would break down and long to see my kids. My schedule was relentless. I had to prepare a timeline for my lawyers of all the work I did in the past ten years and I rarely had any breaks. I want people to think before they EVER label a woman a bad mother … You need to know her circumstances, understand her situation.

Don't ever say, 'Just walk away. It's that simple.'

It's not ever that simple. You love them. You think you can make it work. You are scared to leave them because you fear that they could take your kids away. Your whole support network has gone. And for a hell of a lot of women out there, it's because they don't have the money to leave.

—

After I married Stephen in Egypt, I lost my family. It was not what I wanted. The whole thing was a huge, horrible, ugly drama. For better or for worse I was with him.

He promised to make things better. He went into his best, full-on super-Stephen mode. He was going to sort things out with Phoenix, he was going to look after me, he was going to get our lives in order. He was going to get a family therapist to help us and – even better – he was going to come up with a reality TV-show format to put our new, happy, wacky, hilarious life on the telly.

By now, it was 2009. All the people who had been so close to me ever since I'd been in LA had gone from my life. I was kept busy with endless jobs – designing cupcakes (what the hell … I have never pretended to be Mary Poppins or Mary Berry), shoes, fashion lines – all sorts of things that were 'good for my image'.

I had no adults close to me – except Stephen. Then, when a neat, handsome man in his fifties arrived at our beautiful, five-bedroom, all-white house in Mount Olympus where we moved shortly after Stephen and I got married with its private pool, dark wooden decks and views over the Hollywood Hills, I had no idea I was meeting someone who was going to become my guardian angel.

—

Stephen had gone to the top. He'd appointed the most well-known and respected family therapist in Los Angeles whose client list included Michael Jackson, Paris Hilton and Elliot Rodger (the 22-year-old son of the assistant director of Hunger Games) who killed six people and shot himself in a shooting in California in May 2014.

Stephen went outside the house – lord of the manor – to greet him because this, he thought, was going to be his guy. Dr Sophy recalls that first meeting somewhat differently. Years later as we sat on the rooftop of a private hospital watching the sun set over LA, he told me, 'I knew straightaway something was off. There was a dog (Lordy) barking and barking because it was trapped on this forecourt, and he was screaming at the dog. He then pointed up at the roof and told me he'd had a putting green installed up there to shoot golf balls. I could see immediately that he was trying to over-power me.

'And then we walked in and I saw you. I knew you were a Spice Girl, I knew you were Mel B. You were very quiet; you gave nothing away but all I could see in your face and your body language was damage. Stephen did not stop talking, over me, over you – it was completely disorientating. The whole situation was extreme. The word going round my head was "powerless".'

Of course, I didn't see any of that. All I saw was a man brought in by Stephen who would sit in front of us while my husband either laughed at me, slagged me off or said how much he loved me and how much I needed to change and do exactly what he said. I sat there and barely opened my mouth. I found it uncomfortable. I didn't like talking about my problems, particularly to one of Stephen's people.

We had so many issues going on. My family were out of the picture and now there were disagreements with Jim, despite the fact that we had worked out a civil arrangement with Phoenix after I first moved to LA. A year after the row with my parents, after Stephen tried every way he could to stop him seeing his daughter, Jim instigated a battle to regain official visiting rights to Phoenix. He succeeded and he allowed my parents to call her when he was with her, but things were still very rocky between him and Stephen.

I wanted my life to get back to normal, I wanted to make things right. If Dr Sophy could do anything to save my family, I would sit there and take whatever.

We were sitting in our huge bedroom. I could see the lights over the city behind him. Stephen was talking, telling him I was a mess as a mother, that I needed to listen to him because he was smarter, he was my husband. 'She sits and drinks all the time, she doesn't talk, she looks like a weirdo,' he was telling him.

I could see him looking at Stephen. Dr Sophy had one leg crossed over the other, the raised foot tapping slowly, slowly. I could see him breathing in and out. I watched his eyes narrow slightly as Stephen talked and talked and talked. 'This guy isn't buying it,' I thought. But I wasn't sure. He was still Stephen's guy. I was wrong, he was my guy. I didn't know for sure back then.

—

On that Christmas Day in 2014 – some five years later – it was Dr Sophy who convinced me to get on the plane and to go back to Stephen for the sake of my children. And when we said goodbye at the airport, he said to me, 'You go back. You sort things out. And then you make some decisions.' Those words were going round and round in my head that day as I chewed on that Christmas turkey. It was going to take three more years.

27
PHOENIX CHI GULZAR BROWN

—

PHOENIX'S STORY

The first time I set eyes on Stephen, I didn't like him. My mom had just had a baby and I was with my grandma in our hotel room when this big, loud dude appeared, being super-friendly and all over her and Angel.

I wasn't that spoiled, bratty kid who never wanted to share her mom. I loved Eddie as soon as I met him. He was just cool. He didn't even try to be funny (and he's very funny, obviously). He was just kind of relaxed and interested. Nice.

And then Stephen was around all the time. He was driving me to school, living in our house, telling me when I could have something to eat and drink, telling me when I saw this giant ring on his finger that him and my mom were getting married.

That was a few months before the Egypt wedding, and it was the first I knew of it. My mom played down the whole Vegas thing. She was building up to telling me about Egypt, but he couldn't wait to be the one to break the news when she wasn't there. 'Are you serious?' I asked her when I got back from school. 'You're marrying that guy?'

By then I was nearly ten years old and I'd woken up to the fact that life can just suddenly turn into a pile of crap. I'd had it so good for years. I had this amazing, funny, strong mother. I had this great family in Leeds. I had a dad who was my best friend. I had this movie-perfect life in Los Angeles, with sunshine, loads of great people in our lives and my dog, Lordy. I had the best parties as a kid. My mom knew every single thing I loved, from the Harlem Globe Trotters to baggy shorts and chocolate frosting. When Eddie came along, things got even better. He treated me like one of his kids and I started doing really well in school. And then it was like someone just switched the channel to this total shitstorm show. *The Stephen Show*.

Stephen didn't like me. Not in a grown up 'I disapprove of you' way. He was like a kid, a bigger, sneakier kid. He beat up my dog, and laughed when Lordy got so ill he had to be put down. 'Now you don't have to walk him.' He left shit in my room. He would start screaming about something like me leaving food on my plate, and go so ballistic it was as if I'd committed a crime and had to be seriously punished.

I couldn't talk to my mom; someone else who looked like her was in her body. She believed every word he said. She loved him. I could tell. This might be the way it was when your mom got married. Maybe I had to suck it up. I didn't want to ruin it for her.

I remember finding Stephen's gun. I was on my own in the house. He was always talking about his gun. I was snooping around in their bedroom. I found it in a box which opened as soon as I pressed on it. I took it out and looked at it. I saw the bullets in the barrel. I pointed it at my head and said, 'Bang.' Then I put it back. I'd held a gun. It was sort of cool and sort of scary.

I thought if I told my grandma how mean he was to me she'd be able to do something. I always felt like I was in trouble. He told me I was retarded and ugly. He cursed at me and shouted so close to my face I'd get spit all over me. I was being grounded for nothing. My mom didn't even know the word *grounded* until Stephen came along. I told Grandma about the gun. And I put a bullet through my whole world. And my mom's. I think that broke my family, and it was my fault.

—

I was still a kid back then. I hadn't learned to block my emotions. Stephen seemed to hate my dad. It used to make me cry and it made me confused. Every time I saw my dad, there was a drama. It got so I didn't even want to go. And then I did something so bad it still breaks my heart today. I was maybe ten. I was in a mood when I got to my dad's, and I started yelling so much he locked me in the bedroom to calm me down. I called my mom and said he'd locked me in a room. Stephen shouted, 'Call the police.' I did.

They busted into the house and arrested my dad in front of me. It was horrific. He was crying. I was crying. I never really got to see my dad again for what seemed like forever. It was the second time he'd been arrested in front of my face. It had happened before at school. They both turned up to pick me up and Stephen was screaming at me to get into his car. I did because I was pretty terrified. My dad went wild and Stephen called the police, who took my dad away.

I don't think Stephen really got to me because I taught myself to shut him out. I made myself stop crying, stop acting scared, stop shaking. I didn't care what he said to me. I did care when he'd scream at my mom, talking to her like she was an idiot. I'd listen at their door and hear her crying. My mom is this crazily tough woman, but I knew she was scared of him. She was a mess.

I think my mom started drinking a couple of years after they got married. They both drank. A lot.

I hated it when I got dragged into their rows. It was so messed up. And then I'd get angry and tell him to stop giving her drink. I'd scream at him, 'Why do you let this happen to her? Do something. Send her to rehab. Stop videoing her.'

He was the one who used to buy it, he was the one who used to say, 'Let's go out. Come on, babe, have a drink.' And he was the one pouring her the drinks and then going bat-shit crazy when she got off her face.

It was all so out of control. I tried to do my own thing. Then he'd get into my friends. None of them understood my life. I don't think

I was ever in danger, but I know my grandma was scared for me. I can look after myself. I don't get emotional except around my mom. I get really emotional with my mom. When she was in hospital in England, I knew something bad had happened. I knew things were getting worse and worse with them. I got picked up from school by her security. I guessed straightaway what had happened.

I wanted it to stop. My mom kept telling me she was going to leave him. I think we actually left a couple of times. But she always went back.

I kept Angel and Maddie away from most of it. I'd take them away. Back to their bedrooms.

I think in a lot of ways I had a pretty normal life. I have lots of friends. I go to school. I had a job in a hairdressing salon when I was sixteen, sweeping up hair and making teas and coffees. My mom is part crazy and part really down to earth. She wants me to work for a living. She came from nothing and has worked all her life. She has single-handedly supported all of us. In a weird way, I think when Stephen got most mad with her was when she was back to being the mom I knew. She'd have these phases of getting really fit. She can stop drinking, stop partying in the click of a finger, and then she will be super-focused on exercising, weighing her food, checking in on everyone.

—

I've seen a lot of arguments. One time in the Mount Olympus house the police came. On lots of occasions my mom would sleep in my room.

I didn't ever know what to do. Maybe I could have done something more. I would get texts from her at times, saying, 'I can't do this.' I would be out at friends' or at home and I wouldn't know what to say.

I'd hear her crying in her bathroom or her bedroom. She'd say she would divorce him, but nothing ever happened until we finally all left in March 2017. I couldn't speak to my grandma because I didn't have her number and because I would probably cause another world of trouble. I couldn't speak to my dad because there was nothing he could do. If I asked my mum what was wrong, she would say, 'Life is hard.'

I didn't think I was angry with Stephen. I thought I was over him. Over what happened. Then I was with my friends eight months after we left him. I was leaving my house and I saw him. He was picking up Maddie and he got out of the car and he was smiling and waving at me, saying, 'Hey, Phoenix.' I can't repeat what I said, but I had to be dragged back into the car by my friends. I don't think I'd do that again.

I do think I'm over him. I'm so glad my mom has left. I just want life to move on …

28
DEATH AND LIFE

—

They call it the circle of life. Nature's way of taking and then giving life back. And it took the death of my father at 3.15 p.m. on 4 March, 2017 to get my life back.

I had left Stephen on several previous occasions. There were times I would call my mother's home number and sob down the phone. 'Melanie, Melanie,' she would say. 'Talk to me. Are you hurt? Where are you?' I said nothing, just sobbed. And there were times, I'm ashamed to say now, when Stephen would goad me into screaming, abusive phone calls to her, fuelled by drink and paranoia and the ever-present burning pain of an abandoned child.

I felt I had to choose between my family and him. I began to think that they had betrayed me or were trying to ruin me, that they hated me and only ever wanted me for my money. I mentioned before the power of what is called gaslighting, when your idea of reality is manipulated. And he got to me. I felt isolated from my family and isolated within my own family as my ability as a mother was endlessly mocked and berated.

'I want to take the kids to the park,' I'd say.

'No, it's too dangerous,' he'd say, shutting the conversation down.

Like what? I'd think. I'd travelled the world, I'd knocked out girls twice my size who called me a 'Paki' at Intake High School, and I'd faced down some of the toughest sharks in the music industry, all before he'd even left New Jersey.

I'd even put Prince Charles in his place when I was sitting a few seats down from him at the *Spice World* movie premiere in December

1997, when he brought Prince William along. We were all squished into the seats and there were loads of famous people there because we'd persuaded people like Roger Moore, Jools Holland, Stephen Fry and the lovely Richard E Grant to be in the movie with us. Halfway through, I noticed Charles, who was sitting next to Geri (she was always his favourite); he was laughing his head off. I was thrilled. I leaned across and said, 'I'm so happy you're enjoying it.'

Charles turned and looked and me. 'I'm a very good actor,' he said.

I was totally enraged. 'That's rude,' I said loudly, leaving it to Geri to smooth it all over (her role was always the diplomat). But it was rude and I told him so.

'It's not a good idea for you to take the kids,' Stephen would say. 'Why don't you go and have a rest instead?' In the early days of our marriage, I tried to make sure that I was always the one who made the arrangements for Angel and Phoenix. I'd tell nannies to leave them with friends or take them to the tennis club to be picked up by me from there. Eventually, though, there was no doubt who was making the decisions in the house.

And I always went back to him. I had too much to lose and no-one to run to. I didn't have numbers or email addresses for a lot of my old friends anymore as my phone had been changed so many times that their contact numbers had been lost. It was too embarrassing to pitch up at someone's door, and there was no chance I could do anything with my family. If I went back to them then Stephen would take it as a sign the marriage was over. 'Just one click' he would say, holding out his phone. If those videos were made public my poor, proud dad would never be able to hold up his head up again. I would have ruined his life. I could not do that to him.

I did, however, have Dr Sophy. Every week, he would come to the house and we would sit in a room and he would listen. He saw Phoenix and – with her grades slipping at school – diagnosed that she was suffering from ADHD. I was also diagnosed and medicated for the same disorder (although Stephen did not want me taking any medication). It made so much sense. The kid my family called 'The Wind' because she could never sit still, the pupil who teachers despaired of because she never paid attention and could not make head nor tail of maths. Dr Sophy tried to explain the condition to Stephen who complained that I 'never listened', 'lost everything' and 'made no sense to him'. But, as Dr Sophy, says, 'No-one can tell Stephen anything. Every time I tried to explain he would talk over me, interrupt, tell me I didn't know what I was doing, that he would get me sacked.' Like me, Dr Sophy found those sessions with Stephen traumatic.

It took me years – probably that moment in my hotel room at The Grove in Watford when he told me he would help me – to finally trust Dr Sophy. My life was a series of secrets, and I didn't like the idea of discussing my private thoughts or those secrets in front of either him or Stephen. Most of the time I didn't really know what my thoughts were because I couldn't make sense of my life myself.

Dr Sophy would arrange meetings and I would either cancel or disengage. Then if things got really bad, if me and Stephen were rowing and fighting, I would call him in desperation, asking for his help. Then, more often than not, I would not bother to return his calls the next day. My marriage was something I needed to handle myself. Stephen told me he was only being nice to me because I was a Spice Girl and he wanted me to make him famous. But, as many barriers as I put up, as many meetings as I cancelled, Dr Sophy never gave up on me.

I asked him later, sitting in the house he helped me find after I left Stephen, why he never gave up on me. He said the thought of me always frightened him because he was worried about what was going to happen to me. He said he saw only two clear modes in my behaviour – either I sat there mute while Stephen berated me and talked about how I was nothing without him, or I went into anger mode and fought back at anything he said. Even though I never actually spelt out what was really going on between us he sensed there was a real problem. To him, we were a Molotov cocktail waiting to blow and he knew he had to be around to pick up the pieces. I felt he thought one morning he would wake up and read in a newspaper a headline: 'Mel B is dead'. He wanted to save me.

I always knew there was only one man who could save me. Martin Brown. My dad. That thought was like a neon light in the fog of my brain throughout the final year of my marriage. I hadn't spoken to him since that awful row at our old house in Leeds in December 2014, and the anger and disappointment I saw in his eyes stabbed at my heart like a knife. Despite all of that, I was his daughter, the little girl he had adored more than life itself. He might hate me, but I knew that his love still burned away underneath. The bloodline between Black Grandma, my dad and me ran deep; we were connected on a primal, instinctive level. And in the end, it was my dad who gave me the strength to leave Stephen.

—

When Madison was born on a beautiful sunny day in September 2011, all I thought about was Dad. Phoenix was in the delivery room and I said she could name the baby. I suggested 'Sydney' because I was – and still am – so in love with that city and the whole of Australia. But when this tiny ball of black curls popped out, Phoenix said, 'Madison'. She cut the cord and was the first person to hold her sister, and she looked out for her and her other sister Angel from the moment they were born.

I thought of my dad because Madison is my double. I looked at her and I thought of a hundred pictures I'd seen of my dad holding this cute little, round bundle with brown eyes, wild hair and a cheeky smile. I thought of how much I missed him. I thought of the moment my sister had been born in Hyde Hospital, Leeds, on 4 June 1980.

I came back from school so excited to see this new baby sister and then so horrified when I leaned into the little cot. 'But she looks like me,' I spluttered in disbelief to my mum. 'I wanted a sister with white skin and blonde hair. And she's brown.'

And now I was a mother of three beautiful brown girls and so proud of my heritage, and proud that every single time a mixed-race girl would come up to me and tell me that seeing me as a Spice Girl, seeing me standing there onstage with my afro curls (I always refused to have my hair straightened because I didn't want to hide my race), helped them believe they could achieve their dreams.

I loved being a role model for mixed-race girls and made sure I spoke up about the difficulties I'd faced, the racism I'd encountered, and it meant a lot to me as a little kid when I saw posters of Terri Seymour modelling the clothes of C&A where my mum worked. There were never any brown people on television or in magazines. I hated the black-and-white movies Black Grandma always wanted me to watch with her when I went to her house because all the black people in them were servants. I still don't like old black-and-white movies for that reason. Terri has now become a good friend of mine because she is on the American entertainment show 'Extra' and is a great friend of Simon Cowell. She laughs when I tell her that she was my first role model (followed by Neneh Cherry), but she was. It was such a big deal to a young brown girl who spent the first few years of her life wondering when she'd turn white.

I think that's why I was so shocked in 2018 when, on social media, my skin colour became another issue. I was accused of whitening my skin because I looked pale in photographs. And I was pale. Brown skin does go pale. I had spent many months at home, not really going out, shuffling between legal meetings, court appearances and working on 'America's Got Talent', and looking after my kids. I wasn't out in the sun, hiking, sunbathing, swimming. My skin was reflecting the time I was going through. But the idea that people would believe I was wanting to 'go white' appalled me to such a degree that on top of spray tans, I started going out and sunbathing in my back garden. I have never, ever wanted to change my roots. My colour comes from my dad. The first love of my life.

Unbeknown to Stephen, by the end of 2015, I was planning my exit. My father had been diagnosed with multiple myeloma cancer in 2012 after an operation on his spine led to further medical investigations. In 2013 he had a stem-cell transplant, which was traumatic for him and also for me because he wouldn't speak to me when I called the hospital. 'Face it. He doesn't give a fuck about you,' Stephen told me, as I cried myself to sleep.

Ever since I had returned to Los Angeles at Christmas 2014, Dr Sophy had been telling me, on the rare occasions we got the chance to speak in private, 'You have to make tough decisions, and you have to get sober so you can do this properly with a clean exit.' I was working on it, just as Stephen seemed to be working to get me institutionalized for being crazy. I had to get sober, I had to plan, I had to be smart.

In 2016 I bought Stephen a restaurant on Sunset Boulevard. He was – to be fair – a great cook, and it was a dream of his to own his own place. I didn't even think about the money it cost to buy a restaurant – to me it is never about the money. There was a reason. Running a restaurant is a full-on job. He liked to be there every night – the king of his castle – and that meant when I was working away, he wouldn't be able to come with me and check on my every move. If he was in his restaurant – running his own show – he wouldn't always be there with me on my shows, especially when I had to leave the country for work. I was paying for weeks of freedom.

I went to Australia with the girls to film 'The X Factor'. We were so happy. Then I went to the UK to shoot with the brilliant Bear Grylls (anyone who thinks I was still drinking at this point should consider hanging off a rock with a hangover). As I was always paranoid about my phone being monitored, I called Phoenix in LA and asked her to tell my mother to come and meet me where we were filming near Wales. My mother got the call after work and drove through the traffic to arrive at a tiny hotel in the middle of nowhere, late at night. We walked around the garden in the near dark and – despite not having seen each other for eight years – neither of us really said anything. She cried and I kept repeating I was OK, and that the girls were OK. I'd lost the ability to do anything other than block all emotions. She didn't mention Stephen's name and neither did I. In a film, it would be a moment of lots of outpourings, with me sitting there telling her my plans, but it wasn't like that. Neither of us knew how to be with the other, and maybe each of us was expecting a dramatic gesture. But I had seen her, she had seen me. 'I love you, Melanie,' she said in the early hours of the morning as I was leaving to start filming. 'I love you too, Mother.'

—

'When my dad dies, I'm divorcing you,' I told Stephen by the end of 2016. He laughed, but I think he was nervous. I had stopped answering all his calls. He could sense I didn't care.

I went back to England to meet up with Geri and Emma to discuss a Spice Girl reunion in March. I was losing the fear. I was slowly starting to take back control. Making decisions. Being a mother.

Phoenix was in trouble at school with her grades, and there had been an incident when she crashed my car. She was at Beverly Hills High, mixing with all sorts of kids with too much money and too many privileges, and I was only too well aware of what she had witnessed with Stephen and me. I had told her that time in hospital that there was no way I wanted her ever to drink or take drugs, and – harnessing every ounce of my strict Black Grandma's spirit – I took her out of school and checked her into the Diamond Ranch in Utah, which is hardcore therapy and education for troubled teenagers. I then went back to work in New York, where, since December, I'd been playing Roxie Hart in *Chicago* on Broadway.

When I left LA for New York, Stephen knew it was all over bar the shouting. I kept telling him, 'My dad is getting worse and then I'm leaving you. I don't care what you do then.' Initially there was no shouting. I couldn't wait to get to New York with Madison and Angel. I hosted the New Year's Eve Ball Drop with Carson Daly and had worked my backside off to get in shape for *Chicago*. I identified with the impetuous, free-spirited Roxy, and New York took me back to happier times.

It was there where I first met Janet, my old assistant, when I was appearing in *Rent*. We were introduced through a mutual friend and went out for a night, and like two classic Northern girls, we got absolutely smashed and then somehow rode our rented bikes back to my hotel. Janet's bike got stolen and the next day she woke up hungover and certain she would never be trusted as a PA. 'You've got the job,' I remember screaming at her when she appeared in my dressing room later that morning.

'Are you sure?' she said. 'I made a right tit of myself last night.' She looked really wrecked. I laughed out loud. I knew she was going to be a friend for life.

Performing in *Chicago* was a surreal time. I impressed the critics (I had put in the work to make sure I would) and I was away from Stephen. Every night, however, I would get messages from my sister telling me how ill my dad was. He was admitted to St James's University Hospital in Leeds. As January wore on, he was getting weaker and weaker, and by the beginning of February the few words he could say were, 'Where's my daughter?' I knew I had to go, but I had to finish the run of the show, which ended on 19 February. Otherwise I would be sued because it was in my contract, and also – I have to admit – I needed to finish the job. I also knew that my dad would wait for me and would understand I had to finish it. This was a man who'd never taken a sick day in his life.

When the show ended, I felt the strangest mix of emotions. I felt strong, focused and fearless. 'I'm going back to England, my dad is dying, and then we're getting a divorce,' I told Stephen.

However, I realized that my passport was missing. I arranged for an emergency passport and drove with Angel to the British Embassy, where a kind woman took pity on me. 'I need a letter from your father's doctor, and your dad has to also sign a letter.'

I knew he could barely write because he had wanted to write a letter to me but couldn't. I called my sister and waited there until an email arrived with a letter from the doctor, scanned with my dad's signature – a thin, wobbly line in black biro – which churned through the printer to be officially stamped for a temporary passport. Then I took Angel home and arranged for a friend I'd met in Australia when Stephen was stuck in LA looking after the restaurant to come and look after her and Madison. I got back in my car and drove to Utah to pick up Phoenix. I could not go back to my father without my daughter. His first beloved grandchild.

'My dad's dying. We're going to go and see him. And then I'm leaving Stephen,' I told my daughter as she rushed to get in the car.

'OK, Mom,' was all she said. Which is why I love her. Even through everything, we don't need words. We have a bond which Stephen could bury but not break.

We drove to LA airport and took the first flight to Heathrow. 'Dad, I'm coming home,' I whispered as the plane took off.

29
GOODBYE. I LOVE YOU

—

Phoenix and I stood in Heathrow Airport. After weeks and weeks of being able to carry on singing and smiling on Broadway and telling myself, 'There is still time,' suddenly I had to be right by his side.

I had booked train tickets but reckoned I wouldn't be arriving at St James's hospital in Leeds for at least four more hours. Driving would take longer because of the traffic. 'I'm going to hire a jet,' I told Phoenix, who looked at me open-mouthed.

I have been on private jets, but I had no idea how to go about hiring one. I went up to a help desk and said, 'Where do I go to get a private jet?' The woman looked at me, took one glimpse at my leopard-print suitcase, realized who I was and said, 'I'll take you to the right desk, Miss Brown.' She probably thought this was the way I always behaved. Despite the circumstances, I actually giggled at the thought. This was so not me.

I still shop in Target and Primark, and, in the early days of the Spice Girls, I used to put all my things in a plastic Morrison's bag like the one my dad used to have hanging over his bicycle handles. 'Where's Melanie's placcy bag?' Mel C used to yell as we unloaded from cars, planes, jets and tour buses. I didn't want a designer handbag; it took years before they felt comfortable on my arm, so I'd chuck everything – keys, money, jewellery, phones, diaries, tampons and cigarettes – into my Morrison's bag and take it everywhere with me. It reminded me of Leeds, of my dad. Of who I am and always will be.

It took twenty-seven minutes to get from London to Leeds and Bradford airport. On the flight, I'd put makeup on Phoenix. She looked beautiful. Once we were on my home soil, I felt weird again. Scared. I was about to see my dad. My big, strong dad on his deathbed. I would have to see all my family who probably all hated me. I would have to say goodbye. 'Let's go and get UK SIM cards and leave our bags in a hotel and then go to the hospital,' I told Phoenix. 'And I need to get Black Grandma on a flight from Nevis. I'm going to book her a first-class ticket.' (I finally had my own credit card attached to a shared bank account with Stephen, and I was going to make the most of it.) Phoenix shook her head. She knew exactly how I was feeling, exactly what I was doing. I was delaying again. Fear makes me delay facing reality. A reality I don't want to see.

'We are going to the hospital,' she said.

—

I felt more nervous than I ever had in my life as we walked into the massive university hospital. More terrified than going on stage in front of a hundred thousand people, or stepping out of those taxis at the Olympics, or going up onstage.

The last time I'd been in the hospital was when I'd taken an overdose at fourteen. I clung onto Phoenix, who had already texted my mum to say we were on our way. My dad's sisters, Auntie Beverly and Auntie Kathleen, were there already. As I opened the door to my dad's room, I grabbed Phoenix's hand. Planet Radio's Magic Soul was playing the classic songs my dad loved. There were flowers and food in the room, the sort of things you'd have at a party, and there he was on the bed. It was hard to look at him. The machines around him were beeping, and he was making an awful gurgling sound because he was struggling to breathe. I was shocked at how thin and frail he looked. He looked like a stick man I used to draw in those hangman games me and dad used to play together. I was stricken. I felt completely decimated seeing him like that. 'He can't speak now, Melanie love,' my mum said.

I hugged her and my aunts, and then all of them, except my mum, left the room. I sat by the bed, looking at my dad's beautiful face, which is more familiar to me than my own. Tears were running down my face. 'It's Melanie, Martin,' my mum said.

'Dad, it's me.' He opened his eyes and looked at me. Phoenix was by my side, but I barely even noticed she was there.

'I love you.' The words came out in the faintest croaking whisper. I held his hand, my heart breaking. I was actually terrified he was going to die right there and then, he looked so unbelievably frail.

'He hasn't been able to say anything at all for weeks,' said my mum.

'Phoenix is here,' I said, and saw my dad's thin right arm move slightly. Phoenix took his hand. My dad could no longer speak, but neither could I. What the hell had happened in my life that my daughter and her granddad would only meet on his deathbed? My dad, my good strong dad. We had broken each other's hearts. I heard Phoenix saying, 'Hey Grandad, it's me. I love you. And Angel and Madison want you to know they love you too. Madison looks just like Mom …' She talked on and on, as if it was the most natural thing in the world. In that moment I loved her so much I thought I was going to burst with all the emotions flooding through me.

The doctors said he had only days left. I went – as I do – into organizational mode. I gave him Reiki healing, something he would have dismissed as 'mumbo jumbo', but I could feel it helping him. I wanted him moved to a hospice because he was in too much pain, and the wonderful St Gemma's told us they had a bed. I cannot speak highly enough of the staff in the NHS, and particularly those at St Gemma's Hospice. He had a beautiful room, Danielle and I arranged new flowers, Magic Soul was switched back on, and – because hospices are all about pain management and palliative care – he looked more comfortable. Anyone who has sat around the bed of a dying relative will know how strange and special that atmosphere is, how your hours slow down, you learn about every fluid and medication going in and out of your loved one's body, and every card, every flower, every word becomes so precious and meaningful.

Add to that the fact that I was back with my family who I had been estranged from for so long – you might think there was difficult tension and added emotional heights. There wasn't. In times like that, everything other than what is in that room seems pointless and unreal. We all slotted into our old roles. Danielle seemed almost relieved that her big bossy sister was back. Time was running out and I knew my dad would want to be prepared. 'We need to cut his hair,' I said on his second day in the hospice. 'Let's find a beautiful, comfortable shirt for him to wear.' My mother shaved him, my sister brushed his teeth. Each task filled hours of the day.

We talked, we laughed, we sang along to soul classics like 'Sitting On the Dock of a Bay' and 'Heard It Through The Grapevine'. My mum's sisters came in and out, along with streams of cousins and family friends. And Black Grandma arrived in a dark fitted suit and hat. Danielle and I had to keep leaving the room to howl with laughter as she told us how she refused all food and drink on the plane and sat upright all the way. She would not lie back in the first-class reclined seats. I'd arranged for someone to meet her with a wheelchair when she landed in London because she has a bad leg, but she wouldn't get in it. She walked on her own to baggage claim, even though it took her three times as long it would have done with assistance. But that's my grandma.

When White Grandad was dying, my mum had spoon-fed him a couple of sips of his favourite beer. I remembered the story and told Danielle we needed to get some Special Brew. Dad couldn't even swallow, so we wiped it over his lips with some cotton wool. He would have appreciated what we were trying to do. I told him I was leaving Stephen and I felt his hand tighten slightly on mine. On Saturday, 4 March 2017, I knew it would be his time to go. It was his favourite day of the week – football on the telly and no need to get up with the lark.

One of the nurses told us that some people wait for their family to leave before they die. They choose to die on their own because that, to them, makes it easier on their family.

I told Danielle we needed to pray and then leave the room for seven minutes in case he needed to be on his own to die. Seven is a magical number. But he didn't. In the end we were all in the room, everyone was talking, and the Stylistics were singing 'You Are Everything' on the radio. It was 3.15 p.m. I leaned over him. 'Dad. You've had your hair cut and a shave. You've got a beautiful fresh shirt on. We have prayed. We are ready. You are ready. But I can't start my divorce until you die.'

His eyes opened for a second, we looked at each other, and there was a moment which I felt every ounce of pain that had ever passed between us disappear. Then he took one last very slow breath. 'He's gone,' I announced to the room. They all stood around the bed in disbelief. I didn't want to cry. My dad was out of pain. He was free. We had made our peace and I had made him a promise. Now, I needed to go and do what my father wanted me to do: get Stephen out of my life. I said goodbye to my family and took the first plane back to LA.

—

My dad once told me he was proud of me. Only once that I can remember. But it was my dad, mind, and emotions were a pretty big deal for him.

It was in 1995 before 'Wannabe' came out and all of us Spice Girls organized a showcase for our parents, who really didn't have much of a clue about what we were doing (rehearsing like crazy, trying to find a manager and writing songs together). We hired a room in the Holiday Inn in Borehamwood, Hertfordshire, and that's where we performed for them. I think that for the first time in his life, my dad saw I had something.

A few days later, he wrote me a letter, which I keep in a special box in my bedroom. The letter reads:

I feel proud you have turned out so level-headed, self-sufficient, generous and a lovely girl. I hope in times to come you don't change. I don't know what the future holds for you and your group, but I think you will make it big time and I am keeping my fingers crossed. Whatever happens, take in all the experience, all the travel, the people etc and enjoy it to the full.

You will make mistakes along the way, everybody does. The way to gain experience is to learn from your mistakes. Always take a camera with you and take lots of photos. When you are an old and married woman not only will you have your memories but also photos to show your kids.

When you make it big and have lots and lots of money, do not ever forget your background or where you were born and brought up. Your family and friends are the ones who have been there for you and always will.

I know you didn't have a happy teenage life and mainly that was due to my strictness. That was my way of showing how much I love and care for you. I wanted to protect you from the dangers of life. I pushed you too hard with your education. I thought education was the most important thing for you to achieve.

I love you very much and I am very proud of you. No matter what happens in the future I will always be here for you.

I know he is, and every day I feel him by my side. It was his strength I drew on in the darkest days of my court case with Stephen, his spirit I feel close to me at so many times of the night and day, and it is because of him I'm getting my life back to make him proud of me again.

30
FREEDOM

—

I drove down Sunset Boulevard with Phoenix, past the Art Deco Sunset Tower Hotel where a giant poster of me, Heidi, Simon and Howie Mandel loomed over the passing cars, promoting the latest series of 'America's Got Talent'. I took the turn on the corner by Soho House, towards the Hollywood Hills. It would take a matter of minutes before we arrived at Cordell Drive, our home for the previous few years where Stephen would be waiting.

I pulled up on the steep hill outside the house with its unassuming white entrance directly on the street. If you lived in that house, you would expect to experience a little thrill whenever you opened the door. Once inside, you looked down a vast white staircase which opened out onto a huge, modern living area with a state-of-the-art kitchen and floor-to-ceiling windows. The windows opened onto a balcony overlooking the hills of Los Angeles and our glistening turquoise swimming pool two floors below. Stephen had gutted and rebuilt this house to a top-spec design with artworks on the walls, Italian marble in the six bathrooms, a gym, a private cinema and an outdoor entertainment centre. As always, we had a separate upstairs floor containing a palatial bedroom, bathroom – with a white porcelain bath you could fill to overflowing and the water would disappear into drains hidden in the floor – and two dressing rooms for ourselves, as well as a security and electronics system to rival the White House.

But as I stood outside holding my key, all I was thinking was,

I want to get away from this place as fast as possible. I walked inside and up to the bedroom and started to unpack. I texted Dr Sophy. We had arranged for him to come and talk, with Stephen and I, to the kids about the divorce. Dr Sophy could not believe this was finally happening. 'This has to be done properly, Melanie,' he had told me. I thought about my dad. This was his final wish. I was going to live my life without fear, disrespect and shame.

I sat on the bed and cried but not for long. Stephen made me feel like there was no point in me crying, that my dad had never liked me. And that was it. My tears stopped. My emotions were blocked – the biggest lesson I learned from that marriage. The next few days were spent in endless discussions. 'America's Got Talent' was starting again with the judges' auditions being taped in the Pasadena Civic Auditorium. In Leeds, my mum and sister were arranging my dad's funeral. I wanted to help my sister make a video for the day with special music and photos of us and all our kids. I could feel the tension rising with Stephen as he began insisting we make a podcast to talk about our divorce. My mum then told me she'd had a late-night call from Stephen while I was doing *Chicago* in New York. He'd been screaming and ranting. My mum had put the phone down. Still, it made me feel completely sick. I was out the other side with an entirely different perspective. But he was still the same Stephen.

I didn't go to my father's funeral. I found a house and a divorce lawyer. I moved myself and my children out and asked a judge to put a restraining order on Stephen. On the day before my dad's funeral, we missed the flight from Los Angeles. I was already uneasy because I did not have official permission from Stephen to take Madison out of the country. Missing the flight seemed like a sign. I called my mum from the airport. The next available flight would get us in after the funeral had ended.

My mum remembers telling me that she didn't want to put me through any more grief. 'You have said goodbye,' she told me. 'Take the girls home and have a peaceful day remembering your dad. We know you are with us in spirit.' I spent the rest of the day in the calm of my new house lighting candles for my dad, saying prayers and thinking of the man whose death had given me a new life.

—

When I left Stephen, I walked away with nothing but $936 in a bank account (the only one I had access to) and suitcases full of clothes, books and toys. I didn't care. I was happy. My kids were happy. I put on my music full blast (sorry to my neighbours) and danced around my house, which was decorated in a very over-the-top Versace style – not my style at all. But I was free. Finally, after ten years, I was free.

The thing is, I was on my own. Apart from Dr Sophy, I had no friends. All the people who used to be in my life, like Kim Deck, like Charlotte, like Janet, were long gone.

I wanted to celebrate, to open some champagne. The realization of what I had lost and who I had lost hit me. But I am nothing if not proactive, and I have never been someone who wastes time on self-pity. I set about tracking down old friends. I had no idea whether people still cared enough about me, whether they had lost faith, given up on me for good. 'Melanie, you're back,' was largely the response I got. Charlotte flew into Los Angeles from Leeds with her daughter, Tillie Amartey, who I hadn't seen since she was little. Tillie is now all grown up and looks unbelievably like I did when I was a teenager, and she can sing, dance and act like a total star. Friends from years back came over to the house. I got my own phone and my own computer. I linked myself back to the world. I felt amazing.

Strange and inexplicable things happened. Serendipitous things (another new word in my Thesaurus). My estate agent turned up a few days after we moved in with Mrs Lynch, Eddie's mother, who happened to be one of her closest friends. She looked spectacular in a fabulous outfit and perfectly braided hair. 'I'd like to take my grand-daughter out to lunch,' she announced as she came into the house. Angel was aware that Eddie was her father (her step-sister, Giselle, had told her years before), but it was something we never discussed as Stephen encouraged her to think of him as her father. When she was a small child, we all used to go as a family to various events at 'Uncle Eddie's' house, but then we stopped going.

I took Angel out into the garden. Angel is a special child. She is incredibly intelligent and a real old soul. 'You know Uncle Eddie,' I began slowly. She looked at me with her huge brown eyes and nodded. 'You do know he's actually your dad, don't you?' She nodded again, and I realized I had to say it quickly because Angel's brain works faster than anyone else's. 'Well, your grandma is here and she wants to take you to lunch.' Angel looked over my shoulder at Mrs Lynch, who was standing patiently in the kitchen, and she frowned. The only 'grandma' she had ever seen (in photographs) was my mum. 'That's Eddie's mum,' I said. 'She's really lovely and now you can start to get to know her.' Angel grinned and walked into the kitchen. She spends weekends with Eddie now, and that she is getting to know the man she so reminds me of is one of the greatest joys of my life.

I would like to say that once you leave a toxic relationship, your life is suddenly perfect, as if you are living in a Disney movie with birds tweeting and flowers blooming. Actually, it did feel like that for a while. The kids were beside themselves with excitement the first time we all sat down at the kitchen table and ate in our new house. 'It's so great to eat at a table, Mummy,' Madi grinned. What a thing for a kid to say.

We loved our new lives. We got pets (our French bulldogs named Zeus and Axl by Angel and my hilarious fainting goats Phyllis and Stanley named by me). I lit Palo Santo sticks throughout the house (Palo Santo is a tree with mystical healing properties that grows in South America, and the scent is known for cleansing the energy around you – and I had a lot of energy to cleanse). I started practising Reiki again (I am a fully trained Reiki master), something I hadn't done regularly since the age of nineteen.

I signed the girls up for dance and gymnastics, invited their friends over to the house, burned sausages on the barbecue and dive-bombed in the pool with the girls – all of us howling with laughter. I bought crystals and music speakers that changed colour depending on the soundwaves. I made a shrine with my Spice Girls outfits on dressmakers' models in my room – I did this to remind myself that I came from nothing and I burst onto the world stage with my four wannabe friends screaming and yelling for Girl Power.

But I couldn't keep the reality of my situation completely away from my new world. The story was out in the press and all over the papers and social media. I refused hundreds of thousands of pounds to do a 'tell all' interview. It's not my style. It wasn't the time. I needed to hunker down with my kids, mend bonds that had been broken with my family. I had to deal with lawyers over the divorce. And I needed to heal.

I didn't realize how much I needed to heal back then. I didn't understand about post-traumatic stress syndrome and the aftershocks that keep on coming like invisible waves when you least expect them. I'm a very practical person. I was out of my marriage; I had to move on. I didn't realize how many times I would fall again and have to pick myself back up. How I would still make mistakes and how much I would need my family and friends to support me. I had been desperate, powerless and suicidal. Now I could be happy and fearless once again. I wanted, as everyone does, to get my life back to how it was before. Friends, family, laughter, work, and people in and out of my house drinking wine, having barbecues, having play-dates, like it was in our home in Los Feliz, like it was in Leeds, where I grew up surrounded by my aunts, cousins and all my mum's mates.

And so I did things which I thought at the time made absolute sense. As everyone knows, I am an extremely sexual person, but for ten years I had only had sex with one man. I hadn't mixed socially with any straight guys for years. The idea of sex with Stephen repulsed me so much; I felt physically sick at the thought of him. 'You need to have sex with a nice, normal guy,' said one gay friend (I still love my gay friends because it's so much easier to talk about sex with them). 'To get over a man, you have to get under another one. Just get out there, girl. It's not like you don't know what to do.'

Who the hell was I going to have sex with? I didn't want to go on a date, I didn't want another relationship, and I couldn't exactly go on the pull in a bar in LA. Another gay friend, who is very well connected in the entertainment industry, had the solution. He told me he could show me a secret website where famous unattached guys looking for a discreet hook-up put up images. I was sitting in Soho House on a night out with a couple of girlfriends when the images came through. I couldn't believe what I was looking at. The site was filled with images of men's erect privates, each one lined up against a milk or juice carton so you could gauge the size. I shut my laptop. Then, obviously, opened it again. My friends and I spent the next few hours laughing and gawping through the images. I called my friend and said, 'Now what?'

'You choose one and I will make a discreet introduction,' he answered. I did. A few days later, I met him (young, handsome and very famous) in a hotel room wearing just my underwear. It was horribly awkward and nothing happened (it was obviously easier with a milk carton). I tried again with another famous penis in another hotel room. Same result. Aaarghhhh. Mortifying. I'd have had better luck on a night out in Leeds with a local builder. I gave up on famous penises and had a few encounters with some very normal, regular guys. Way better.

—

I went to a cosmetic surgeon. When I was married to Stephen, I had surgery on my boobs and there were complications, but I didn't have them corrected. I contacted the brilliant Dr Kao, and in the space of a matter of months arranged to have a whole series of small surgeries on my face, eyes, boobs and stomach. I heard about a man called Dr Matlock who specializes in vagina rejuvenation. I called him up, made an appointment and explained I wanted to have surgery straightaway. He told me I didn't need it and that for a woman with three children, I was in exceptionally good shape. But I knew I wanted this done.

A week later, I was sitting in the roof-top bar of the SLS Hotel in Beverly Hills, where there is a special recovery centre for people who have had surgery. A girlfriend had flown from England to see me, and she sat and listened to me talk about my surgery – I always go into eye-watering detail. She sat nodding, sipped on her gin and tonic and then looked at me and said, 'You know, Melanie, when people have been through trauma, they often scrub themselves till they bleed or use horrible things like bleach on themselves. It's a primal thing, an instinct. You're a famous woman, you live in Hollywood where all this is normal, but you have to think why you did this. Are you trying to erase every trace? Are you trying to turn back the clock to the point before Stephen was even in your life?'

I opened my mouth to say, 'No.' And then it dawned on me that what she was saying was true. I didn't know what to think because I didn't want to go down a dark path. I wanted light and laughter from now on. And then you realize how long that path to recovery is. Whether you try and run down it or dance down it, that road just keeps getting longer … And along the way there will be bouts of depression, panic attacks, insomnia and paranoia, and your throat will be gripped in turn by guilt, fear and shame.

Along the way you may do things that seem shocking to the rest of the world – like when I decided to have Stephen's name cut from the tattoo I'd had inked down my ribcage a few years after we got married. 'Stephen, till death do us part, you own my heart.' I didn't have it lasered off. I had the piece of skin with his name on cut out by a surgeon and I will burn that piece of flesh or bury it when I am ready. The skin has healed. I am still healing. I still have a long way to go.

There were things that I was ignoring. I think other women in this situation are similar because they are so intent of everything being all right. For all my genuine happiness and the thrill I got from the smallest things like cooking pancakes for my girls or jumping in the waves at the beach with Heidi, I couldn't sleep without having an armed man downstairs guarding the house. I couldn't go out to Soho House (where I knew Stephen was never able to get his own membership, something for which I am eternally grateful to them for) without worrying that the man on his own by the bar was someone sent to spy on me or listen in to my conversations. 'Let's move over there,' I'd say to my friends, who had already changed seats three times in less than an hour. The landline in my rented Versace Palace in Coldwater Canyon rang at least twice a day. I would answer and the line would just crackle with the faint sound of someone's breath. Was it Stephen? I will never know. A year in, it stopped bothering me. I would just laugh into the virtual silence when I picked the phone up.

In the midst of all this, I was also fighting a court case that was getting messier by the day. I wanted to stand up and fight for all women, but the law is the law. You need proof of things it is impossible to prove, perfect recall of times and places you have blocked from your mind. If you are a celebrity, the court battle spills into the media, where with every single headline your reputation is damaged chip by chip. You will be faced by unfair decisions, impossible choices and soul-destroying compromises. You will be criticized by people who have no clue what you have been through and why you behaved in the way that you did. You will meet people who give you good advice and bad advice, and you will listen to both. You will make mistakes.

You will have regrets. You will trust the wrong people and you will be betrayed. You will hide in your room and block out the world. Your body will fall back into hardwired ways to numb your pain. You will go out into that world in loud, bright, colourful dresses with your hair dyed every shade of the rainbow to show other women you still have a message of joy in your heart and you still want to share it. You will carry on.

Legal battles are like living with a team of builders permanently in your house. They make a mess, they cost a fortune, and, whatever you ask them to do, there is always a problem. A legal problem. I would advise anyone in my position coming out of a seriously corrosive relationship to try to wait till they have let some time pass before they turn to lawyers. Of course if there are children involved, it's a process you have to go through. It's a process I'm still going through.

In the past twenty something years of my life, I have made more than £80 million. When I met my second husband, I had a house and a loft apartment in Los Angeles and a good career. When I left him, I had less than $1,000 in the bank. I have continued to work on 'America's Got Talent' (thank you, Simon and Paul Telegdy for your loyalty), and I have reunited with Simon Fuller, Geri, Vic, Emma and Mel C to work on Spice Girl projects. I have to continue to pay my ex-husband a substantial monthly payment. I have legal bills to pay and my three children to support, I pay my own way, as I have done all my life. I have moved from my mansions to an apartment in the centre of Los Angeles. I am not complaining. Life is what life is. I have my girls; I carry on working. I have never thought anything other than 'I am lucky to do what I do.'

EPILOGUE

—

THIS IS NOT THE END

The comedians Dave Chapelle and Iliza Schlesinger (a genius). The Scarlett Johansson movie *Rough Night* with its catchphrase 'swimming in dicks'. Peter Kay's 'Live at the Top of the Tower'. Dancing in my dressing room with Heidi Klum. Yorkshire puddings cooked on a barbecue in Wandsworth (thank you James, Charlie, Billy and Daisy). Going to a spa in Arizona with my lovely Gary and a whole bunch of pensioners. Forcing Gary to make me turkey sandwiches at midnight because the kitchen closed at 8 p.m. sharp. Hoovering (making perfect hoover lines in my carpets), cleaning out my kitchen cupboards. Watching Geri and Emma being so polite to guys coming over and asking for autographs when I tell them to leave us alone. Dancing with Madison and Angel. Going on television for the very first time with Phoenix; she dressed me up like Sandy from *Grease*. Laughing so much in the back of a London cab that drove off without my friend, who had to run behind us until the cabbie realized we were screaming, 'Stop!'. Giggling with guests at my cousin John's wedding in Leeds.

These are just some of the things and some of the moments where I have felt myself again. Melanie Brown.

I pray, I meditate, I do my Reiki, but the healing power of laughter is possibly one of the greatest of all. I surround myself with my family and friends, and I remind myself who I am, what I do. I can perform.

I am not scared of anyone. I can face all of the things that continue to be thrown at me. I am still a work in progress, but believe me, I am doing everything I can to progress. I think of the things I have done, the incredible people I have met. People who have passed away. George Michael. I remember sitting with him and Geri and passing time, laughing and joking.

Prince. I remember being pregnant with Phoenix and having to interview him at his Purple Palace in Minneapolis. I was in awe of him as an artist, but he didn't intimidate me as a man. He took me round his great big mad complex and showed me his doves and his recording studio. He flirted outrageously and I flirted back. He told me I was incredibly sexy, and I told him he was married and to stop trying to make a move on me. He told me that most of all he liked to laugh. And so do I.

I can laugh at good things that happened. I can laugh at bad things too. My family is the same. I am from slave stock and I am from Yorkshire. I am resilient. I am always looking for the punch-line. We were brought up NEVER to swear. If my mum even said so much as 'Bloody hell' then me and Danielle used to tell my dad on her. 'No swearing in this house,' he would say. 'And never in front of the children.'

My mother told me recently of a time when Stephen made one of his threatening, abusive calls to her. It was in the middle of an afternoon, when she was out in Leeds. At one point, she heard herself 'yell as loud as possible, "WHY DON'T YOU JUST FUCK OFF!" And then I looked around,' she says, 'and everyone was staring at me. I was in the middle of the chilled aisle in Morrison's holding a packet of butter. I had to put all my shopping down and run out of the shop.'

I laughed until I cried. And then I asked Mother, 'Did you ever go back?'

'Oh yes,' she said. 'I'm not going to let him stop me shopping at Morrison's. I went back the next day.'

I laughed so much I almost choked on my soda.

—

I am not going to let anyone stop me living a happy life. I read books about PTSD and emotional abuse. I watch documentaries on cults and marvel at how so many people can end up being sucked into situations they have no control over, at how it all starts, little by little, heating that frog up gently until it burns.

Every now and again I get stopped in my tracks, like when I started watching Benedict Cumberbatch in the Sky Atlantic drama *Patrick Melrose*, and there was a scene where Jennifer Jason Leigh plays a drunken, drugged-up mother who is stopped from comforting her distraught son by her manipulative, domineering husband. It made me feel ill. But it made me think that we are living in much more en-lightened times because these issues that shame and demonize women are being opened up, explored and shown for what they really are.

In the BBC's brilliant and award-winning series 'Doctor Foster', Simon criticizes his wife Gemma (played by the superb Suranne Jones), saying that she is a terrible mother, that she is going mad. He makes her feel that she is imagining things and that she is completely deluded. In other words he gaslights her. It made me feel sick because in many respects I feel like I've been there. But it made me feel glad because so many women responded to that show, in particular those episodes. And so many articles were written about gaslighting afterwards, opening up something we need to be aware of and need to talk about more and more.

I don't listen to it (and I have to confess I'd never even heard of it), but in BBC Radio 4's 'The Archers' in 2016, they had a storyline about an emotionally abusive, coercive relationship between Helen Archer and Rob Titchener. It may have been fiction, but it brought the whole subject – including gaslighting and questions over Helen's ability as a mother – to the attention of millions of women.

Mental health is an issue, abuse is an issue for men and for women, and equality for gay, lesbian, transgender, gender-fluid and queer people is something we talk about and celebrate. We still have a long way to go, but little brown girls in playgrounds see other brown girls in magazines, on television, in business and on stages. Movements like #MeToo and #TimesUp are about real empowerment, about breaking silence and standing strong and united as a female force. Girl Power has grown up, and I want to learn from my past and grow with it.

My rollercoaster life is far from over. There will be more twists and turns and falls and rises as every year goes by. But I welcome that. I am an imperfect woman who has made mistakes, but I believe the truth sets you free. If my honesty enables another woman to share her story or feel less shame then I am happy.

My story is yet to end.

15 SIGNS OF DOMESTIC ABUSE

—

Domestic violence doesn't look the same in every relationship because every relationship is different. But one thing most abusive relationships have in common is that the abusive partner does many different kinds of things to have more power and control over their partner. Some of the signs of an abusive relationship can include a partner who:

- Tells you that you can never do anything right
- Shows extreme jealousy of your friends and time spent away
- Keeps you or discourages you from seeing friends or family members
- Insults, demeans or shames you with put-downs
- Controls every penny spent in the household
- Takes your money or refuses to give you money for necessary expenses
- Looks at you or acts in ways that scare you
- Controls who you see, where you go, or what you do
- Prevents you from making your own decisions
- Tells you that you are a bad parent or threatens to harm or take away your children
- Prevents you from working or attending school
- Destroys your property or threatens to hurt or kill your pets
- Intimidates you with guns, knives or other weapons
- Pressures you to have sex when you don't want to or do things sexually you're not comfortable with
- Pressures you to use drugs or alcohol

www.thehotline.org www.womensrefuge.org,uk